EXAM ESSENTIALS PRACTICE TESTS

Cambridge English: Advanced (CAE)

Charles Osbourne
with Carol Nuttall
with new material by Tom Bradbury
and Claire Morris

NATIONAL GEOGRAPHIC
LEARNING

Australia · Brazil · Mexico · Singapore · United Kingdom · United States

NATIONAL GEOGRAPHIC
LEARNING

Exam Essentials Practice Tests 1
Cambridge English: Advanced (CAE)
(with key)

Charles Osbourne with some new material
by Tom Bradbury, Claire Morris and
Carol Nuttall

Publisher: Gavin McLean

Publishing Consultant: Karen Spiller

Editorial Project Manager: Stephanie Parker

Development Editor: Andrew Reid

Strategic Marketing Manager: Charlotte Ellis

Project Editor: Tom Relf

Manufacturing Buyer: Eyvett Davis

Cover design: Oliver Hutton

Compositor: Cenveo® Publisher Services

National Geographic Liaison:
Wesley Della Volla

Audio: Martin Williamson,
Prolingua Productions

DVD-ROM: Tom, Dick and Debbie Ltd

Contributing writer: Susan Yokes
(video materials)

For product information and technology assistance, contact us at
Cengage Learning Customer & Sales Support, cengage.com/contact
For permission to use material from this text or product,
submit all requests online at **cengage.com/permissions**
Further permissions questions can be emailed to
permissionrequest@cengage.com

ISBN: 978-1-285-74497-1

National Geographic Learning
Cheriton House, North Way, Andover, Hampshire, SP10 5BE
United Kingdom

National Geographic Learning, a Cengage Learning Company, has a mission to bring the world to the classroom and the classroom to life. With our English language programs, students learn about their world by experiencing it. Through our partnerships with National Geographic and TED Talks, they develop the language and skills they need to be successful global citizens and leaders.

Locate your local office at **international.cengage.com/region**

Visit National Geographic Learning online at **NGL.Cengage.com/ELT**
Visit our corporate website at **www.cengage.com**

Photos
pp 52 l (Juniors Bildarchiv GmbH/Alamy), 169 t (Eric Fougere/Vip Images/Corbis UK Ltd), 169 c (Dan Wooller/Rex Features), 169 br (Imagebroker/Alamy), 170 t (Monkey Business Images/Shutterstock), 170 c (Radius Images/Alamy), 170 b (Bartosz Hadyniak/Getty Images), 172 t (Adam Blasberg/Getty Images), 172 c (Marco Kesseler/Alamy), 172 b (OJO Images Ltd/Alamy), 173 t (Aurora Photos/Alamy), 173 c (117717/Getty Images), 173 b (Image Source/Getty Images), 175 t (F1online digitale Bildagentur GmbH/Alamy), 175 bl (Chad Ehlers/Alamy), 175 br (NASA Photo/Alamy), 176 t (PhotosIndia.com LLC/Alamy), 176 c (Stockbroker/Alamy), 176 b (Ryan Smith/Somos Images/Corbis UK Ltd), 178 t (Robert Harding Picture Library Ltd/Alamy), 178 c (Leo Mason sports photos/Alamy), 178 b (Imagebroker/Alamy), 179 t (CL Studio/Alamy), 179 c (Krzysztof Slusarczyk/Shutterstock), 179 b (Getty Images), 181 t (Corbis UK Ltd), 181 c (Paul Brown/Alamy), 181 b (David Grossman/Alamy), 182 t (ZSSD/Getty Images), 182 bl (Marmaduke St. John/Alamy), 182 br (Auremar/Shutterstock), 184 t (Svetikd/Getty Images), 184 bl (Picture Partners/Alamy), 184 br (Vicki Beaver/Alamy), 185 t (Prodakszyn/Shutterstock), 185 bl (Jupiter Images/Getty Images), 185 br (Leungchopan/Shutterstock), 187 t (Ocean/Corbis UK Ltd), 187 c (Blend Images/Alamy), 187 b (ZUMA Press, Inc./Alamy), 188 t (Zigy Kaluzny/Getty Images), 188 c (lightpoet/Shutterstock), 188 bl (Scottish Viewpoint/Alamy), 190 t (Pascal Saez/Alamy), 190 c (Michael S. Yamashita/Corbis UK Ltd), 190 b (Photodisc/Getty Images), 191 c (Christopher Pillitz/Getty Images), 191 c (Reuters/Corbis UK Ltd), 191 b (Paul Glendell/Alamy),

Texts
Adapted from 'Peach of an idea: The founders of Innocent Drinks' by Richard Wray, The Guardian, 7 August 2004, Copyright Guardian News & Media Ltd 2004. Adapted from 'Language jobs that translate globally' by Kate Hilpern, The Independent, 16 October 2011, copyright The Independent. Adapted from 'Satellite Archaeology' by Hannah Bloch, http://ngm.nationalgeographic.com/2013/02/explore/satellite-archaeology. Adapted from 'Mind your languages' by Matthew Brace, Geographical, Vol.71, No.11, November 1999, Copyright © Geographical 1999. Adapted from 'Citizen Scientists' by A. R. Williams, http://ngm.nationalgeographic.com/2013/03/explore/citizen-scientists. Adapted from 'Read it and weep! Research shows modern day books contain 14% less emotion than books published at the beginning of the 1900s... but are far more paranoid' by Nick McDermott, Daily Mail online, 20 March 2013, reproduced with permission from Solo Syndication. Adapted from 'Back to basics' by Ashley Seager, The Guardian, 13 July 2004, Copyright Guardian News & Media Ltd 2004. Adapted from 'Close encounters of the wild kind' by Christian Amodeo, Geographical, Vol.76, No.2, February 2004, © Geographical 2004. Adapted from 'Missing Out: In Praise Of The Unlived Life, By Adam Phillips' by Christina Patterson, 16 June 2012, http://www.independent.co.uk/arts-entertainment/books/reviews/missing-out-in-praise-of-the-unlived-life-by-adam-phillips-7851441.html#, copyright The Independent. Adapted from 'Wired for Culture' by Tom Chivers, The Telegraph, 6 March 2012, © Telegraph Media Group Limited 2012. Adapted from 'Teach Us To Sit Still by Tim Parks' review by John Preston, The Telegraph, 11 July 2010, © Telegraph Media Group Limited 2010. Adapted from 'The Antidote by Oliver Burkeman' by B. J. Epstein, http://www.walesartsreview.org/the-antidote-by-oliver-burkeman/, with permission from Wales Art Review. Adapted from 'Field science: When your degree takes you to the jungle' by Tamara Williams, 27 February 2013, http://www.independent.co.uk/student/student-life/field-science-when-your-degree-takes-you-to-the-jungle-8512656.html?origin=internalSearch#, copyright The Independent. Adapted from 'Bred to Soar' by Jeffrey P. Cohn, published in Américas Magazine (Volume 56, #5, 2004) © 2004 Organization of American States. Reprinted from Américas Magazine, the official publication of the Organization of American States (OAS). Adapted from 'Scientists and their emotions: the highs and the lows' by Ewan Birney, The Observer, 10 February 2013, Copyright Guardian News & Media Ltd. 2013. Adapted from 'Why the humble mushroom is being hailed as a superfood' by Angela Epstein, The Mail on Sunday, 19 October 2008, reproduced with permission from Solo Syndication. Adapted from 'How sound and smell can create perfect harmony' by Cassie Barton, The Guardian, 22 October 2012, Copyright Guardian News & Media Ltd 2012. Adapted from 'Neolithic discovery: why Orkney is the centre of ancient Britain' by Robin McKie, The Observer, 7 October 2012, Copyright Guardian News & Media Ltd 2012. Adapted from 'David Hockney, Philip Pullman, Kirsty Wark: my favourite masterpiece' by Jonathan Jones, The Guardian, 13 October 2011, Copyright Guardian News & Media Ltd 2011.

Although every effort has been made to contact copyright holders before publication, this has not always been possible. If notified, the publisher will undertake to rectify any errors or omissions at the earliest opportunity. Note that the sample answer sheets in the Practice tests are not the updated official answer sheets provided by Cambridge as these were not available at the time of publication.

Printed in China by RR Donnelley
Print Number: 07   Print Year: 2019

Contents

CAMBRIDGE ENGLISH: ADVANCED

Paper 1: READING AND USE OF ENGLISH (1 hour 30 minutes)

Part	Task type and focus	Number of questions	Task format
1	**Multiple-choice cloze** Task focus: vocabulary	8	A multiple-choice cloze text with eight gaps, followed by eight four-option questions.
2	**Open cloze** Task focus: grammar and some vocabulary	8	A modified cloze text with eight gaps which you fill with the appropriate word.
3	**Word formation** Task focus: vocabulary	8	A text with eight gaps. You are asked to complete the text by making an appropriate word from the word prompt you are given for each gap.
4	**Key word transformations** Task focus: grammar and vocabulary	6	This task consists of six discrete key word transformations. You are asked to complete a sentence which means the same as the given sentence using the key word.
5	**Multiple choice** Task focus: reading for detailed understanding of a text, gist, opinion, attitude, tone, purpose, main idea, meaning from context, implication, text organisation features	6	You answer six four-option multiple-choice questions on a text.
6	**Short texts** Task focus: reading to understand meaning across different texts.	4	You read four short texts by different writers on a similar topic, and with a similar purpose. Reading across the texts, you identify similarities and differences in the themes and opinions of the writers.
7	**Missing paragraphs** Task focus: close reading of a text, identifying references and meanings across discourse.	6	You read a text from which six paragraphs have been removed. There is one extra paragraph. You decide which paragraphs complete each gap in the text.
8	**Multiple matching** Task focus: reading for specific information in a text, detail, opinion, attitude	10	You match ten questions to different texts or different sections of a text.

Paper 2: WRITING (1 hour 30 minutes)

Part	Task type and focus	Number of questions	Task format
1	**Question 1** Essay	Part 1 is compulsory. 220–260 words	You write an essay based on a given title and accompanying ideas, including one of your own.
2	**Questions 2–4** may include an email/a letter, a report, a review or a proposal	You have a choice from three tasks. 220–260 words	You carry out a writing task, using the appropriate style and format.

Paper 3: LISTENING (40 minutes approximately)

Part	Task type and focus	Number of questions	Task format
1	**Multiple choice** Task focus: understanding gist, detail, function, purpose, feeling, attitude, opinion, genre, agreement, etc.	6	A series of short unrelated extracts, from monologues or exchanges between interacting speakers. There is one three-option question for each extract.
2	**Sentence completion** Task focus: detail, specific information, stated opinion	8	A monologue. The task consists of eight gapped sentences.
3	**Multiple choice** Task focus: understanding attitude and opinion, main idea, specific information and gist	6	A listening text involving interacting speakers. You have six four-option multiple-choice questions, and need to decide what the correct answer is.
4	**Multiple matching** Task focus: understanding mood and attitude, main ideas, specific information and context	10	Five short monologues, all on a similar theme. You listen once and match each speaker to information from two separate lists.

Paper 4: SPEAKING (15 minutes approximately)

Part	Task type and focus	Input	Task format
1 **Interview** (2 mins)	The interlocutor asks each candidate to say a little about themselves.	Verbal questions	You must be able to • give personal information. • talk about present circumstances / past experiences. • talk about future plans.
2 **Individual long turn** (4 mins)	Each candidate talks about a pair of photographs for 1 minute, followed by a 30-second response from the second candidate.	Visual stimuli, with verbal and written instructions	You must be able to • give information. • express your opinions. • relate photos to yourself and your own experience.
3 **Two-way collaborative task** (4 mins)	The interlocutor asks candidates to carry out a task based on written prompts.	A written question with written stimuli and verbal instructions	You must be able to • exchange information and opinions. • express and justify opinions. • agree, disagree or partly agree. • suggest and speculate.
4 **Discussion** (5 mins)	The interlocutor asks candidates general opinion questions related to the topic covered in Part 3.	Verbal prompts	You must be able to • exchange information and opinions. • express and justify opinions. • agree, disagree or partly agree.

Exam Essentials Practice Tests is a series of materials published by National Geographic Learning for students preparing for the major EFL/ESL examinations: Cambridge English: First (FCE); Cambridge English: Advanced (CAE); and International English Language Testing System (IELTS). The series is characterised by the close attention each component pays to developing a detailed knowledge of the skills and strategies needed for success in each paper or part of the exams.

Cambridge English: Advanced (CAE) Practice Tests helps learners become aware of the Cambridge English: Advanced (CAE) exam requirements, offers details about the format and language in the exam, and helps learners develop exam skills necessary for success. The book also provides extensive practice in all parts of the exam, using the actual test format.

Taking the Exam

Cambridge English: Advanced is one of a series of five Cambridge English exams corresponding to different levels of the Common European Framework of Reference for Languages (CEFR):

• Cambridge English: Key (KET) CEFR Level A2

• Cambridge English: Preliminary (PET) CEFR Level B1

• Cambridge English: First (FCE) CEFR Level B2

• Cambridge English: Advanced (CAE) CEFR Level C1

• Cambridge English: Proficiency (CPE) CEFR Level C2

Cambridge English: Advanced is widely recognised by universities and similar educational institutions, and in commerce and industry, as proof that the holder of this qualification can take a course of study in English at university level, and also carry out managerial and professional work effectively. It can also be used as proof of English skills when applying for employment in English-speaking environments.

The exam can be taken on many dates during a year, and can be taken on paper or on a computer. It consists of four Papers.

Paper 1 Reading and Use of English (1 hour 30 minutes)

• Part 1 is a multiple-choice cloze task. You read a text with eight gaps. This is followed by eight four-option multiple-choice questions. You need to complete each gap with the correct option. Part 1 tests your knowledge of vocabulary, including idioms, fixed phrases, phrasal verbs, collocations and shades of meaning.

• Part 2 is an open cloze task. You read a text with eight gaps. You need to complete each gap with an appropriate word. Part 2 tests your knowledge of the structure of the language – grammar and some vocabulary.

• Part 3 is a word formation task. You read a short text with eight gaps. You need to complete each gap with an appropriate word formed from a prompt word in capitals that appears to the right of the text on the same line as the gap. Part 3 tests your knowledge of how words are formed from other words.

• Part 4 consists of six sentences, each of which is followed by a word and a gapped sentence. You need to complete the gapped sentence so that its meaning is the same as the first sentence using three to six words, including the word given. Part 4 tests your knowledge of vocabulary and grammar.

• Part 5 consists of a long text with six four-option multiple-choice questions. Part 5 tests your ability to read for detail, gist, opinion, attitude, purpose, implication and text organisation features such as reference and comparison.

• Part 6 consists of four short texts written by four different people about the same subject, together with four questions. The questions test your ability to understand the opinions and attitudes expressed in the texts and to identify when writers agree and disagree with each other.

• Part 7 consists of a long text from which six paragraphs have been removed and placed in jumbled order after the text. You have to decide from where in the text the paragraphs have been removed. Part 7 tests your understanding of how a text is structured.

• Part 8 consists of a long text with several sections or several short texts. There are 10 questions which require you to decide which section of the long text or which short text each one refers to. Part 8 tests your ability to read for specific information, detail, opinion and attitude.

Paper 2 Writing (1 hour 30 minutes)

- Part 1 is compulsory. You are required to write an essay in 220–260 words. Before you write your answer, you must read the instructions as well as an input text or texts. Part 1 focuses on your ability to evaluate, express opinions, hypothesise, etc. Persuasion is always an important element in your writing in Part 1.

- There are three questions to choose from in Part 2. For questions 2–4, you are required to write an email/letter, a proposal, a report or a review in 220–260 words. Part 2 focuses on your ability to give opinions, persuade, justify, give advice, compare, etc.

- Both parts of the Writing Paper test your ability to write a text according to instructions in an appropriate style and register for a given purpose and target reader. Effective text organisation, accuracy and a good range of vocabulary are also important.

Paper 3 Listening (approximately 40 minutes)

- Part 1 consists of three short monologues or texts involving interacting speakers. You are required to answer two three-option multiple-choice questions for each extract. Part 1 tests your ability to understand feeling, attitude, opinion, purpose, function, agreement, course of action, general gist, detail, etc.

- Part 2 consists of a long monologue. You are required to complete eight gapped sentences with information you hear on the recording. Each gap is completed by one, two or three words or a number. Part 2 tests your ability to understand specific information and stated opinion.

- Part 3 consists of a text involving interacting speakers. You are required to answer six four-option multiple-choice questions. Part 3 tests your ability to understand attitude and opinion.

- Part 4 consists of five short monologues on a related theme. There are two tasks in this part. Both tasks require you choose from a list of options the opinion that each speaker expresses. Part 4 tests your ability to understand gist, attitude and main point and to interpret context.

Paper 4 Speaking (approximately 15 minutes)

The Speaking Paper generally involves two candidates and two examiners.

- In Part 1 you have a brief conversation with the examiner. Part 1 tests your ability to give personal information and use social and interactional language.

- In Part 2 the examiner gives you and the other candidate visual and written prompts. Each candidate is required to use the prompts he/she is given to talk for a minute. He/She is also required to answer a question based on the other candidate's prompts in 30 seconds. Part 2 tests your ability to organise a larger unit of discourse to compare, describe, express opinions and speculate.

- In Part 3 the examiner gives you and the other candidate visual and written prompts. You are required to use the prompts to have a conversation with the other candidate. Part 3 tests your ability to sustain an interaction, exchange ideas, express and justify opinions, agree and/ or disagree, suggest, evaluate, reach a decision through negotiation, etc.

- In Part 4 the examiner asks you questions based on the topics you talked about in Part 3. You are required to have a three-way discussion with the examiner and the other candidate. Part 4 tests your ability to exchange information, express and justify opinions, agree and/or disagree.

Preparing for the exam

In preparing for the four Papers, the following points should be taken into account.

Reading and Use of English

To prepare for the **Use of English** (Parts 1, 2, 3 and 4), you need to develop your awareness and use of both grammatical structures and vocabulary. You need to know how structures such as verb forms, modal and auxiliary verbs, pronouns, prepositions, conjunctions, modifiers and determiners are used correctly in a variety of different types of text. You also need a good knowledge of vocabulary, so learn whole phrases rather than single words in isolation, how words and phrases are used in combination with other words, how words can have different meanings and uses, and how different words can be formed from a root. It helps to read widely and to pay attention to grammar and vocabulary as you read. Make use of dictionaries and grammar books (except when doing the tests), and develop an efficient system for recording the new vocabulary and grammar you encounter.

To prepare for the **Reading** (Parts 5, 6, 7 and 8), you should read from a range of material: newspapers, magazines, journals, novels, leaflets, brochures, etc. When you read, pay attention to text organisation features, train yourself to recognise the author's purpose in writing and his or her tone, and learn to read between the lines for what is implied rather than stated explicitly. It is important to practise different reading strategies that can be used for different parts of the Reading Paper, for example skimming for the main idea and gist, scanning to locate specific information or reading closely to determine the writer's precise meaning.

Writing

You need to be familiar with all the text types you may be required to write in the exam. You should also be aware of the criteria that will be used in marking your texts.

- Has the candidate achieved the purpose stated in the instructions?
- Does the text have a positive general effect on the target reader?
- Does the text cover all the content points?
- Is the text organised effectively and are ideas linked appropriately?
- Has language been used accurately?
- Does the text have a good range of vocabulary and grammatical features?
- Is the register appropriate for the task?
- Is the layout appropriate?

Listening

You should practise listening to a wide variety of spoken English: announcements, speeches, lectures, talks, radio broadcasts, anecdotes, radio interviews, discussions, etc. You should also practise listening for different purposes: to understand gist, identify context or attitude or find specific information.

Speaking

You should practise speaking English as much as possible. It is important to master conversational skills such as turn taking and the appropriate way to participate in a discussion, giving full but natural answers to questions and requesting clarification.

Further information can be obtained from the Cambridge English website: www.cambridgeenglish.org

Practice Tests: contents

Cambridge English: Advanced (CAE) in the *Exam Essentials Practice Tests* series prepares candidates for the Cambridge English: Advanced examination by providing **eight full practice tests,** which accurately reflect the latest exam specifications.

There are **three guided tests** at the beginning, which feature **essential tips** to practise exam strategy. These tips offer guidance and general strategies for approaching each task. Other tips offer advice relevant to specific questions in the guided tests. These guided tests will help students prepare for each paper, while the following five **tests (without guidance)** will offer students thorough practice at a realistic exam level.

The **DVD-ROM** accompanying the book includes the audio materials for all the Listening Papers. These accurately reflect the exam in both style and content. Moreover, the audio materials for Tests 1 and 2 have been recorded with the repetitions and full pauses, exactly as in the exam itself.

A **writing bank** includes **sample answers** for the kinds of tasks that occur in Paper 2 (Writing), writing tips in the form of notes and **useful phrases** for the different task types. Varied **visual materials** for Paper 4 (Speaking) have also been included, while a **language bank** supplies useful phrases and expressions for use in the Speaking Paper.

There is also a **glossary** for each test, explaining vocabulary that is likely to be unfamiliar to students.

Clear and straightforward design simplifies use of the book. **Exam overview** tables ensure that key information is readily accessible, while a specially designed menu makes it easy to navigate through the different parts and papers of each practice test.

You will find **sample exam answer sheets** on pages 166–168 which you can photocopy and use to note down your answers. These will help you practise using the answer sheets you will be given in the real exam.

For more practice, there is also an additional book of tests for this exam: *Exam Essentials Practice Tests 2 Cambridge English: Advanced (CAE).*

Practice Tests: principles

In writing this book, three guiding principles have been observed.

Firstly, that it should be useful for teachers, students sitting the Cambridge English: Advanced exam for the first time or re-sitting the exam, whether they are working alone or in a class. Students approaching the exam for the first time would be best advised to work through the book linearly, developing their skills and confidence; those re-sitting the exam can consult the Exam overview tables to concentrate on particular areas for targeted revision. The **without key** edition can be used by students working in a class, while the **with key** edition includes a detailed **answer key and all the audio scripts,** ensuring that students working alone can benefit from support while attempting these tests.

The second principle is that the questions should accurately reflect the range of questions found in the Cambridge English: Advanced exam. Thus students obtain guidance concerning the general content and the best way of approaching the tasks from the questions themselves. Seeing the questions in this light – as instructions to the candidate from the examiner rather than intimidating challenges – also helps students feel less daunted by the whole experience of sitting a major exam like this.

The third principle is that the texts used in the practice tests should be not only representative of those used in the exam, but also varied and interesting. Everyone finds it easier to learn if the subject matter is relevant to his or her lifestyle and interests. In choosing, editing and creating the texts here, we have done our utmost to ensure that the experience of working with this book is as stimulating and rewarding as possible.

This edition of *Exam Essentials* for students of Cambridge English: Advanced (CAE) includes a brand new DVD-ROM which focuses on the Speaking test component of the Cambridge English: Advanced examination. The DVD-ROM includes two videos:

• a complete Cambridge English: Advanced Speaking test.
• a short clip giving valuable advice about the Cambridge English: Advanced Speaking test.

To maximise learning from the complete Cambridge English: Advanced Speaking test, the following PDFs are also available on the DVD-ROM:

• a worksheet for individual or class use.
• an answer key for the worksheet.
• the complete script of the Speaking test.

A complete Speaking test

A full Cambridge English: Advanced Speaking test interview is approximately 15 minutes in length. Please note that the interview shown on this DVD-ROM is a slightly extended version of the Speaking test. This allows for a wide range of language and types of response to be included. This interview also features high-level candidates whose performance would achieve a good pass in the exam. The video therefore provides a good model to follow. Don't worry if you feel you may not perform to this high standard in every area of the test. You will need to demonstrate a good level, but you will not need to use every structure or item of vocabulary perfectly in order to pass the test.

The video clearly details:

• the role of the examiners.
• the timings of the test.
• the four parts of the test and what is involved in each one.

The role of the examiners

There are two examiners in the test room. Examiner 1 (the interlocutor) asks the candidates questions and handles the tasks. He or she has to keep to very strict timings and has a script to follow. Unscripted conversation or questions are therefore not possible. This is to ensure that each candidate receives equal treatment. Examiner 2 (the assessor) does not usually speak in the test, except to greet the candidates. However, Examiner 2 will make notes. Both examiners give marks to the candidates.

The timings of the test

Part 1: Interview – 2 minutes (3 minutes for groups of three)

Part 2: Individual long turn – 4 minutes (6 minutes for groups of three)

Part 3: Collaborative task – 4 minutes (6 minutes for groups of three)

Part 4: Discussion – 5 minutes (8 minutes for groups of three)

The four parts of the test

Part 1: Interview – this includes greeting the candidates, introducing the examiners and general questions about yourself.

Part 2: Individual long turn – this involves talking about two out of three pictures and briefly answering a question about your partner's pictures after he/she has spoken.

Part 3: Collaborative task – this is where both candidates talk about prompts on a diagram, and reach a decision through negotiation.

Part 4: Discussion – the interlocutor leads a discussion by asking candidates questions. Candidates exchange information and opinions related to the topic in Part 3.

How each part of the test should be answered

The video offers tips for improving candidates' performance in each of the four parts. In Part 1, candidates need to give personal information, talk about their present circumstances, talk about past experiences and future plans as well as express opinions. In Part 2, candidates need to express their opinions through comparing, hypothesising and speculating on the pictures given. In Part 3, candidates need to work together to exchange ideas and opinions, agree or disagree, suggest, speculate, evaluate and reach a decision through negotiation. In Part 4, candidates express and justify their opinions and agree and disagree.

Tips and advice

Following the Speaking test, there is a short clip to supplement the speaking tips given in the book. In this section, which is about five minutes long, an examiner gives some tips and advice about how to do well in the Cambridge English: Advanced Speaking test.

The worksheet

This printable worksheet accompanies the complete Cambridge English: Advanced Speaking test. Although primarily designed for self-study, the worksheet can also be used in the classroom. It provides in-depth information about the Speaking test and focuses on the language each candidate uses in the video.

The worksheet is divided into four sections which relate to each part of the Speaking test. It includes activities which:

- draw students' attention to key features of the candidate's response.
- relate these features to the marking criteria used by the examiners.
- give the student practice in developing their own answers for similar questions.

A separate answer key and a full video script are also provided.

PAPER 1	Reading and ▶	Part 1
	Use of English	Part 2
PAPER 2	Writing	Part 3
		Part 4
PAPER 3	Listening	Part 5
PAPER 4	Speaking	Part 6
		Part 7
		Part 8

For questions **1–8**, read the text below and decide which answer (**A, B, C** or **D**) best fits each gap. There is an example at the beginning (**0**).

Mark your answers **on the separate answer sheet**.

Example:

| 0 | **A** | event | **B** | aspect | **C** | field | **D** | division |

| 0 | A | B | C | D |

Essential tips

▶ Read through the whole text to get a general idea of what it is about.

▶ The correct option must have the correct meaning. It can also be part of a phrase, collocation, idiom, phrasal verb or expression.

▶ The correct option must fit in the sentence structurally. All the four options will be the right part of speech (noun, adjective, verb, adverb, etc.), but only one will be correct in the context of the sentence. For instance, the correct option may be the only word that is followed by a preposition that comes after the gap. So, check the words on either side of the gap carefully to see what collocates with them.

Question 2: One of the options does not collocate with *time*. Of the other three options, only one has the correct meaning of 'best'.

Question 3: Only one of the options forms a fixed expression with *what is* and has the meaning of 'in addition' or 'moreover'.

Question 4: All four options can form phrasal verbs with *out*, but only one collocates with *activities* to mean 'perform activities'.

Question 6: Only one option collocates with *convinced*.

Nature's clocks

Our biological clocks govern almost every (**0**) …….. of our lives. Our sensitivity to stimuli (**1**) …….. over the course of the day, and our ability to perform certain functions is subject to fluctuations. The middle of the day, for example, is the (**2**) …….. time for tasks such as making decisions. Anything that demands physical co-ordination, on the other hand, is best attempted in the early evening. What is (**3**) …….., there is a dramatic drop in performance if these activities are (**4**) …….. out at other times. The risk of accident in a factory, for example, is 20% higher during the night (**5**) …….. .

Primitive humans lived in tune with the daily cycle of light and dark. Today, we are (**6**) …….. convinced that we can impose schedules on our lives at will. Sooner or later, however, we pay a (**7**) …….. for ignoring our natural rhythms. A good example is jet lag, caused when we confuse our body's biological clocks by (**8**) …….. several time zones. Jet lag often lasts for several days and can badly affect our decision-making ability.

1	**A** modifies	**B** ranges	**C** varies	**D** wavers
2	**A** peak	**B** summit	**C** maximum	**D** optimum
3	**A** more	**B** else	**C** different	**D** besides
4	**A** made	**B** gone	**C** carried	**D** set
5	**A** labour	**B** work	**C** duty	**D** shift
6	**A** powerfully	**B** firmly	**C** steadily	**D** highly
7	**A** price	**B** fine	**C** fee	**D** cost
8	**A** landing	**B** penetrating	**C** crossing	**D** travelling

PAPER 1	Reading and ▸		Part 1
	Use of English		**Part 2**
PAPER 2	Writing		Part 3
			Part 4
PAPER 3	Listening		Part 5
PAPER 4	Speaking		Part 6
			Part 7
			Part 8

For questions **9–16**, read the text below and think of the word which best fits each gap. Use only **one** word in each gap. There is an example at the beginning (**0**).

Write your answers **IN CAPITAL LETTERS on the separate answer sheet.**

Example: | 0 | I | N | | | | | | | | | | | | | | | | | | | |

Antarctica in danger

The last 20 years have seen a dramatic increase (**0**) …….. the numbers of visitors to Antarctica. These (**9**) …….. only include scientists who are researching (**10**) …….. crucial issues as climate change and its impact on the polar regions, but also more and more tourists. Some tourists simply want to see the last unspoiled continent. Some, on the (**11**) …….. hand, seek more active pursuits like adventure sports. However, environmentalists are concerned that the growing tourist industry may (**12**) …….. endangering the Antarctic environment and sowing the seeds of its destruction.

(**13**) …….. of the problems facing the area is pollution resulting from tourism. Careless visitors throw rubbish into the sea, without realising (**14**) …….. harmful this can be to wildlife. Just (**15**) …….. damaging, perhaps more so, is oil spilt from ships insufficiently reinforced to withstand collisions (**16**) …….. icebergs. Oil from even a small spill can remain an environmental hazard for many years, and there are increasing numbers of icebergs breaking off the continental ice sheet due to global warming.

Essential tips

▸ Read through the whole text to get a general idea of what it is about.

▸ Decide what word(s) in the sentence are grammatically related to the gapped word. This will help you decide what part of speech is needed (auxiliary verb, pronoun, article, preposition, etc.).

▸ Read the whole sentence to see if the word you need is part of a longer phrase, such as *either ... or ...* .

▸ It may be that two (or even three) words could fit in the gap, so do not assume the word you are thinking of is wrong if you can also think of one or two alternatives.

Question 9: Read the whole sentence carefully. Notice *but also* in the last part of the sentence. Think of the structure *... only ... but also.*

Question 10: Look carefully at the words either side of the gap. Climate change is an example of a crucial issue. Can you think of a word to go with *as* to indicate an example?

Question 11: The gapped word is part of a phrase: *on the ... hand.* Read the previous sentence before deciding on the word for the gap.

Question 12: Which verb usually comes before a continuous (*-ing*) verb form? Which verb form comes after *may* and other modal verbs?

PAPER 1 Reading and ▸   Part 1
         Use of English   Part 2

PAPER 2 Writing   **Part 3**
                             Part 4
PAPER 3 Listening   Part 5
                             Part 6
PAPER 4 Speaking
                             Part 7
                             Part 8

For questions **17–24**, read the text below. Use the word given in capitals at the end of some of the lines to form a word that fits in the gap **in the same line**. There is an example at the beginning (**0**).

Write your answers **IN CAPITAL LETTERS on the separate answer sheet.**

Example: | 0 | A | C | T | I | V | I | T | Y | | | | | | | |

Essential tips

▸ Read through the whole text to get a general idea of what it is about.

▸ Decide what type of word is needed in each gap (e.g. verb, noun, adjective or adverb).

▸ Look at the word in capital letters. You may need to change its form to fit the gap.

▸ Think about what prefixes and suffixes you could add.

▸ Some words will need more than one change.

▸ Check the spelling carefully and consider whether the word should be singular or plural.

Question 17: Think carefully about the type of word you need here. You will need to add both a prefix and a suffix.

Question 19: The gapped word forms part of the expression *in ... with*, which means 'matching something'.

Question 22: You need to make a verb from a noun here. Make sure you use the correct verb form. There are two ways of spelling this word, and both can be correct.

Elephant training

If you are travelling in Thailand, you can now take part in
an (**0**) .... of an unusual kind. For a sum of money which   **ACTIVE**
is (**17**) .... modest, you can spend a few days at   **CREDIBLE**
an elephant-conservation centre training to be a
mahout (elephant driver).

Primarily set up in an endeavour to preserve the (**18**) ....   **MAJESTY**
Thai elephant, the centre welcomes tourism as a means
of funding itself. Nevertheless, its programme remains
strictly in (**19**) .... with the traditions of *Kachasart*, the ancient   **KEEP**
method of studying elephants, and the *mahouts* build up very
close relationships with their elephants. Training is believed
to be (**20**) .... to the elephants, providing them with physical **BENEFIT**
and mental (**21**) .... Their well-being is considered of   **STIMULATE**
utmost importance.

The elephants are captive, of course, and the centre
has been (**22**) .... for not allowing them to go free.   **CRITIC**
The reality, however, is that (**23**) .... deforestation has   **EXTEND**
left wild elephants struggling to survive in habitats that
are shrinking almost on a (**24**) .... basis, and the centre   **DAY**
offers them a sanctuary – for the time being at least.

For questions **25–30**, complete the second sentence so that it has a similar meaning to the first sentence, using the word given. **Do not change the word given.** You must use between **three** and **six** words, including the word given. Here is an example (**0**).

Example:

0   Jane regretted speaking so rudely to the old lady.

   MORE

   Jane .... politely to the old lady.

Example: | 0 | WISHED SHE HAD SPOKEN MORE |

Write **only** the missing words **IN CAPITAL LETTERS on the separate answer sheet**.

---

25   Pop in for a chat whenever you are in town.

   HAPPEN

   If .... in town, pop in for a chat.

26   Paula had just reached the gate when it began to rain.

   THAN

   No sooner .... it began to rain.

27   'Mark wrote that poem, not Ian,' said Helen.

   IT

   According to Helen, ... that poem, not Ian.

28   Even if it is expensive, they want to stay in the hotel by the beach.

   MAY

   Expensive ...., they want to stay in the hotel by the beach.

29   Unless you tell the truth, the school trip will be cancelled.

   MEAN

   Your failure .... the cancellation of the school trip.

30   Noriko has never been here before, so it is possible that she has got lost.

   HAVE

   Noriko .... it is the first time she has ever been here.

Essential tips

▶   For each question, read both sentences carefully. The second sentence must convey the same information as the first sentence, but in different words.

▶   The key word in capital letters must be used without changing its form in any way.

▶   You may need to change the order in which you give the information, and the form of some words from the first sentence.

▶   Some questions may require you to change from a negative sentence to a positive one, or from a passive structure to an active one (or the other way round – be prepared for this!).

▶   You must use between three and six words in your answer. If you write too few words or too many, you will lose marks.

Question 26: Think about the word order here. Certain negative structures at the start of a sentence are followed by inversion (e.g. *Never **before had** Caroline seen such a beautiful garden*).

Question 27: How can you use *it* to emphasise that Mark, not Ian, wrote the poem?

Question 30: How can you express the idea of possibility? You need a structure with a modal verb (more than one modal verb is possible). You will also need a suitable linking word.

PAPER 1	Reading and ▶	Part 1
	Use of English	Part 2
PAPER 2	Writing	Part 3
		Part 4
PAPER 3	Listening	**Part 5**
PAPER 4	Speaking	Part 6
		Part 7
		Part 8

You are going to read a magazine article. For questions **31–36**, choose the answer (**A**, **B**, **C** or **D**) which you think fits best according to the text.

Mark your answers **on the separate answer sheet**.

The beauties of the stone age

Jane Howard reviews some ancient works of art.

I have just come home after viewing some astonishing works of art that were recently discovered in Church Hole cave in Nottinghamshire. They are not drawings, as one would expect, but etchings – shapes cut into the rock – and they depict a huge range of wild animals. The artists who created them lived around 13,000 years ago, and the images are remarkable on a variety of counts. First of all, their sheer number is staggering: there are 90 in all. Moreover, 58 of them are on the ceiling. This is extremely rare in cave art, according to a leading expert, Dr Wilbur Samson of Central Midlands University. 'Wall pictures are the norm,' he says. 'But more importantly, the Church Hole etchings are an incredible artistic achievement. They can hold their own in comparison with the best found in continental Europe.' I am not a student of the subject, so I have to take his word for it. However, you do not have to be an expert to appreciate their beauty.

In fact, it is the wider significance of the etchings that is likely to attract most attention in academic circles, since they radically alter our view of life in Britain during this epoch. It had previously been thought that ice-age hunters in this country were isolated from people in more central areas of Europe, but the Church Hole images prove that ancient Britons were part of a way of living, thinking and seeing the world that had spread right across the continent. And they were at least as sophisticated as their counterparts on the mainland.

News of such exciting discoveries spreads rapidly, and thanks to the internet and mobile phones, a great many people probably knew about this discovery within hours of the initial expedition returning. As a result, some etchings may already have been adversely affected, albeit inadvertently, by eager visitors. In a regrettably late response, the site has been cordoned off with a high, rather intimidating fence, and warning notices have been posted.

An initial survey of the site last year failed to reveal the presence of the etchings. The reason lies in the expectations of the researchers. They had been looking for the usual type of cave drawing or painting, which shows up best under direct light. Consequently, they used powerful torches, shining them straight onto the rock face. However, the Church Hole images are modifications of the rock itself, and show up best when seen from a certain angle in the natural light of early morning. Having been fortunate to see them at this hour, I can only say that I was deeply – and unexpectedly – moved. While most cave art often seems to have been created in a shadowy past very remote from us, these somehow convey the impression that they were made yesterday.

Dr Samson feels that the lighting factor provides important information about the likely function of these works of art. 'I think the artists knew very well that the etchings would hardly be visible except early in the morning. We can therefore deduce that the chamber was used for rituals involving animal worship, and that they were conducted just after dawn, as a preliminary to the day's hunting.'

However, such ideas are controversial in the world of archaeology and human origins. Dr Olivia Caruthers of the Reardon Institute remains unconvinced that the function of the etchings at Church Hole can be determined with any certainty. 'When we know so little about the social life of early humans, it would be foolish to insist on any rigid interpretation. We should, in my view, begin by tentatively assuming that their creators were motivated in part by aesthetic considerations – while of course being prepared to modify this verdict at a later date, if and when new evidence emerges.'

To which I can only add that I felt deeply privileged to have been able to view Church Hole. It is a site of tremendous importance culturally and is part of the heritage, not only of this country, but the world as a whole.

▶ This part of the exam tests your detailed understanding of a text, including the views and attitudes expressed.

▶ Read through the text quickly to get a general idea of what it is about. Do not worry if there are words or phrases you don't understand.

▶ The questions follow the order of the text. Read each question or question stem carefully and underline the key words.

▶ Look in the text for the answer to the question. One of the options will express the same idea, but don't expect that it will do so in the words of the text.

Question 31: An option can only be correct if all the information contained in it is accurate. Look at option A: are the images in Church Hole 'unique examples of ceiling art'? The text says they are 'extremely rare in cave art'. Is this the same? Look at option B: are the images in Church Hole 'particularly beautiful'? And are they 'paintings'?

Question 33: Look at option A. What does the writer say about the discovery of the images being made public? Look at option B. If something is 'vulnerable to damage', what might happen to it? Look at option C. The text says 'many people probably knew about the discovery within hours of the initial expedition returning'. Is this the same as saying 'many people visited the cave within hours'? Look at option D. Were the measures definitely ineffective?

Question 35: Sometimes you will find words from the options in the text. Be careful: the meaning in the text is not necessarily the same as that in the answer options. Here, option D says the hunters 'kept animals in the cave', but the text says the cave was used for 'rituals involving animal worship', which is not the same thing.

31 According to the text, the images in Church Hole cave are
  A unique examples of ceiling art.
  B particularly beautiful cave paintings.
  C superior in quality to other cave art in Britain.
  D aesthetically exceptional in their own right.

32 What is the cultural significance of these images?
  A They indicate that people from central Europe had settled in Britain.
  B They prove that ancient Britons hunted over large areas.
  C They reveal the existence of a single ice-age culture in Europe.
  D They suggest that people in Europe were more advanced than Britons.

33 According to the text,
  A the discovery of the images should not have been made public.
  B the images in the cave are vulnerable to damage.
  C many people visited the cave within hours of its discovery.
  D the measures taken to protect the images have proved ineffective.

34 Why were the images not discovered during the initial survey?
  A They were not viewed from the right direction.
  B People were not expecting to find any images.
  C The search took place at the wrong time of day.
  D The torches used were too bright.

35 What conclusion does Dr Samson draw from the lighting factor?
  A Rituals were common in animal worship.
  B The artists never intended to make the images visible.
  C The images were intended to be seen at a certain time of day.
  D Ice-age hunters kept animals in the cave.

36 According to Dr Caruthers,
  A we cannot make inferences from cave art.
  B the images in Church Hole do not serve any particular purpose.
  C experts know absolutely nothing about life 13,000 years ago.
  D the reasons such images were created are open to question.

PAPER 1 Reading and
         Use of English

PAPER 2 Writing

PAPER 3 Listening

PAPER 4 Speaking

Part 1
Part 2
Part 3
Part 4
Part 5
Part 6
Part 7
Part 8

You are going to read four contributions to a debate about the value of sending people into space. For questions **37–40**, choose from the contributions **A–D**. The contributions may be chosen more than once.

Mark your answers **on the separate answer sheet**.

Manned space missions

Is it a good idea to send people into space? Four scientists give their views.

A

What are we looking for out in space? That's the question that needs asking. The only thing we bring back is knowledge, and robots outperform astronauts in that respect. They are cheaper to put into space, they can stay there longer and they can collect and retain far more information. The early manned space flights generated genuine interest around the world, but who really cares nowadays, apart from a minority in whose interest it is that vast sums should continue to be invested? Who really believes it will ever be feasible to ship back large quantities of valuable materials from the moon, Mars or another planet, let alone migrate to these places in the event of a catastrophe? What is the priority? To try to create a station on Mars which could accommodate a handful of people, or to do something here to try to resolve global warming?

B

Space exploration, whether manned or not, is hugely expensive, and this is probably a key reason why it seems to have lost its appeal for many people. The fact is, however, that our galaxy is littered with giant meteors like the one that struck the Earth 16 million years ago, wiped out the dinosaurs and precipitated an ice age. Other cosmic dangers exist, as do threats on Earth itself, and one day the human species may only survive by settling in a new home. If we are to form colonies on the moon or other places in space, we have no alternative but to go there ourselves and do it, and that requires preparation. Robots tend to be good at certain tasks like collecting data, but their ability to think critically and creatively and to engage in problem-solving is limited. Some experiments that can only be conducted in space require physical and intellectual dexterity and these are skills that only humans possess.

C

People with a vested interest will say that for humans to travel beyond the Earth is important for the prestige and glamour of space exploration, and for the way it draws young minds into science and technology. However, for the cost of putting a few people into space for a few days, science education in schools could be transformed by creating smaller classes, new laboratories and equipment. Now, wouldn't that be exciting! So much of the investment in manned missions goes into keeping astronauts alive and safe, and the really useful science takes second place. The idea that humans will ever be able to (or want to) settle on the moon or anywhere else in space is unthinkable, so investment for that purpose is ludicrous, but the technological stimulus gained from the development of robotics and computer programmes that can deal with things in real time without people around has immense value on Earth, as well as in space.

D

Manned space flight is not primarily about science. The truth is that developments in science and computer design mean that satellites, robots and other technology are probably better than astronauts at collecting information from space which we can use on Earth. But people do not get excited when they see robots launched into space. Computers attached to a rocket don't stimulate the imagination or the enthusiasm for space exploration. And we do need to explore space, whatever the financial implications. In the long term, we need to find out whether we can survive outside the Earth's orbit. It's a question of our species' survival. Astrophysicists have worked out that at some point in the future – we do not know when – the sun will engulf the Earth, and for the species to continue, when that happens, we need to be elsewhere.

Which writer

has a different opinion from the others about the inspirational significance of manned space missions?	**37**
has a similar view to writer B about the importance of establishing whether humans can live on other planets?	**38**
expresses a different view from the others regarding the relative efficiency of manned missions for carrying out research?	**39**
shares writer A's opinion about the cost effectiveness of sending people into space?	**40**

Essential tips

- This part of the exam tests your ability to understand opinions and attitudes expressed in different texts and to identify whether different writers agree or disagree with each other. There are always four short texts by different writers, and the four texts are all on the same subject.

- Read the main title and the four texts quickly to get a general idea of what they are about. Don't worry if there are words or phrases you don't understand.

- Look carefully at the four questions, highlighting the key words in each.

- Read the first text and highlight the sections of the text that refer to each of the questions. Write the question numbers next to the relevant parts of the text. Then do the same for each text.

- Then look across the four texts and compare the sections that refer to Question 37. Read them carefully and decide which ones express similar views and which have different views.

Question 37: The key words in this question are *different opinion from the others* and *inspirational significance*. All the questions are about 'manned space missions' so there is no need to highlight that. You need to find three views that are similar and one that is different. The relevant part of Text A is: *The early manned space flights generated genuine interest around the world, but who really cares nowadays ...?* The relevant part in text B is: *it seems to have lost its appeal for many people.* Are they similar or different opinions? Now, go through the same process with texts C and D.

Question 40: The key words here are: *shares writer A's opinion* and *cost effectiveness*. All the texts are about sending people into space so there is no point highlighting that. The relevant part of text A is: *They are cheaper to put into space, they can stay there longer and they can collect and retain far more information.* If you look at the previous sentence, it is clear that *they* refers to 'robots'. So, writer A believes that robots are more cost-effective than humans in space. Now, look through the other three texts and highlight references to cost. Which one expresses a similar view to that of writer A?

PAPER 1   Reading and ▸   Part 1
            Use of English   Part 2
                             Part 3
PAPER 2   Writing   Part 4
                             Part 5
PAPER 3   Listening   Part 6
PAPER 4   Speaking   Part 7
                             Part 8

You are going to read a newspaper about a company that makes fruit drinks. Six paragraphs have been removed from the article. Choose from the paragraphs **A–G** the one which fits each gap (**41–46**). There is one extra paragraph which you do not need to use.

Mark your answers **on the separate answer sheet**.

Peach of an idea

At the end of the 1990s, three friends in their mid-20s, Adam Balon, Richard Reed and Jon Wright were thinking of starting a business. They took £500 worth of fruit to a music festival in west London, made a huge batch of smoothies – fruit drinks blended with milk and yoghurt – and asked their customers for a verdict.

| 41 |

Looking back, they now admit that they were amazingly naïve, thinking it would just take off once they had the recipes and packaging figured out. In fact, the three budding entrepreneurs had nine months living on credit cards and overdrafts before they sold their first smoothie.

| 42 |

Only five years later, though, Innocent had become Britain's leading brand of smoothie, selling about 40% of the 50 million downed annually by British drinkers. Eight years after that, Innocent employed 250 staff, were selling over 200 million smoothies per week around the world, and a majority stake in the company had been bought up by the international giant, Coca Cola. What was the recipe for this startling success?

| 43 |

Innocent's refusal to compromise on this point presented them with some problems when they first started talking to potential suppliers, Adam says. This was when they discovered the truth about the majority of so-called natural fruit drinks.

| 44 |

'Naïvety', adds Richard, who is always ready with a soundbite, 'can be a great asset in business because you challenge the status quo.' Although Innocent's drinks are fiendishly healthy, the company has always been very careful not to preach. 'Everyone knows what they're supposed to do,' says Richard. 'But people just don't, especially when they live in a city. We just thought, "Wouldn't it be great to make it easy to get hold of this natural fresh goodness?" Then at least you've got one healthy habit in a world of bad ones.'

| 45 |

'In essence,' explains Jon, 'we simply froze some of our smoothies and threw in a bit of egg to make it all stick together.' To help testers make up their minds about which combinations worked, they dusted off the old "yes" and "no" bins and put them out again. And once again their methods proved fruitful.

| 46 |

'We didn't rule it out completely,' says Richard. 'But the three of us have always gone away once every three months to talk about what we want out of the business and we've always been in the same place. So as long as we're excited and challenged and proud of the business, we're going to want to be a part of it.'

A Most are made from concentrated juice with water – and perhaps sweeteners, colours and preservatives – added. 'We didn't even know about that when we started,' Adam explains. 'It was when we started talking to people and they said, "OK, we'll use orange concentrate," and we said, "What's *concentrate*?" and they explained it and we said, "No, we want orange juice."'

B Probably something to do with pure, unadulterated ingredients with a dash of quirky advertising. As one campaign put it, their drinks are not made *from* fruit, they *are* fruit.

C 'We decided to keep it simple,' says Richard. We had a bin that said "yes" and a bin that said "no", and at the end of the weekend the "yes" bin was full of empty bottles. We quit our jobs the next day.'

D Their early years of success coincided with increasing consumer concerns about healthy eating, and Innocent soon became worth a lot of money to potential buyers. Was there ever a temptation in those early years to sell up and go and live on a desert island?

E They also seem to have managed to stay friends, and the fact that each member of the team brings a different and complementary set of skills to Innocent seems to have helped them avoid any big bust-ups over strategy.

F So, at another festival in 2004, the Innocent team tried extending their range of products into desserts. 'For us there was this problem of Sunday evenings, sitting down to watch a film with a big tub of ice cream – it's nice to munch through it, but very bad for you,' Richard adds.

G They found that the finances were the basic stumbling block. But they eventually had a lucky break when Maurice Pinto, a wealthy American businessman, decided to invest in them. In total, it took 15 months from the initial idea to taking the product to market.

Essential tips

▶ This part of the exam tests your understanding of how a text is organised and how paragraphs relate to each other. For example, a paragraph might give details about an idea mentioned previously, or it may present another side of an argument.

▶ Read through the text quickly to get a general idea of what it is about. Don't worry if there are words you don't understand.

▶ Look for links between the main text and the gapped paragraphs. The gapped paragraph may have links either to the paragraph before it or to the paragraph after it, or even to both.

▶ Look for theme and language links. For example:

• references to people, places and times;

• words or phrases that refer back or forward to another word, phrase or idea in the text. For example, if the first line of a paragraph says something like *This becomes clear when we look at ...* then *this* refers back to something expressed in the previous paragraph.

• linking devices such as *firstly, secondly, furthermore, on the other hand, however*. These will help you to find connections between paragraphs.

▶ When you have found a paragraph that may fill a gap, read the paragraph that comes before it and the one that comes after it to see that they fit together.

▶ Re-read the completed text and make sure it makes sense.

Question 41: The last sentence in the previous paragraph describes how Balon, Reed and Wright 'asked their customers for a verdict'. Which gapped paragraph describes how customers gave their opinion?

Question 43: The previous paragraph ends with the question *What was the recipe for this startling success?* Look for a gapped paragraph which seems to answer this question.

Question 44: The previous paragraph ends with the sentence. *This was when they discovered the truth about the majority of so-called 'natural fruit drinks'.* Look for a gapped paragraph which describes this 'truth'.

You are going to read a magazine article in which four people talk about careers involving foreign languages. For questions **47–56**, choose from the people (**A–D**).

Mark your answers **on the separate answer sheet**.

Which person

mentions being discouraged from studying languages?	47
expresses sympathy for those who find language learning difficult?	48
points out a common misconception about what it takes to learn a language?	49
enjoys the respect shown due to their language skills?	50
emphasises the impact learning a foreign language can have on mother-tongue use?	51
describes suffering embarrassment through ignorance of a language?	52
admits to having been unaware of their abilities?	53
mentions the excitement experienced when working with languages?	54
points out what language skills can indicate about someone's personality?	55
claims that a lack of career focus is common among language students?	56

Essential tips

▶ In this part of the exam, you are required to read several short texts to find specific information, which may include an opinion or the expression of an attitude.

▶ Read the instructions, the title and the questions.

▶ Skim through the texts quickly to get a general idea of what they are about. Don't worry if there are words you don't understand.

▶ Read each question again and make sure you understand what it is asking. Underline the key words in the questions (the words that show you what you should look for in the text).

▶ Scan the texts for ideas or words that relate to the question. Read the relevant parts of the texts carefully.

▶ Remember that the part of the text that gives the answer for each question will almost certainly not use the same words; instead, it will express the idea in a different way.

▶ All the texts are about the same topic, so similar points may be made in two or three texts. When you match a question with a text, make sure it reflects exactly what is in that text.

Question 47: The word *discouraged* is used in the question. Look for other words in the texts that express the same idea. Then check that the part of the text you find also expresses the idea of studying languages.

Question 48: Think of other words or phrases that express the same idea as *find language learning difficult*. Then scan the texts for references to this. Make sure the one you choose contains the idea that the writer expresses sympathy.

Question 49: If the statement is expressed in difficult language, you need to examine it carefully. What is meant by 'a common misconception'? '*Mis-*' refers to something wrong and *conception* means an idea, so 'a wrong idea'. Then think carefully about the meaning of 'what it takes to learn a language'. There may be more than one 'wrong idea' in the texts, and there may be more than one reference to learning languages.

Careers with foreign languages

A Jack Reynolds – interpreter in the UK

Most of my friends studied subjects like business or engineering, and I suspect they thought learning foreign languages was pointless, especially if your first language is English. That changed when I became the interpreter for a couple of Brazilian footballers who'd joined Manchester United. When my friends realised who I was spending time with, my coolness rating definitely shot up, which has been nice. I've always been interested in languages. I did French and Spanish at school and then added Portuguese at university. To be honest, I've never seen myself as a brilliant linguist – I was never the best in my class – but I've worked at it, and when I went to Brazil after university I decided to forget any shyness I might have, and immerse myself in the local culture. When I came back to the UK, I was good enough to qualify as an interpreter. Apart from the sports work, I interpret at conferences. That gets my adrenaline going more than being with the footballers, actually.

B Ana Ramirez – educational consultant

I did a degree in English and Russian at university in Spain. I enjoyed it but I'm ashamed to admit that I had no idea what I was going to do with it when I finished. I was by no means the only one from my course in that position, and there's a similar thing in other countries, from what I've seen. After a few false starts, I ended up working for a Europe-wide organisation which administers various educational projects. I travel around Europe and Russia a lot, so I get to practise my languages. Part of our brief is to promote language learning and I genuinely believe in it. Interestingly, one thing it's given me, apart from a job and the opportunity to meet people around the world, is a greater awareness of my strengths and weaknesses in Spanish. Unfortunately, I hear lots of people saying 'I'd like to have another language, but it's beyond my abilities.' The truth is, though, that anyone can learn a language. We all learn our mother tongue, after all. You just need the right conditions and attitude. I absolutely believe that.

C Helen Murdoch – IT project manager

I'm naturally curious and hate not understanding people, and that's what's always attracted me to languages. It works the other way round, too. When we're recruiting for a challenging IT project, I always think the candidates who are multilingual tend to be more adaptable and open-minded, which certainly helps us. I went to university in the 1980s, and in those days, languages were seen as no more than a 'nice-to-have'. When I told my father I'd decided to study French, he said, 'Are you sure? Wouldn't something more substantial be better?' So, I combined it with a management degree. With the increasingly competitive marketplace, I think that view's changed. My work has taken me to different countries, and helped me improve my French and pick up Arabic and Turkish, an opportunity not available to everyone sadly. I've seen at first-hand the difference that knowing a language can make. I once committed a major blunder in an office in Japan. Had I spoken Japanese, I would have known not to do it, and would have avoided a couple of very awkward days afterwards.

D Timo Heikkinen – student

I'm in my final year at university. I'm studying Chinese but I also speak English, Swedish, Russian, German and French, and Greek because my mum's half-Greek, and Finnish as I'm from Finland. I recently won a prize for achievement in learning languages. To be honest, I hadn't considered myself unusual because I've picked up languages from going to different countries with my parents who work for international companies. I realise now, however, that I do have a flair for languages; I've been told I even write well in Finnish and Greek. I'm not sure what I'll be doing next year. I've had a few offers but I'm not very decisive. Quite a lot of people I know are really good at their subjects – maths, physics or whatever – but languages defeat them and that seriously narrows their options. I'm glad I'm not in their shoes.

PAPER 1 Reading and
Use of English

PAPER 2 Writing

PAPER 3 Listening

PAPER 4 Speaking

Essential tips

▸ In Paper 2, you must answer two questions. The question in Part 1 is compulsory. In Part 2, there are three questions, and you have to answer one of them.

▸ In Part 1, you will be asked to write an essay for a particular purpose and target reader.

▸ Part 1 tests your ability to respond to the input material in an appropriate style, evaluating information, expressing opinions, etc. All tasks require you to be persuasive. Read the instructions carefully and underline the key words that tell you what you are being asked to do.

▸ The input information in Part 1 may be from a variety of different texts: notes, letters, reports, advertisements, diagrams, etc. Make sure you read it carefully and understand what information it conveys before you start writing.

▸ Think about the appropriate register for your writing: formal, semi-formal, neutral or informal.

▸ Don't try to write out your answer in a rough draft before you produce a final draft; you will not have enough time. Instead, plan what you will say in each section/ paragraph of your writing.

▸ Divide your writing into three sections: introduction, main body and conclusion. Think about what you will say in each part. Plan approximately how many words should be in each section of your writing.

▸ Write your essay. Use your own words as far as possible; don't copy the information from the input texts.

▸ When you have finished, check your spelling and punctuation. Make sure the examiner can read your writing.

▸ See the **Writing bank** on pages 193–205 for examples of different types of writing.

PAPER 1   Reading and
           Use of English

PAPER 2   Writing ▶   Part 1
                       Part 2
PAPER 3   Listening

PAPER 4   Speaking

You **must** answer this question. Write your answer in **220–260** words in an appropriate style on the separate answer sheet.

1   Your class has attended a lecture on what governments could do to minimise the use of fossil fuels. You have made the notes below.

> **Methods of minimising the use of fossil fuels**
>
> • recycling
> • increaing taxes on petrol
> • increasing use of nuclear energy

> **Some opinions expressed in the discussion:**
>
> 'Is the technology for recycling adequately developed?'
>
> 'Increased taxation will not be a sufficient deterrent.'
>
> 'Nuclear energy is too risky.'

Write an **essay** for your tutor discussing **two** of the methods in your notes. You should **explain which method you think is more important** for governments to consider, and provide reasons to support your opinion.

You may, if you wish, make use of the opinions expressed in the discussion, but you should use your own words as far as possible.

Essential tips

▶ When you write an essay, think about the appropriate register and tone for the question you are answering. Who is going to read your essay?

▶ In your essay, you must describe the general idea What information should you give? Is it necessary to mention who 'you' are in this essay?

▶ What is the reason for writing the essay? What effect do you want it to have on the reader? What do you hope to achieve by writing it? Do you want to convince the reader about anything? Think about the language you will need to achieve this goal.

▶ The notes and opinions provide you with information, and you can develop your own arguments around them.

PAPER 1 Reading and
Use of English

PAPER 2 Writing ▶ | Part 1 |

PAPER 3 Listening | **Part 2** |

PAPER 4 Speaking

Write an answer to **one** of the questions **2–4** in this part. Write your answer in **220–260** words in an appropriate style on the separate answer sheet. Put the question number in the box at the top of the page.

2 You would like to start a radio station at the college where you are a student. You have decided to send a proposal to the principal, asking for permission and practical assistance. Your proposal should include the following:
- why you think the radio station would be beneficial
- what sort of programmes you would begin with
- what sort of support, practical and financial, you would need.

Write your **proposal**.

3 You have seen the following blog in an online magazine for young people.

> I live in a small village and long to move into the city. I am 18 years old and have just left school. What are the good things about city life? What about the disadvantages? Would I be mad to leave my village, or would I be opening up great new opportunities?
>
> Paul

Write your **email** to Paul giving your views.

4 A British television channel is interested in making a documentary about public transport in different parts of the world. You have been asked to write a report for the channel, addressing the following questions.
- What means of public transport in your region are the most popular?
- What is being done to improve these facilities and encourage the use of public transport?
- What more could be done?

Write your **report**.

Essential tips

- In Part 2, you must choose one task. However, you should be familiar with all the possible types of text you might need to write.

- Read each question carefully. Before you choose a question, ask yourself if you know enough vocabulary on the subject and can employ it in the required register and text type.

- In Part 2 questions, you have more freedom to use your imagination and come up with information that is not in the input material.

  If you are writing a report or proposal, consider whether to use headings and bullet points or numbered lists.

Question 2
- What style would be appropriate for this proposal? Bear in mind that the proposal is written by a college student to the principal of the college.

- Consider your three sections: introduction, main body and conclusion. The introduction could state simply what you want, and the conclusion could repeat this request, perhaps with some extra force or promise of success. The words 'Introduction' and 'Conclusion' could also be headings. What will the main body contain? What will the heading(s) be?

- Don't worry about precise figures, for example, how much money would be needed to start the radio station. You are not expected to know this.

Question 3 : You are writing to a young person, so use a lively, informal style, bringing in anecdotes and advice related to your experience.

Question 4
- In order to answer this question, you must be familiar with the format of a report. You need to write clear paragraphs and use headings. You may also want to use other features such as bullet points or numbered lists.

- Remember that a report must have a clear introduction and conclusion as well. In your introduction, state what the report is about and who it is for. In your conclusion, summarise the information contained in your report. See the Writing bank on page 200.

- You need to include information about the public transport in your region. At the same time, your task is to produce a good piece of writing, so as long as the points you make sound reasonable, they do not all have to be factually correct. For instance, if you want to say that most people in your region travel to work by car, you could invent a survey that shows 25% of workers say they travel to work by car. It doesn't matter if this survey was never actually carried out.

- The question asks you to give your opinion about how the situation may change in the future. Therefore, you can use the first person to say what you think.

Essential tips

▶ Before you listen to each extract, you will be given time (15 seconds) to read the questions. Make good use of this time, and try to predict what you are going to hear.

▶ Listen carefully before choosing the answer. The options may contain words you hear on the recording, but the meaning of the sentence may be different!

▶ Some questions ask you about the speaker's feelings or attitude to something. Listen to the speaker's tone of voice and the way he/she speaks. It may be necessary to listen to the whole extract before making your choice.

Question 1: More than one option may seem possible here. Why did Nigel join the project?

Question 2: Listen carefully to Jenny's tone of voice.

Questions 3 and 4: Some of the vocabulary is specialised, but you can understand the meaning from the rest of the text.

Track 1

You will hear three different extracts. For questions **1–6**, choose the answer (**A**, **B** or **C**) which fits best according to what you hear. There are two questions for each extract.

Extract One

You hear two friends talking about an experience one of them had as a volunteer.

1 Nigel joined the Blue Ventures project because
   A a friend of his encouraged him to do volunteer work.
   B he had always dreamed of going to Madagascar.
   C he thought the experience would be useful to him.

2 Which word best describes Jenny's reaction to Nigel's account?
   A enthusiasm
   B disinterest
   C envy

Extract Two

You hear two students at law school talking about possible future jobs.

3 When Rich finishes his course, he
   A would like to work in commerce.
   B will join a top firm of solicitors.
   C intends to do postgraduate study.

4 Jenny will work in the area of
   A criminal law.
   B property law.
   C human rights law.

Extract Three

You hear two friends talking about a football match they have just watched.

5 Tracy thinks that England
   A deserved to lose.
   B were not confident enough.
   C were unfortunate.

6 According to Dave,
   A Gerrard was unfairly treated.
   B England played badly.
   C Russia didn't play well.

PAPER 1 Reading and
Use of English

PAPER 2 Writing

PAPER 3 Listening ▶
Part 1
Part 2
Part 3
Part 4

PAPER 4 Speaking

 Track 2

You will hear a writer talking about a book she has written on the subject of aspirin. For questions **7–14**, complete the sentences with a word or a short phrase.

THE STORY OF ASPIRIN

Doctors in (**7**) .... treated their patients with a
medicine derived from the bark of the willow.

Edward Stone believed that (**8**) .... was similar to
quinine.

The active ingredient of aspirin was isolated in (**9**) ....

Unfortunately, salicylic acid can affect the (**10**) ....
quite badly.

The first commercially available aspirins were made by Bayer, a
(**11**) ....

However, there was little (**12**) .... into the way aspirin
works for nearly 70 years.

Some scientists think that people over (**13**) .... should
take aspirin to prevent certain diseases.

It appears that (**14**) .... grown without artificial
chemicals also contain the active ingredients of aspirin.

Essential tips

▶ Read the instructions and find out the subject of the recording.

▶ Read the questions carefully and think about the sort of information you might need to complete the gaps.

▶ Each gap is completed by one, two or three words, or a number.

▶ Decide what grammatical form the gapped word or words should have.

▶ You will hear the words you need on the recording, but not in the same sentences as the questions. You need to listen for the ideas expressed on the recording.

▶ You will hear the recording twice, so you will have a chance to fill in any gaps you miss the first time.

Question 7: What sort of word could come after *in*: a time, a place, or an expression with the preposition *in*? Listen for any of these.

Question 10: The recording is about a medicine, and this sentence mentions an acid that can affect something or somebody quite badly. Who or what could this be?

Question 12: The sentence is about something that happened or lasted for nearly 70 years, so you should listen for information about this period. Also consider what could fit with the phrase 'into the way aspirin works'.

Question 14: The gapped word must describe something like a plant, which can be grown without artificial chemicals, so listen for a word with this meaning.

PAPER 1 Reading and
Use of English

PAPER 2 Writing

PAPER 3 Listening ▶
PAPER 4 Speaking

Part 1
Part 2
Part 3
Part 4

 Track 3

You will hear part of an interview with Stan Levin, a dance critic, about a modern ballet production involving animals. For questions **15–20**, choose the answer (**A, B, C** or **D**) which fits best according to what you hear.

Essential tips

This part of the exam is usually a multiple-choice task, but it could also be a sentence-completion task. If it is a sentence-completion task, look back at the tips for Parts 1 and 2. If it is a multiple-choice task, read the following tips.

▸ Read the instructions and find out the subject of the recording.

▸ Read the questions or question stems carefully and underline the key words.

▸ The questions follow the order of the recording, but the final question may be about the recording as a whole.

Question 15: Option A suggests most people, especially the critics, liked the ballet; option B implies some people liked it and some didn't; option C implies most people didn't like it; and option D implies that people who love animals liked the ballet. Which of these ideas does the recording convey?

Question 18: Think about different ways to express that something 'is of greatest interest to audiences'. You should also be prepared for the information to be given in a different order. For example, the speaker may describe something that happened and then say afterwards that it interested audiences.

Question 19: The question tells you that Stan will talk about something that went wrong when he saw the ballet. Which option best describes what happened?

15 We gather that the ballet being discussed here
   A   has received general critical acclaim.
   B   has caused considerable controversy.
   C   has not been well received on the whole.
   D   has become popular with animals-lovers.

16 It appears that the function of the dogs in the ballet is to
   A   reflect what happens to the human characters.
   B   act as a contrast to the human characters.
   C   show how wild animals behave in a civilised society.
   D   symbolise homeless people.

17 How does Stan feel about the increasing use of technology in dance?
   A   He thinks this trend has gone too far.
   B   He prefers more traditional approaches to dance.
   C   He does not approve of it in principle.
   D   He believes it is creating a new art form.

18 What aspect of the ballet is of greatest interest to audiences?
   A   the way the dogs behave during dance sequences
   B   the way the dogs perform their tricks
   C   the sight of the dogs in a pack
   D   the way the dogs copy the actions of one character

19 What caused the lapse in mood during the performance Stan saw?
   A   the inability of the dogs to concentrate
   B   the audience's unwillingness to accept the dogs
   C   the behaviour of a member of the audience
   D   the inability of dogs and humans to work as a team

20 What aspect of the performance made the most powerful impression on Stan?
   A   the implicit potential for violence
   B   the aggression shown by the dogs
   C   the bond between the dogs and the tramp
   D   the primitive appearance of the dogs

Essential tips

- Read the instructions and find out who will be talking and what they will be talking about.

- You have two tasks to think about at the same time, each relating to one type of statement made by the speakers. So the first time you hear each speaker, be prepared for a piece of information that corresponds to an option in the first task; the second time, listen for a piece of information that corresponds to an option in the second task.

- The answer options do not repeat what the speakers say; they express the ideas in different words. Read each option carefully, and be prepared to hear the information expressed in a different form.

- Each task has three options you do not need.

Questions 21–25
Option A: If something has a 'social function', what does it have? How might you express the idea that learning English has a social function?

Option B: What sort of jobs are 'sedentary' and what could be a problem for people working in these jobs?

Option F: What are some examples of 'high-level sporting events', and how are the competitors regarded in the community?

Option H: If this option is correct for one of the speakers, it must mean that the person had 'an injury'. What kinds of things can happen when people have an injury?

Questions 26–30
Option G: What ways are there to express that something is a 'commitment'? If you commit yourself to do something, what do you do or say?

Option H: How else could a speaker talk about 'genetic make-up'?

🎧 **Track 4**

You will hear five short extracts in which people talk about fitness and health.

While you listen, you must complete both tasks.

TASK ONE

For questions **21–25**, choose from list **A–H**, what each person says is his or her reason for attending a gym regularly.

A	The gym has a social function for me.	
		Speaker 1 — `21`
B	I have a sedentary job.	
		Speaker 2 — `22`
C	My company pays for me to attend a gym.	
		Speaker 3 — `23`
D	I'm studying sport science at college.	
		Speaker 4 — `24`
E	Being fit gives me a sense of achievement.	
		Speaker 5 — `25`
F	I compete in high-level sporting events.	
G	I come here with members of my cycling club.	
H	I started exercising regularly after an injury.	

TASK TWO

For questions **26–30**, choose from list **A–H** what opinion each speaker expresses about fitness and health, generally.

A	It is alarming that so many people have an unhealthy lifestyle.	
		Speaker 1 — `26`
B	Being good at sport commands respect.	
		Speaker 2 — `27`
C	I find it hard to commit myself to exercising.	
		Speaker 3 — `28`
D	Diet is as important as exercise.	
		Speaker 4 — `29`
E	Exercise machines are extremely boring.	
		Speaker 5 — `30`
F	Achieving health requires self-sacrifice.	
G	Exercise is necessary to keep weight under control.	
H	Genetic make-up has a lot to do with fitness.	

Essential tips

Part 1

▶ In this part of the exam, you must show that you can use English appropriately to interact with another person using general social language. You will be expected to answer questions about yourself: your family, home, interests, education and future plans.

▶ Make sure you answer the questions you have been asked and don't talk about something different.

▶ Don't try to prepare for this part of the exam by learning a prepared speech – the examiner may ask you something different.

Part 2

▶ In this part of the exam, you have to talk on a subject for about a minute. This is a long time when you have to talk in an exam. Make sure you practise talking for this length of time.

▶ The examiner could ask you to compare things, contrast them, identify them or speculate about them. He/She will give you three pictures and ask you to talk about them.

▶ In this part of the test, you are asked to compare and contrast the pictures, and to speculate about why someone is doing something, or what advantages something might have. Make sure you answer the two questions that you are asked.

▶ While the other candidate is talking, listen carefully. The examiner will ask you an extra question related to what the other candidate has been talking about.

Part 1 (2 minutes)

The examiner will ask you a few questions about yourself and about a general topic. For example, the examiner may ask you:

• Where are you from?
• What do you do here?
• What did you like most about the area where you grew up?

Part 2 (4 minutes)

You will each be asked to talk on your own for about a minute. You will each be given three different pictures to talk about. After your partner has finished speaking, you will be asked a brief question connected with your partner's photographs.

Costumes (compare, contrast and speculate)

Turn to pictures 1–3 on page 169 which show people in costumes.

(*Candidate A*), it's your turn first. Here are your pictures. They show **people in different costumes**.

I'd like you to compare **two** of the pictures and say **why these people are dressed in this way and how the people might be feeling**.

(*Candidate B*), **which of these costumes do you think is most comfortable? Why?**

Working environments (compare, contrast and speculate)

Turn to pictures 1–3 on page **170** which show different working environments.

Now, (*Candidate B*), here are your pictures. **They show different working environments**.

I'd like you to compare **two** of these workplaces, and say **what the advantages and disadvantages of working there might be**.

(*Candidate A*), **which of these environments would you prefer to work in? Why?**

Part 3 (4 minutes)

Look at page 171 which shows some things related to modern life.

Modern times (discuss, evaluate and select)

Here are some aspects of modern life and a question for you to discuss.

First, you have some time to look at the task.

(*Pause 15 seconds*)

Now talk to each other about **the advantages and disadvantages of each aspect of modern life**.

Now you have about a minute to decide **which two aspects best illustrate that modern life has both advantages and disadvantages**.

Part 4 (5 minutes)

The examiner will encourage you to develop the topic of your discussion in Part 3 by asking questions such as:

• Which aspects of life in the past, which no longer exist, do you think were positive? Could they be revived? (Why? / Why not?)

• Should developments in technology be restricted in any way? (Why? / Why not?)

• What sort of difficulties do young people face today, but that previous generations did not have to confront, or not to the same extent?

• Why do older people sometimes become nostalgic about the past?

PAPER 1 Reading and Use of English	Part 1
PAPER 2 Writing	Part 2
	Part 3
PAPER 3 Listening	Part 4
	Part 5
PAPER 4 Speaking	Part 6
	Part 7
	Part 8

For questions **1–8**, read the text below and decide which answer (**A**, **B**, **C** or **D**) best fits each gap. There is an example at the beginning (**0**).

Mark your answers **on the separate answer sheet**.

Example:

| 0 | **A** situation | **B** business | **C** function | **D** case |

| 0 | A | B | C | D |

Essential tips

▶ Read the title and the whole text quickly for general meaning.

▶ Remember – the gapped word may be part of an idiom, expression or phrasal verb. It may collocate with another word, or be part of a fixed phrase.

▶ If you do not know which option to choose, read out the sentence with each of the options in turn. Choose the option that sounds best in context.

▶ Check the clauses and phrases on each side of the gap to see whether the presence of a word here dictates the choice of a word for the gap.

Question 1: The words at the start of the sentence (*There's no getting away from it*) indicate the meaning of the word needed for the gap.

Question 3: Look at the whole sentence. In their research, scientists want satellite images to be as clear and accurate as possible. Which word expresses this idea?

Question 5: The options tell you that this is a phrasal verb with *make*. Which one means 'see' or 'detect'?

Question 7: This is a fixed phrase used to describe a way of learning something: you try something new and you learn something if it goes wrong.

Satellite archaeology

Archaeology is a messy (**0**) .... There's no getting away from it; digging holes in the ground is an (**1**) .... part of archaeological work. But there is a new way to search without a shovel. Satellite images are now used to (**2**) .... buried objects in landscapes with astonishing (**3**) .... In the same way that medical (**4**) .... let doctors examine parts of the body they couldn't otherwise see, satellite images help scientists find and map long-lost rivers, roads and cities, and make (**5**) .... archaeological features in places which are very difficult to survey from the ground. 'There's much we miss on the ground,' emphasises archaeologist Sarah Parcak, a (**6**) .... in using satellite imagery.

Through 'thousands of hours' of trial and (**7**) ...., Parcak has developed techniques using satellite imagery which allow her to detect (**8**) .... changes in the surface of the land caused by objects like bricks buried underground. In 2011, her team discovered evidence of hundreds of dwellings at the 3,000-year-old city of Tanis near the River Nile delta in Egypt. This might have taken a century using traditional methods.

1	**A** inflexible	**B** inevitable	**C** inclusive	**D** infallible
2	**A** disclose	**B** conceive	**C** define	**D** identify
3	**A** attention	**B** measurement	**C** precision	**D** adjustment
4	**A** scans	**B** looks	**C** regards	**D** sights
5	**A** through	**B** out	**C** for	**D** up
6	**A** creator	**B** principal	**C** chief	**D** pioneer
7	**A** failure	**B** mistake	**C** error	**D** fault
8	**A** subtle	**B** thin	**C** mild	**D** soft

For questions **9–16**, read the text below and think of the word which best fits each gap. Use only **one** word in each gap. There is an example at the beginning (**0**).

Write your answers **IN CAPITAL LETTERS on the separate answer sheet**.

Example: | 0 | O R D E R | | | | | | | | | | | | | | |

Essential tips

▸ Remember: the gapped words will probably not be complex or specialised words. Most of them will be structural items like articles, pronouns or prepositions. A few may form a part of common expressions, etc.

▸ Look at the whole sentence, or even bigger sections of the text, to see if the word you need is part of a longer or parallel structure. For example, you might need the word *other* in the expression *on the other hand*, which will be clear if you find *on one hand* in the previous sentence.

Question 12: The structure *as ... as* is often used with adjectives to compare two things that are the same. Can you think of an expression with *as ... as* that has the more abstract meaning of 'to the extent that'?

Question 14: This gap follows the word *insight*, which means 'understanding'. The preposition *of* usually follows *understanding*, but *insight* takes a different preposition.

Question 16: Read the whole sentence. The first part of the sentence must mean something like 'it seems that the Pirahã ...'.

Finding the right word

Do people need words in (**0**) .... to think? A study of a tribe living in the Amazon basin could provide the answer to this age-old question. The Pirahã tribe (**9**) .... be small – there are only about 200 members all told – (**10**) .... they exhibit a fascinating cultural peculiarity. These people have no words for numbers, (**11**) .... from *one*, *two* and *many*. What is more, their words for *one* and *two* are very similar. As (**12**) .... as anyone can tell, this tribe has never had (**13**) .... sort of vocabulary for numbers, but they appear to survive quite well without it.

Could these people perhaps supply an insight (**14**) .... the way our minds work? When asked to count some objects, they could not get beyond two or three before starting to make mistakes. This applies even to adults who appear intelligent in (**15**) .... other way.

So it looks (**16**) .... though the Pirahã are not very good at counting simply because they lack a vocabulary for numbers. This would suggest that human beings cannot think if they have no words to do so.

For questions **17–24**, read the text below. Use the word given in capitals at the end of some of the lines to form a word that fits in the gap **in the same line**. There is an example at the beginning (**0**).

Write your answers **IN CAPITAL LETTERS on the separate answer sheet**.

Example: | 0 | I | N | T | R | I | G | U | I | N | G | | | | | | | | |

Essential tips

Question 19: What part of speech do you need? A verb, noun, or an adjective or adverb? You need to read the whole paragraph in order to be sure of the meaning of this sentence. Does the missing word have a positive or negative meaning? Sometimes it is necessary to make two changes to a word, a prefix and a suffix.

Question 21: *Variable* means 'changeable'. However, the word you need here means 'always'. What part of speech do you need, and what changes do you need to make to *variable* in order to form the missing word?

Question 22: The adjective *new* indicates a noun is needed for the gap. Should it be singular or plural?

Question 23: What word could we use here to mean 'add new information to something'?

The jigsaw history puzzle

Of all the games in the world, the jigsaw puzzle must be among the most widely known. Yet its early history presents an (**0**) …….. puzzle of its own.

INTRIGUE

Officially, the jigsaw puzzle (**17**) …….. in England, and its (**18**) …….. was John Spilsbury, a London engraver and map maker. It is also an apparently (**19**) …….. fact that in 1767 Spilsbury created a puzzle, (**20**) …….. known as a 'dissected map', by mounting one of his maps on a piece of hardwood and cutting around the borders of the countries. His puzzles came to be used in schools to help children learn geography.

ORIGIN
INVENT
DISPUTE
INITIAL

However, as is almost (**21**) …….. the case with inventions, some doubts have been raised about whether Spilsbury's puzzle was the first. This was an age of exploration, and new (**22**) …….. demanded that maps be constantly (**23**) …….. . There is some evidence that two Dutch map makers produced map puzzles ten years before Spilsbury. The evidence is (**24**) …….., however, and advertising for their dissected maps only appears in 1779.

VARIABLE

DISCOVER
DATE

CONCLUDE

PAPER 1	Reading and ▶	Part 1
	Use of English	Part 2
PAPER 2	Writing	Part 3
		Part 4
PAPER 3	Listening	Part 5
		Part 6
PAPER 4	Speaking	Part 7
		Part 8

Essential tips

Question 26: You need a phrasal verb here which means 'think of something'. Be careful. Do you need a two-part or three-part phrasal verb?

Question 27: You need to make two changes to the second sentence. First, you need a causative structure because someone else is decorating the room, not us. Secondly, think about the word you have been given. It is part of an expression that means 'decorated'.

Question 30: Think about the word order here. Certain negative structures at the start of a sentence are followed by inversion.

For questions **25–30**, complete the second sentence so that it has a similar meaning to the first sentence, using the word given. **Do not change the word given.** You must use between **three** and **six** words, including the word given. Here is an example (**0**).

Example:

0   Jane regretted speaking so rudely to the old lady.

   MORE

   Jane .... politely to the old lady.

Example: | **0** | WISHED SHE HAD SPOKEN MORE |

Write **only** the missing words **IN CAPITAL LETTERS on the separate answer sheet**.

---

25   'Do your homework first, and then you can go to the cinema,' said Jamie's mother.

   LONG

   Jamie's mother agreed to let him go to the cinema .... his homework first.

26   Harry thought of throwing a surprise party for Katie's birthday.

   CAME

   Harry .... of throwing a surprise party for Katie's birthday.

27   They are decorating our living room, so the house is a mess.

   DONE

   We are ...., so the house is a mess!

28   I really hate it when people speak to me like that!

   BEING

   I really object .... like that!

29   I was just about to call him when he rang me instead.

   POINT

   I was .... when he rang me instead.

30   The manager gave her secretary strict instructions that no one should be allowed to disturb her.

   CIRCUMSTANCES

   'Under .... to be disturbed!' the manager told her secretary.

PAPER 1 Reading and Use of English ▶	Part 1
	Part 2
PAPER 2 Writing	Part 3
	Part 4
PAPER 3 Listening	**Part 5**
PAPER 4 Speaking	Part 6
	Part 7
	Part 8

You are going to read a magazine article. For questions **31–36**, choose the answer (**A, B, C** or **D**) which you think fits best according to the text.

Mark your answers **on the separate answer sheet**.

The Cinderella story

The basic story is very old indeed and familiar to most of us. The heroine, Cinderella, is treated cruelly by her stepmother and mocked by her two ugly stepsisters. Even though her father loves her, she can't tell him how unhappy she is because her stepmother has bewitched him. One day, Cinderella's stepmother and stepsisters are invited to a ball at the royal palace. Cinderella is told she cannot go and is understandably very unhappy. However, her fairy godmother comes to the rescue and, waving her magic wand, produces some beautiful clothes for Cinderella, as well as a carriage to convey her to the ball. There, she dances with the handsome prince, who falls in love with her, not only because she is beautiful but also because she is good and gracious. Cinderella has been warned that the magic will wear off at midnight, so when the clock strikes 12, she hurries away, leaving behind a glass slipper. Next day, the prince, smitten by her charms, comes looking for the girl whose foot fits the glass slipper. He finds Cinderella and they marry amid general rejoicing.

Just a sweet, pretty tale? Not in the view of Ellen Macintosh, who has written extensively about fairy tales. 'This story features the stock, two-dimensional characters of most fairy tales, and little character development is attempted,' she says. Indeed, although her comment does make one wonder why simplicity of this sort should be out of place in a story for children. Be that as it may, Ellen's main problem is with what the story implies. 'Instead of standing up to her cruel stepmother and absurd stepsisters, Cinderella just waits for a fairy godmother to appear and solve her problems. But wouldn't you want a daughter of yours to show more spirit?'

The story is enduring, whatever its shortcomings, and it doesn't take much in the way of analytical skills to see its influence on a number of recent Hollywood productions, all aimed at girls aged five to 15. In these versions for the silver screen, the Cinderella character no longer has to clean the house and has no siblings to make her life a misery, though she persists in not showing much backbone. The character of the rich and handsome stranger, however, is retained, and in some cases really is a prince. The role of the fairy godmother is often played by coincidence or sheer luck. We live in an enlightened age when even very young children might reject the notion of fairies. The wicked stepmother may be transformed into a villain of some sort. In the majority of film versions, the heroine has a profession and is even permitted to continue working after marrying her prince – this is the 21st century, after all.

Doesn't the success of these films indicate that the story has relevance to children even today? 'Yes,' admits Ellen, who sees its message as being rooted in a fundamental childhood desire for love and attention. 'Most children experience a sense of inner loneliness as they are growing up and empathise with the protagonist who faces some sort of test or challenge. This can be seen in the original story of Cinderella, where the fairy godmother tells the heroine that she must learn to be gracious and confident if she is to go to the ball. She has to grow spiritually, and by maturing, she becomes attractive to the prince, thus ensuring that the ending of the story will be happy. 'In the later versions, this element is missing,' says Ellen, 'and the theme of the story is simply that a girl's role in life is to be more beautiful than other little girls so that she can carry off the prize: the handsome prince. Is this really what we want girls to grow up believing?'

▶ Remember – in this part of the exam, you need to understand the details of a text, as well as the writer's opinion, attitude and purpose.

▶ You can approach this part in two slightly different ways. However, you should begin by reading the instructions and the title of the text. Then you can either skim the text first before you read the questions, or read the questions first before you skim the text.

▶ There will be six questions or question stems. Read each question carefully and, without looking at the options, scan the text for the answer or for a suitable and accurate way to complete the question stem.

▶ Think about the meaning of what you read, and only then see if you can match the relevant section of the text with one of the options.

▶ The correct option is unlikely to use the same words as the text to express an idea.

Question 31: You are being asked about the writer's view, not Ellen MacIntosh's. Look for a section of the text where the writer describes Ellen's ideas and then gives her opinion of these ideas.

Question 33: This question is about films based on the Cinderella story. Look in the text for the word *film* or any other word which means the same thing, for example, *movie*. When you find the relevant section of the text, read it carefully. Then, see which option corresponds precisely to what the text says.

Question 36: Even though you may be nervous and in a hurry, you must think carefully about the meaning of the questions. Which word in the question stem shows you are being asked to find a *difference* between the original story and the modern version?

31 What does the writer imply about fairy tales in the second paragraph?
   A   Fully developed characters would improve them.
   B   The stories lines are very straightforward.
   C   It is unrealistic to expect character development.
   D   It is a mistake to consider them sweet and pretty.

32 What is Ellen's primary objection to the Cinderella story?
   A   The heroine is treated cruelly.
   B   The heroine is not assertive enough.
   C   The ugly stepsisters are figures of ridicule.
   D   The stepmother is not a convincing character.

33 Modern film adaptations of the story tend to present a Cinderella
   A   whose character remains basically unchanged.
   B   who is luckier than she is in the original story.
   C   whose circumstances are unusual.
   D   that many children might find unconvincing.

34 Modern variants on the story generally
   A   portray Cinderella as a successful professional.
   B   imply that Cinderella will become a real princess.
   C   reflect children's beliefs.
   D   make concessions to modern women's lives.

35 In Ellen's view, what makes the Cinderella story so appealing?
   A   Children can identify with the heroine.
   B   Little girls enjoy being challenged.
   C   It has an element of magic.
   D   Cinderella is more beautiful than other girls.

36 Unlike the original tale, modern versions of the Cinderella story
   A   suggest that girls do not need strength of character.
   B   do not require the heroine to develop.
   C   underestimate the power of love.
   D   are aimed solely at young children.

PAPER 1 Reading and ▸   Part 1
        Use of English   Part 2
PAPER 2 Writing   Part 3
                  Part 4
PAPER 3 Listening   Part 5
                  Part 6
PAPER 4 Speaking   Part 7
                  Part 8

You are going to read four reviews of a book about the connection between music and the brain. For questions **37–40**, choose from the reviews **A–D**. The reviews may be chosen more than once.

Mark your answers **on the separate answer sheet**.

This is your brain on music: the science of a human obsession by Daniel Levitin

Four reviewers comment on Daniel Levitin's book about the neuroscience of music.

A

Scientific analysis of difficult concepts regarding how music works and the psychological processes involved in our interactions with it is something few of us are comfortable with, but in trying to keep things simple for a non-specialist audience, as far as technical terms are concerned, Levitin too often ends up dumbing down. A number of small errors obvious to a knowledgeable musician – like the tonic pitch of a scale being referred to as the *root*, when only chords have roots – fuel this sense of irritation. It's a fascinating subject, however, made more so by Levitin's decision to explain it against the background of his own intriguing narrative. A successful rock musician for many years, he switched careers and became a professor of psychology and music. This background shows in his sensitive choice of familiar tunes and songs that he uses to illustrate concepts and theories.

B

We can all enjoy music, yet the theory of it can seem excessively complex, and you'd think the study of its effect on the brain even more so. The success of this book, by a musician and record producer turned neuroscientist, is both that it goes out of its way to make the general reader feel at ease, and that it celebrates our extraordinary capacity for analysing and understanding music. Consider the job the brain has to do in separating and processing even, say, the sound of a cat's purr over a refrigerator's hum, merely by analysing the way that various air molecules cause the eardrum to vibrate. Then go and listen to your favourite piece of orchestral music or even pop music. Levitin's anecdotes about famous musicians he has met and played with are worth passing over, but the rest of this excellent introduction will leave your brain buzzing.

C

Setting jargon aside in favour of everyday terminology, Levitin gives readers enough background to understand what to listen for in music and to connect what they hear to his science. Having been a musician and producer in the music industry before turning to science, Levitin knows about communication, and wisely weaves in stories about music making and working with musicians to make the science easier to relate to. The bulk of the music Levitin talks about, however, is pop. Classical music, or modern music in that tradition, is sometimes referred to in patronising terms, but for the researcher interested in the achievements of the brain, one might think that classical music's larger structures and more complex achievements would provoke greater interest. It is also disappointing to come across flawed accounts of certain aspects of musical acoustics and music theory. But overall, this book is an admirable contribution to popular science.

D

It is to Levitin's credit that this book contains clear, well-informed explanations of a range of musical phenomena and their underlying psychological processes. It should be stimulating and accessible to the non-specialist. His attempt to make the science easier to grasp by regular reference to his own career in music – as a musician, producer and neuroscientist – is well intentioned, but there are times when we could do with fewer funny stories and more attention to detail. This is more than just a stylistic point. There are misleading descriptions of significant research work, for example. The choice of music to illustrate his arguments is refreshingly free of high-art bias but it draws so strongly on Levitin's own musical preferences that some readers who do not share his musical tastes may feel lost. Despite my misgivings, however, Levitin's efforts to show a lay audience how music is at the centre of human experience and evolution are to be applauded.

Which reviewer

has a similar view to reviewer C regarding Levitin's
selection of musical examples?

| 37 | |

takes a different view to the others about the accuracy
of the book's content?

| 38 | |

shares reviewer D's opinion about the extent to which
Levitin includes information about himself?

| 39 | |

has a different opinion from the others regarding the
suitability of the writing style for the target readers?

| 40 | |

Essential tips

▶ Remember – in this part of the exam, you have to decide
whether four different writers have similar or different
opinions and attitudes about a particular subject.

▶ Read the title and the texts quickly for general
understanding.

▶ Highlight the key words in each question.

▶ Read the first text and highlight the sections that are
relevant to each question. Remember to write the
question numbers in the relevant places. Do the same for
each text.

▶ Then look across the four texts and compare the sections
that refer to each question in turn. Read the opinions
carefully and decide which ones are similar and which
are different.

Question 37: The key words in this question are *similar
views to reviewer* C and *selection of musical examples*. The
section of text C referring to 'musical examples' is: *The bulk
of the music Levitin talks about, however, is pop. Classical
music, or modern music in that tradition, is sometimes
referred to in patronising terms, but ... one might think that
its larger structures and more complex achievements would
provoke greater interest and even richer evidence.* This
implies that the reviewer thinks the selection is too limited.
Reviewer A refers to a *sensitive choice of familiar tunes and
songs which he uses to illustrate concepts and theories*,
which is very different from the criticism suggested in C.
Look for what reviewers B and D say about the musical
selection and decide which is similar to reviewer C's
opinion.

Question 38: The key words here are: *different view to
the others* and *accuracy of ... content*. Reviewer A refers
to *a number of small errors obvious to a knowledgeable
musician*. Reviewer B refers to a subject which is
excessively complex but makes no reference to any errors.
So, A and B have different views on the issue of accuracy.
Look carefully at texts C and D, and decide whether they
share reviewer A or reviewer B's view on this.

PAPER 1 Reading and ▶ | Part 1
Use of English | Part 2
PAPER 2 Writing | Part 3
| Part 4
PAPER 3 Listening | Part 5
| Part 6
PAPER 4 Speaking | **Part 7**
| Part 8

You are going to read a magazine article. Six paragraphs have been removed from the article. Choose from the paragraphs **A–G** the one which fits each gap (**41–46**). There is one extra paragraph which you do not need to use.

Mark your answers **on the separate answer sheet**.

Mind your languages

Thousands of the world's languages are dying, taking to the grave not just words but records of civilisations and cultures that we may never fully know or understand. Linguists have calculated that of the 6,000 languages currently spoken worldwide most will disappear over the next 100 years. As many as 1,000 languages have died in the past 400 years. Conversely, the handful of major international languages are forging ahead.

41

But the vast majority of the world never had need of phrases in *Heiltsuk*, a Native Indian language from British Columbia in Canada, which is now dead. Nor will most people be interested in learning any of the 800 languages spoken on the island of Papua New Guinea, many of which are threatened. Frederik Kortlandt, from Leiden University in Holland, is one of several linguists around the world who are determined to document as many of the world's remaining endangered languages as possible.

42

Periodically, linguists and other interested parties meet to discuss their work. One such conference held in Nepal focused on the issue of how to save some Himalayan languages spoken by just a handful of people. A great number of languages in the greater Himalayan region are endangered or have already reached the point of no return.

43

The trouble is, such materials often do not exist. Kortlandt knows a language is disappearing when the younger generation does not use it any more. When a language is spoken by fewer than 40 people, he calculates that it will die out. Occasionally, however,

researchers get lucky. *Kamassian*, a language from the Upper Yenisey region of Russia, was supposed to have died out, until two old women who still spoke it turned up at a conference in Tallinn, Estonia in the early 1970s.

44

'Would you ask this to a biologist looking for disappearing species?' Kortlandt asks. 'Why should languages, the mouthpiece of threatened cultures, be less interesting than unknown species? Language is the defining characteristic of the human species. These people say things to each other which are very different from the things we say, and think very different thoughts, which are often incomprehensible to us.'

45

Take, for example, the vast potential for modern medicine that lies within tropical rainforests. For centuries, forest tribes have known about the healing properties of certain plants, but it is only recently that the outside world has discovered that the rainforests hold potential cures for some of the world's major diseases. All this knowledge could be lost if the tribes and their languages die out without being documented.

46

We will only be able to find them and benefit from their properties through one or more of the 300 languages and dialects spoken on the islands. If the languages die, so too will the medicinal knowledge of naturally occurring tonics, rubs and potions. Science could be left wondering what we might have found.

A This is one of the things worrying linguists working in Fiji in the South Pacific. There are hundreds of known remedies in Fiji's forests. The guava leaf relieves diarrhoea, the udi tree eases sore throats, and hibiscus leaf tea is used by expectant mothers. There are possibly several more yet to be discovered.

B 'I accept this,' says Kortlandt, 'but at the very least, we can record as much as we can of these endangered languages before they die out altogether. Such an undertaking naturally requires support from international organisations.' But what progress is being in this respect?

C Kortlandt elaborates further: 'If you want to understand the human species, you have to take the full range of human thought into consideration. The disappearance of a language means the disappearance of a culture. It is not only words that disappear, but also knowledge about many things.'

D To non-linguists while particular stories like this can be fascinating, it must seem odd to get worked up about the broader issue. Why waste so much time saving languages spoken by so few? Why look back instead of forward?

E For example, Chinese is now spoken by 1,000 million people and English by 350 million. Spanish is spoken by 250 million people and growing fast.

F 'There are about 200 languages spoken in this area, but only a few have been properly described,' says Kortlandt. The problem is it can take years to document a language. 'We are generally happy when we have a group of texts we can read and understand with the help of a reliable grammar and dictionary.'

G This often means trekking to some of the most inaccessible parts of the Earth and can require consummate diplomacy in dealing with remote tribes, some of which may be meeting outsiders for the first time and may be wary of strangers asking for so much information about their language.

Essential tips

▶ Remember – in this part of the exam you need to understand the structure and organisation of a text (how its paragraphs work together). First look at the instructions and the title of the text. Then skim the gapped text for the general meaning and notice how it develops ideas, opinions or events.

▶ You may need to consider more than one gap at a time in order to work out which paragraph goes where. Do not rely simply on recognising repeated names, dates, etc.

Question 41: In the paragraph after the gap, the word *But* shows that a contrast is being described. It is likely that the contrast is between the extinct or threatened languages referred to and the *major international languages* mentioned in the paragraph before the gap.

Question 43: The paragraph before the gap refers to *the greater Himalayan region*. Is there a gapped paragraph which, using different words, refers to a region?

Also, the paragraph after the gap begins with a reference back to 'such materials'. Can you find anything about 'materials' in any of the gapped paragraphs?

Question 44: The paragraph after the gap begins with Kortlandt referring to something that has been asked. Can you find a gapped paragraph with a question in it? Check carefully that it fits the gap.

You are going to read an article in which four people talk about hobbies that turned into careers. For questions **47–56**, choose from the people (**A–D**).

Mark your answers **on the separate answer sheet**.

In which section of the article are the following mentioned?

an enhanced appreciation of other people's work	**47**
thoughts about the future	**48**
the financial necessity for engaging in other ventures as well	**49**
encouragement from a family member	**50**
advice from a specialist	**51**
the value of assessing one's abilities objectively	**52**
identifying potential customers	**53**
an impulsive decision	**54**
a feeling of apprehension about making a major change	**55**
academic qualifications which were never used	**56**

Essential tips

▶ You should begin by reading the instructions and the title of the text. Then you can either skim the text first before you read the questions, or read the questions first before you skim the text. Experiment and see which way works better for you.

▶ Don't waste time reading the text in detail. You only need to match specific information in the text with the questions.

Question 49: Some questions use language which you will need to think about carefully. Here, for example, the question is about the need to do other jobs to make money, but this simple idea is expressed formally. The reverse may also occur: the question may express an idea in simple language but the text will use more formal language.

Question 54: An *impulsive decision* is one taken suddenly without any planning. Which person does this fit best?

Question 55: *Apprehension* means feeling anxious or nervous. The person who experienced this feeling is unlikely to have used exactly these words, but, using other words, they will have described their nervousness before a change.

Turning a hobby into a career

It may seem idealistic or risky to exchange one's regular job for the uncertainty of earning your living from a hobby – but more and more people are attempting to do just that.

A I had piano lessons when I was young, and I did have some talent. But it became obvious I'd never be good enough for a career on the stage. In a way, I was lucky. If I hadn't realised that early on, I probably would have carried on dreaming that my big break would come. As it is, I became a music teacher instead, and in my free time I started to dabble in the technical side of music production. Then an aunt died, leaving me some cash, and I set up my own recording studio! Of course, there is a downside to turning a hobby into a career. I love my job so much that I used to work seven days a week, but after a while, I realised you need to switch off occasionally. My job has definitely added depth to the way I listen to music; now I can really understand why someone's using a certain technique or piece of equipment.

B I studied medicine, but when I finished medical school, I had a sort of crisis. I knew I couldn't go on with it! I'd have been an awful doctor. But I was keen on amateur dramatics and I enjoyed putting on plays at the local youth centre. So I started wondering if I could make a living from teaching drama. A friend suggested I should offer acting lessons for children. It was tricky and at first, I couldn't work out how to find people who would pay for their children to attend the kind of courses I wanted to run. Then someone at an organisation called Business Link, which helps people set up their own businesses, suggested advertising on the internet! I was contacted by a surprising number of interested people and five years down the line, I'm still doing all right. The classes themselves aren't terribly lucrative, but I supplement my income by giving talks to amateur dramatics societies and writing articles for magazines.

C When I left college, I started working in a bank, but my heart was never really in it. The problem was partly the environment: I don't like working in an office. I'm more of an outdoor person – and I'd always been crazy about surfing. One summer while I was on holiday, I got chatting to the owner of a surf shop. It turned out he was good friends with a cousin of mine. He said he wanted to sell up and I jumped at the chance to buy the business from him! Looking back, I can see how lucky I was. It's incredibly difficult to set up a shop like that from scratch. Besides, being an avid surfer myself, I assumed a lot of other people must share that interest – which isn't the case! It took me a while to realise how naive I was. Now that I've learnt the ropes, I'm considering either expanding – more shops, managers and so on – or diversifying, perhaps producing my own surf boards! The second option is more likely because it interests me a lot.

D I wanted to study graphic design when I left school, but I didn't have good enough grades. So I got a job in a garage instead and for the next 10 years, I worked as a car mechanic. But while I was working, I did some evening courses in industrial design. I even built a car of my own from spare parts. Then I got the idea of building a bike – a four-wheel delivery bike – and the next thing I knew, my wife was urging me to set up my own company! I had to take a very deep breath before I finally took the plunge. I'd done my best to prepare for it, taking a course in Business Management in my spare time, and I knew I'd be working longer hours for less money, at least at first. The big difficulty was the uncertainty of not knowing how much would be coming in each month. And things were pretty tough for the first few years – looking back, I can see that I underestimated the amount of paperwork I'd have to do – but I've never regretted it.

Essential tips

▶ In Paper 2, you must answer two questions, so it is essential to use your time effectively. This does not mean you should start writing at once and write as much as you can! You must take the time to prepare before you begin writing.

▶ Make sure you understand the instructions. Read the question several times, underlining the key words that describe your task.

▶ Think about the register of your writing: should it be formal or informal? What layout is appropriate?

▶ Writing Part 2 tasks will include an email or a letter, a proposal, a report, or a review. Your answer for Part 2 must be between 220 and 260 words.

▶ The input for Part 2 questions is much shorter than that for Part 1. You must use the information given, but also use your imagination intelligently to come up with more information. You will need to spend time preparing your answer, as for Part 1.

▶ In Part 2, you must answer one question, so think carefully about the task that you feel most comfortable with. Are you confident you know which register to use and if a particular format or layout is necessary? Do you have a good range of vocabulary relevant to this task? Can you express clear views on the subject (if the question requires you to do so)?

▶ You don't need to write a rough draft – there isn't time for that. Make a plan or an outline instead.

▶ Your writing should normally have three sections: an introduction, the main body and a conclusion. Note down approximately how many words should be in each section.

▶ Note down a few words or phrases to remind yourself what you must say in each section.

▶ Take a few minutes to look at your plan and make sure the information flows well. If it doesn't, you can still change your mind and put something in the conclusion instead of the main body, for instance.

▶ See the Writing bank on page 193–205 for examples of different types of writing and sample answers.

PAPER 1 Reading and
          Use of English

PAPER 2 Writing ▶ **Part 1**
                     Part 2

PAPER 3 Listening

PAPER 4 Speaking

You **must** answer this question. Write your answer in **220–260** words in an appropriate style on the separate answer sheet.

---

1 Your class has attended a lecture on what governments could do to minimise the use of cars in the city centre. You have made the notes below.

> **Methods of reducing use of cars in town:**
>
> - restrict parking
> - cheaper public transport
> - congestion charges

> **Some opinions expressed in the seminar:**
>
> 'People would park illegally.'
>
> 'Travelling by public transport is slow and not suitable for everyone.'
>
> 'It would be expensive to administer congestion charges.'

Write an **essay** for your tutor discussing **two** of the methods in your notes. You should **explain which method you think is better** for the local government to consider, and provide reasons to support your opinion.

You may, if you wish, make use of the opinions expressed in the discussion, but you should use your own words as far as possible.

Essential tips

▶ You could consider the issue from two or more viewpoints, e.g. economic (green), or political (popularity with the townspeople). You could argue for a compromise or come down strongly in favour of one position . Assemble the points you want to make and state them clearly and concisely. Your essay should be thought-provoking and persuasive.

PAPER 1 Reading and
Use of English

PAPER 2 Writing ▶ Part 1

PAPER 3 Listening   Part 2

PAPER 4 Speaking

Essential tips

Question 2

▶ What style would be
appropriate for this report?
Bear in mind that the report
is written for an international
organisation.

▶ When writing a report, you
need to give your paragraphs
headings. Use the details
of the question to help you
organise your answer into
paragraphs with suitable
headings. This will help you
focus on what information
you need to include.

▶ Try to use examples from
your own experience, if
possible.

Question 3

▶ You are writing to a company,
so use a formal, appropriate
style. Remember to answer
each point in the instructions.

Question 4

▶ Begin by giving a general
description of what you are
reviewing. Remember that
the reader may not have
experienced this book or film.
Then, give your opinions on
the film or book. Remember
to phrase these as opinions,
not as facts.

Write an answer to **one** of the questions **2–4** in this part. Write your answer in
220–260 words in an appropriate style on the separate answer sheet. Put the
question number in the box at the top of the page.

2   Read this extract from a letter you received from an international youth
organisation.

> We are conducting a survey on the importance of regional culture to
> young people around the world. Please write a report on this survey,
> describing how young people in your region feel about the history
> and culture of that region, and how you think this may change in the
> future.

Write your **report**.

3   You recently returned from a holiday abroad. On the flight out, the aircraft was
delayed and you missed your onward connection. Your luggage was taken to
the wrong destination and not returned to you for two days. Write a letter to the
airline describing how your holiday was affected. Say how you feel about their
service, and ask for compensation.

Write your **letter**.

4   A website that specialises in film reviews has asked you to write a review of
the film version of a book you have read, comparing the film to the book. You
should comment on the portrayal of the characters, the development of the
main themes, and whether you think the film is as good as the book or not. Give
reasons for your opinions.

Write your **review**.

Essential tips

Question 2: Read the options carefully during the pause before you hear the recording. Then listen to the speaker talking about doing Tai Chi. What does she say takes years of practice?

Question 3: Read the question stem carefully. What information do you have to focus on?

Question 6: All the options may appear possible, but listen carefully to what the speaker actually realised.

🎧 **Track 5**

You will hear three different extracts. For questions **1–6**, choose the answer (**A**, **B** or **C**) which fits best according to what you hear. There are two questions for each extract.

Extract One

You hear part of an interview with a Tai Chi instructor.

1   According to Ruth, Tai Chi
    A   needs to be performed indoors.
    B   is a series of exercises.
    C   represents a way of life.

2   One of the most difficult things about learning Tai Chi is
    A   that you have to do it out of doors.
    B   achieving harmony between your movements.
    C   remembering the complex dance sequences.

Extract Two

You hear two people discussing taking a year off before going to university.

3   Before going to work in China, the man had not expected the job to be
    A   rewarding.
    B   easy.
    C   boring.

4   The woman's experience made her realise that
    A   marketing was a difficult career for women.
    B   working in a hotel was very challenging.
    C   she had made the wrong choice of career.

Extract Three

You hear part of an interview with an illusionist.

5   Daniel's interest in magic arose from his
    A   ambition to become an entertainer.
    B   desire to impress someone.
    C   trips to the cinema as a boy.

6   According to Daniel, one similarity between magic and film-making is
    A   the debt they owe to technology.
    B   the disbelief they arouse in the audience.
    C   the power they have over the audience.

🎧 **Track 6**

You will hear a writer talking about a biography he has written. For questions **7–14**, complete the sentences with a word or a short phrase.

AN INTERESTING CHARACTER

The speaker has written a book about (**7**) ....
                                                    called Robert Tewbridge.

Tewbridge's father was a (**8**) .... in Scotland.

Tewbridge's parents wanted him to become (**9**) ....

Tewbridge earned his living by writing (**10**) ....
                                                        for various publications.

The speaker learnt a great deal about Tewbridge's character
                    from studying his (**11**) ....

It appears that Tewbridge and his (**12**) ....
                                                        were close friends.

Tewbridge spent many years studying (**13**) ....

He lived in (**14**) .... for the last 30 years of his life.

Essential tips

▶ As with all listening tasks, make the best use of the time you are given before you hear the recording. Read the instructions carefully, look at the title and the questions, and imagine what the recording might say.

▶ Remember: you will hear the words you need but not in the same context as the question. Note, however, that you can answer a question with a synonym, or paraphrase an idea, as long as the synonym or paraphrase completes the question appropriately.

▶ Bear in mind the question after the one you are trying to answer, so if you miss the information you need, you can move on to the next question.

Question 7: The word or words you need must describe the person's occupation or role. This sort of information might be given at the beginning of the talk, so make sure you are listening carefully from the very start of the recording!

Question 10: From the context you can guess that the speaker will mention a profession. You might try to imagine which professions a farmer and his wife might aspire to for their son.

Question 11: The speaker will say that he studied something, but remember that another way to say that you did something is to imagine what would have happened if you had not done it.

Question 14: There are many phrases with *in* which might fit here, such as *in luxury*, but that is unlikely. Probably the word you need will be the name of a place. The text may use a different structure, so you might not hear the preposition *in*.

Track 7

You will hear part of an interview with Betsy Boom, owner of a chain of fashion shops. For questions **15–20**, choose the answer (**A**, **B**, **C** or **D**) which fits best according to what you hear.

15 What aspect of shopping does Betsy enjoy most?
  A   experimenting with different styles
  B   finding a bargain
  C   comparing items in different shops
  D   being given advice

16 What does she dislike about expensive clothes shops?
  A   There isn't a wide selection of goods.
  B   The assistants are unfriendly.
  C   Customers are ignored.
  D   Customers are expected to spend a lot of money.

17 When people first went into one of Betsy's shops, they often felt
  A   flattered.
  B   amused.
  C   awkward.
  D   dizzy.

18 The members of staff in Betsy's shop
  A   were offended at the demands Betsy made.
  B   found it hard to adjust to the new surroundings.
  C   disliked dealing with shy and difficult customers.
  D   came to enjoy the atmosphere after a while.

19 What is the most rewarding aspect of the business for Betsy?
  A   seeing customers overcome their inhibitions
  B   proving to others that her idea was a good one
  C   watching the staff relax in their new roles
  D   being able to provide fashionable clothes at low prices

20 What does Betsy feel is the danger she faces now?
  A   becoming complacent
  B   growing arrogant
  C   being afraid to try something new
  D   suffering financially if fashions change

Essential tips

▶ Prepare for what you will hear on the recording: read the instructions and think about the subject. Consider who the speakers will be.

▶ Remember: you will not hear the exact words of the question in the recording, so concentrate on the ideas expressed.

▶ The questions follow the order of the recording, but the final question may be about the recording as a whole.

Question 16: The question refers to Betsy's feelings about expensive shops. If you hear one of the words in the options, check that Betsy is using it to talk about expensive clothes shops.

Question 17: To prepare for this question, think how you would explain the feelings in the options. In the recording you will hear one of these feelings expressed in different words.

Question 19: How might Betsy express *most rewarding* in other words? Now think about the meaning of the options. What does *overcome their inhibitions* in option A mean, for example?

PAPER 1 Reading and
         Use of English

PAPER 2 Writing

PAPER 3 Listening ▶
                              Part 1
                              Part 2
PAPER 4 Speaking   Part 3
                              Part 4

🎧 **Track 8**

You will hear five short extracts in which people talk about environmental issues in the workplace.

While you listen, you must complete both tasks.

TASK ONE

For questions **21–25**, choose from list **A–H**, the person who is speaking.

A a public health officer	
	Speaker 1 **21**
B a sales representative	
	Speaker 2 **22**
C the company manager	
	Speaker 3 **23**
D a company's customer	
	Speaker 4 **24**
E a careers advice officer	
	Speaker 5 **25**
F a marketing executive	
G an environmental activist	
H an office cleaner	

Essential tips

▶ Read the instructions carefully. Look at the options for Task One, and consider what each person's job entails before you attempt this task.

▶ Aim to complete Task One the first time you listen, and Task Two the second time. Then check that you feel happy with your choices for Task One. On listening the second time, you may notice something you missed the first time.

Question 22: Listen carefully to what the speaker says. She mentions helping 'university students'. Who might she be?

Question 24: The speaker says that 'Here at Head Office, we show our employees exactly how much energy can be saved by adopting particular practices.' Who would be likely to talk about the company and its staff in this way?

Question 26: Listen to everything the speaker says before making your choice. What point does he make about workers' awareness?

Question 29: The speaker talks about how the company goes further than simply imposing new regulations at work. What do they do?

TASK TWO

For questions **26–30**, choose from list **A–H** what view each speaker is expressing.

A Consumers should put more pressure on companies to adopt environmental schemes.	
	Speaker 1 **26**
B Few companies prioritise conservation.	
	Speaker 2 **27**
C We should be more optimistic about what companies are doing about the environment.	
	Speaker 3 **28**
D Few office workers realise how much they could do to conserve energy.	
	Speaker 4 **29**
E Companies need to explain environmental initiatives to their employees.	
	Speaker 5 **30**
F Young people don't buy from companies without sound environmental policies.	
G The provision of incentives will encourage staff to adopt company schemes.	
H Young job seekers demand a work environment that reflects their values.	

PAPER 1 Reading and
           Use of English

PAPER 2 Writing

PAPER 3 Listening

PAPER 4 Speaking

Essential tips

Part 3

▶ In this part of the exam, you and the other candidate have to work together to perform a task, such as exchanging ideas or reaching a decision.

▶ Listen carefully to the examiner's instructions.

▶ You have to talk for two minutes, so it is important that you really discuss the issue. You must ask your partner about his/her views and not only give your own.

▶ There is no right or wrong answer. The only important thing is to exchange ideas and express your opinions. However, don't try too hard to persuade your partner. It is acceptable if you each come to different conclusions.

Part 4

▶ In this part of the exam, you will be asked to discuss topics related to the task in Part 3. The focus is on expressing your opinions and agreeing/disagreeing.

▶ Make sure you don't just give one-word responses to the examiner's questions. Include expressions like 'In my opinion', 'It seems to me' or 'I'm not sure that I agree'.

▶ You should listen carefully to your partner because the examiner will ask you if you agree, or have another opinion.

Part 1 (2 minutes)

The examiner will ask you a few questions about yourself and about a general topic. For example, the examiner may ask you:

• What kind of outdoor activities do you enjoy?
• Which sports are popular in your region?
• Which sports do you enjoy watching and playing, and which do you find boring?

Part 2 (4 minutes)

You will each be asked to talk on your own for about a minute. You will each be given three different pictures to talk about. After your partner has finished speaking, you will be asked a brief question connected with your partner's photographs.

> **Anticipation** (compare, contrast and speculate)

Turn to pictures 1–3 on page 172 which show people waiting for something. (*Candidate A*), it's your turn first. Here are your pictures. They show **people anticipating something**.

I'd like you to compare and contrast **two** of the pictures and say **what these people could be anticipating that makes them look this way. How do you think they are feeling?**

(*Candidate B*), **which person do you think is the most nervous? Why?**

> **Being alone** (compare, contrast and speculate)

Turn to pictures 1–3 on page **173** which show people spending time alone.

Now, (*Candidate B*), here are your pictures. **They show people alone.**

I'd like you to compare and contrast **two** of these pictures, and say **why the people are alone, and how you think they are feeling.**

(*Candidate A*), **in which picture do you think the person is least able to cope with being alone? Why?**

Part 3 (4 minutes)

Look at page 174 which shows some situations where people need motivation.

> **Motivation** (discuss, evaluate and select)

Here are some situations where people need motivation and a question for you to discuss.

First, you have some time to look at the task.

(*Pause 15 seconds*)

Now talk to each other about **why people need motivation in these situations.**

Now you have about a minute to decide **which situation needs the most motivation.**

Part 4 (5 minutes)

The examiner will encourage you to develop the topic of your discussion in Part 3 by asking questions such as:

• When do you think it is important for people to be motivated? Are there any times when being motivated is undesirable?
• It is often said that motivation is important in education. Do you agree? (Why? / Why not?)
• What factors motivate people to achieve something?
• How can people motivate themselves?

PAPER 1	Reading and ▶	Part 1
	Use of English	Part 2
PAPER 2	Writing	Part 3
		Part 4
PAPER 3	Listening	Part 5
PAPER 4	Speaking	Part 6
		Part 7
		Part 8

For questions **1–8**, read the text below and decide which answer (**A**, **B**, **C** or **D**) best fits each gap. There is an example at the beginning (**0**).

Mark your answers **on the separate answer sheet**.

Example:

0 **A** bothered **B** feared **C** cared **D** wondered

| 0 | A | B | C | D |

Essential tips

Question 3: The word *sighting* after the gap refers to someone having seen one of these insects. For others to know about the sighting, it must have been written down. Which word best fits the idea of it being written down?

Question 7: The word after the gap, *up*, tells you that this is a phrasal verb. The idea here is recruiting or getting people to help.

Question 8: This is an example of collocation. Which verb is normally used with *a part* to mean 'helped' or 'participated'?

Citizen scientists

Experts (**0**) .... that the nine-spotted ladybug, or ladybird as it is known in some countries, was becoming extinct. Then, in 2011, Peter Priolo, a volunteer ladybug hunter, (**1**) .... one sitting on a sunflower in New York. The ladybug population had once been so (**2**) .... in the state of New York that it was the 'official state insect', but the last (**3**) .... sighting of one had been almost 30 years before. Priolo was thrilled. So was the Lost Ladybug Project, which studies different species of North American ladybugs with the assistance of ordinary people, a (**4**) .... known as 'crowdsourcing'. One reason for the ladybug's (**5**) .... may be that other imported insects have (**6**) .... its habitat and are eating its food.

'In future, crowdsourcing may help us stop this happening,' says the project's director, John Losey from Cornell University.

(**7**) .... up ordinary citizens isn't new to science. Amateur astronomers, weather watchers, and other hobbyists going back to the 1700s have all (**8**) .... a part in the development of science. What's different today is the internet, which has helped recruit hundreds of thousands of volunteers over the past decade or so.

1	**A** regarded	**B** glanced	**C** observed	**D** considered
2	**A** widespread	**B** thorough	**C** overall	**D** comprehensive
3	**A** accounted	**B** recorded	**C** marked	**D** entered
4	**A** ritual	**B** habit	**C** manner	**D** practice
5	**A** recession	**B** drop	**C** decline	**D** letdown
6	**A** interfered	**B** invaded	**C** interrupted	**D** involved
7	**A** Signing	**B** Drawing	**C** Bringing	**D** Meeting
8	**A** put	**B** done	**C** added	**D** played

PAPER 1	Reading and Use of English	Part 1
		Part 2
PAPER 2	Writing	Part 3
		Part 4
PAPER 3	Listening	Part 5
		Part 6
PAPER 4	Speaking	Part 7
		Part 8

Essential tips

Question 9: If you look at the whole sentence, you will see that professional builders and members of the public are being grouped together. Can you think of a structure to join the two elements?

Question 13: Can you think of a phrase that means 'generally'?

Question 15: This is a fixed phrase. Both *on* and *lookout* are part of this phrase, which means 'looking for'. Which word is needed to complete it?

For questions **9–16**, read the text below and think of the word which best fits each gap. Use only **one** word in each gap. There is an example at the beginning (**0**).

Write your answers **IN CAPITAL LETTERS on the separate answer sheet.**

Example: 0 | W | H | O | | | | | | | | | | | | | | | | | | |

Second-hand but better than new

Many people (**0**) …….. are building their own homes or renovating existing buildings these days prefer to buy certain things like doors and fireplaces second-hand. A lot of businesses will supply second-hand materials, (**9**) …….. only to professional builders, but also to ordinary members of the public. People wishing to indulge (**10**) …….. a spot of DIY will be able to find reclamation material, (**11**) …….. second-hand building supplies are known, if they are prepared to look for it, in most parts of the country.

Searching for second-hand goods can be time-consuming, of course, so (**12**) …….. bother? Well, on the (**13**) ……..**,** it makes good financial sense. A second-hand oak door in good condition will be considerably cheaper than a new one, even (**14**) …….. it is only a few years old. Many people, however, are on (**15**) …….. lookout for very old items, ones which can be hundreds of years old. (**16**) …….. articles as these will be expensive, of course, but many are ready to pay high prices for genuine antiques.

PAPER 1 Reading and ▸ Part 1
         Use of English   Part 2
                           Part 3
PAPER 2 Writing   Part 4
PAPER 3 Listening   Part 5
PAPER 4 Speaking   Part 6
                          Part 7
                          Part 8

For questions **17–24**, read the text below. Use the word given in capitals at the end of some of the lines to form a word that fits in the gap **in the same line**. There is an example at the beginning (**0**).

Write your answers **IN CAPITAL LETTERS on the separate answer sheet**.

Example: | 0 | P | O | P | U | L | A | R | I | T | Y | | | | | | | | |

Essential tips

Question 17: The gapped word comes before an adjective. What part of speech do you need?

Question 19: The gapped word is an adjective. Does it have a positive or negative meaning?

Question 21: The gapped word follows an article, so it must be a noun. How do you make a noun from *grow*?

Product placement

The rise in the (**0**) …….. of product placement has been	**POPULAR**
one of the most interesting trends in advertising in the	
last couple of decades. Branded products are promoted	
indirectly by using them in films, and the success of this	
is making it (**17**) …….. desirable. Demand for product	**INCREASE**
placement stemmed, at least (**18**) …….., from regulations	**ORIGIN**
banning the advertising of certain products deemed	
(**19**) …….. for TV commercials. Films are not subject to	**SUIT**
the same sort of (**20**) …….. as television.	**CENSOR**

Other factors have contributed to the (**21**) …….. of product	**GROW**
placement. One is these is the (**22**) …….. of consumers, exposed	**TEND**
to an advertisement over a period of time, to become more	
(**23**) …….. in their response to it. They become tired of 'the	**CRITIC**
same old thing' and advertisers are being forced to recognise	
a (**24**) …….. in their customers which did not exist in the past.	**SOPHISTICATED**
People these days are more likely to be influenced by watching	
film star role models using a product. This is true of consumers	
in general, but it is particularly applicable to younger people.	

Essential tips

Question 26: Two structural changes are needed here. First, *The wishes of the residents* is now the subject of the sentence so a passive structure is needed. Secondly, a phrase including *into* is required which means the same as 'consider'. Can you think of one?

Question 27: You need a phrase with *placed*. What word can be used with *place* to mean that something is someone's fault?

Question 28: You need a phrasal verb which means 'regret saying something'.

For questions **25–30**, complete the second sentence so that it has a similar meaning to the first sentence, using the word given. **Do not change the word given**. You must use between **three** and **six** words, including the word given. Here is an example (**0**).

Example:

0 Jane regretted speaking so rudely to the old lady.

MORE

Jane .... politely to the old lady.

Example: | **0** | WISHED SHE HAD SPOKEN MORE |

Write **only** the missing words **IN CAPITAL LETTERS on the separate answer sheet**.

---

25 Although he studies hard, Christoph never does well in his exams.

MATTER

Christoph never does well in his exams, ... he studies.

26 The town council rarely seem to consider the wishes of the residents.

INTO

The wishes of the residents rarely .... by the town council.

27 John's mum said it was his own fault the party was ruined.

PLACED

John's mum .... for the party being ruined.

28 I'm sorry I said that your new hat looked like a lampshade.

BACK

I .... about your new hat looking like a lampshade.

29 There were a lot of people at the resort, but Mandy still had a great time.

FACT

Mandy had a great time at the resort .... crowded.

30 'You left my MP3 player on the bus, Joe!' shouted Olivier.

ACCUSED

Olivier .... MP3 player on the bus.

PAPER 1 Reading and ▶   Part 1
         Use of English   Part 2
PAPER 2 Writing   Part 3
                            Part 4
PAPER 3 Listening   **Part 5**
                            Part 6
PAPER 4 Speaking   Part 7
                            Part 8

You are going to read a review of a book. For questions **31–36**, choose the answer (**A**, **B**, **C** or **D**) which you think fits best according to the text.

Mark your answers **on the separate answer sheet**.

Book review: Jesse Prinz's *Beyond Human Nature*

Jesse Prinz's book *Beyond Human Nature: How Culture and Experience Shape the Human Mind* is a valuable exploration of the age-old 'nature or nuture' debate – whether individual human beings are the product of the genetic features they are born with or of what they experience as they grow up. The book is also firmly part of what we might call the 'neuro-backlash'. In the last decade or so, a host of accessible books have appeared which are fun and provocative, and supplied startling messages about psychology and neuroscience that promised to empower us by decoding the inner workings of human life. But it was really only a matter of time before the re-evaluation of this popular science writing took off.

The controversy over the work of the American journalist Jonah Lehrer only accelerated the widespread reaction. The discovery that, in writing his celebrated books and magazine pieces on neuroscience, Lehrer had been a bit too careless with his facts, quotes, arguments, and conclusions gave way to cries that the simplification of science, in particular of neuroscience, often by science journalists, was once again to blame. The truth is, though, this trend was due to run out of steam. Even some of the best of these books — and there are certainly many worthwhile ones — have begun to seem formulaic.

With any luck, we will now get more books like Jesse Prinz's. While too many of the popular neuroscience authors write as though they are angling for more high-profile speaking work, Prinz is clearly only interested in trying to leave his mark on the nature-versus-nurture debate. Obviously, as Prinz says, we are shaped by both nature and nurture. But while Steven Pinker's influential book, *The Blank Slate,* provides a compelling defence for 'team nature', Prinz identifies himself as an unashamed 'nurturist'.

As such, he is committed to demonstrating that our interactions with our environment — our upbringing, early experiences, culture — have a lot more to do with the way we think, learn language, acquire knowledge, and make moral judgments than anything we are born with. This position has real implications for such big issues as the influence of genetics on intelligence and the effect of biology on gender inequality. And while it might not seem an exciting approach in the manner we have come to expect from recent popular cognitive science books, in the academic world today, it is a minority view—and in terms of certain established theories, very controversial.

Take the debate about language. For years, the field of linguistics has been heavily influenced by Noam Chomsky's notion of a *universal grammar*. Kids might learn a particular language from experience, Chomsky and his followers say, but they are drawing on a set of pre-programmed grammatical rules that we are all born with. It's why, even at a very young age, we are able to create an impressive array of unique, grammatically correct sentences. It's also a prime example of a 'nature' rather than 'nurture' argument.

Prinz takes us through the research that has been done, meticulously examining the logic behind the conclusions of Chomsky and his supporters, and suggests a different explanation. He defends a lesser-known theory that 'children might learn language statistically,' by unconsciously remembering the patterns in the sentences they hear and 'using these to generalise to new cases.' Instead of going for the hard sell, Prinz admits that all he hopes to do is raise the possibility that this alternative theory might be true. This lends his work an air of maturity.

This book should be seen as a notable example of science writing done right. Before discussing the role of genes in the manifestation of different traits, for instance, Prinz spends several pages explaining what genes are, how they work, and how we should think about them. We also get a useful walk through intellectual history as he shows how the nature/nurture pendulum has swung back and forth over thousands of years, and how Prinz's particular approach to these issues descends directly from the 18th-century philosopher David Hume. Although the author seems to want to win the argument, he's generous when it comes to providing evidence for the opposing side – making sure that readers will finish the book with a more thorough understanding of some major debates in science.

▶ Remember – in this part of the exam you need to understand the writer's opinion, attitude and purpose in a text. You also need to understand details of a text – not just what it says but also how it is organised and how different parts of the text relate to each other.

▶ Either skim read the text first before you read the questions, or read the questions first before you skim the text.

▶ Then read the questions carefully. There should be something in each question to help you locate which part of the text it is about. For example, Question 31 here refers to the first paragraph; Question 32 here mentions 'Johan Lehrer's work' and it should be easy to find Johan Lehrer in the second paragraph.

Question 31: This is an example of a question focusing on understanding the organisation of the text. The inverted commas around *neuro-backlash* and the options indicate that these phrases are in the text. It may help you to underline or highlight them in the text. If you do not know what this word means, look in the text for clues to help you. For example, the word *neuroscience* comes halfway through the third sentence. Secondly, what can the word *back* mean? Think about the meaning of *go back* or *give back*. Is this sense of *back* suggested in any of the options? The read the first paragraph carefully and think about how it is organised.

Question 33: This question focuses on understanding a different kind of detail – the attitude expressed by the writer

31 What does the 'neuro-backlash' in the first paragraph refer to?
   A   a host of accessible books
   B   the inner workings of human life
   C   a new vocabulary of buzz words
   D   the re-evaluation of this popular science writing

32 According to the reviewer, the discovery of problems in Jonah Lehrer's work
   A   stemmed from a wider access to information about science.
   B   triggered a new way of thinking about neuroscience.
   C   confirmed a shift in many people's opinions.
   D   led to exaggerated criticism of him.

33 In which of these phrases from the third paragraph does the writer express disapproval?
   A   'angling for high-profile speaking work'
   B   'trying to leave his mark'
   C   'provides a compelling defence'
   D   'identifies himself as an unashamed 'nurturist'

34 The reviewer refers to 'Chomsky's notion of a universal grammar' as an example of
   A   a big issue
   B   an exciting approach
   C   a minority view
   D   an established theory

35 What view of Prinz's work does the reviewer express in the sixth paragraph?
   A   He shows appropriate caution in putting forward his own ideas.
   B   He spends too much time challenging other people's work.
   C   His explanation of difficult concepts is very clear.
   D   His analysis goes into too much detail at times.

36 What point does the reviewer make in the final paragraph?
   A   The book reveals new information about the issues it covers.
   B   Certain theories have always gone in and out of fashion.
   C   The views Prinz puts forward are rather old-fashioned.
   D   Science writers should consider their readers more.

in his choice of certain words. Questions like this may well include vocabulary you do not know (e.g. *angling, leave his mark, compelling, unashamed*). To find out the attitude expressed in a word, you should read the text around each phrase (you should do this even if you think you know the word). For example, you may not know

unashamed nurturist in option D, but there is an explanation of the word *nurture* earlier in the text, so you should be able to work out what a *nurturist* is. Then, consider what the writer says about Prinz elsewhere in the text and whether he is likely to describe him with a word that expresses *disapproval*.

PAPER 1 Reading and
         Use of English
PAPER 2 Writing
PAPER 3 Listening
PAPER 4 Speaking

Part 1
Part 2
Part 3
Part 4
Part 5
Part 6
Part 7
Part 8

You are going to read four contributions to a debate about whether economic growth is always a good thing. For questions **37–40**, choose from the contributions **A–D**. The contributions may be chosen more than once.

Mark your answers **on the separate answer sheet**.

Economic growth and prosperity

Will more economic growth deliver prosperity and well-being? Or, with natural resources running out and the threat of climate change, should developed countries abandon the idea of endless growth? Four economists give their views.

A

In the advanced economies of the world, there is mounting evidence that ever-increasing consumption adds little to human well-being. In fact, increasing stress levels, obesity and other social ills suggest it positively impedes it. More urgently, it is now clear that the ecosystems which sustain our economies are collapsing under the impact of this consumption. Economists argue that the environmental impact of an economy, relative to its income, falls as it gets richer – wealthier nations tend to have stricter environmental regulations, for example. There is no alternative but to opt out of further growth. However, the bottom line is that economic growth inevitably leads to increases in greenhouse gas emissions, which accelerates climate change. The implications are complex but include a need to fundamentally rethink the uses to which we put our technological expertise and much tighter regulation of advertising, which incites wholly superfluous consumption.

B

It has become received wisdom that prosperity and economic growth do not go together. More 'stuff', we are told, damages the environment and makes us miserable. Hence, we should limit growth, raise taxes to redistribute affluence, invest in welfare rather than wealth creation, and control or even eliminate commercial advertising, a key trigger of consumption. Frankly, it is tragic that growth has such a bad name. In the space of about two centuries, substantial increases in economic output have brought enormous benefits: longer, healthier lives, shorter working hours, miraculous inventions, the ability to reshape the environment for our own benefit and, surely, greater general well-being. The world is not perfect, of course, and climate change is an issue. But to tackle it, we need more resources and technology, rather than less. We should invest in high-tech energy production, sea walls to resist flooding and other engineering-based solutions, rather than cheap moralising.

C

Economic progress has brought huge benefits for humanity, but in some countries, we appear to have reached the stage where the costs of growth have started to outweigh the benefits. The more we have, the less satisfied we are, and we are running up against natural limits on a finite planet as resources are depleted, biodiversity falls sharply and climate change threatens to destroy us. Should we now give up on economic progress and focus instead on well-being and protecting the planet? While the idea has a certain utopian appeal, the reality for the majority is unimaginable. Even wholesale reform of aspects of modern economies like advertising, the cheerleader for consumerism, is unlikely to be accepted. There is a middle way: to pursue, determinedly, existing environmental policies and to apply our technological expertise to overcome our difficulties, with massive projects to harness solar, wind and wave power, for example.

D

The world is heading for catastrophic climate change, and life in some of the world's most technologically advanced nations, while abounding in consumer products, has evidently not been enhanced in terms of personal relationships, meaningful work and other key values for well-being – indeed, it's quite the opposite. So, should the growth model be dropped? In *The Moral Consequences of Economic Growth*, Benjamin Friedman convincingly argues that rising standards of material prosperity foster opportunity, tolerance, fairness and democracy, and to give up on growth is unlikely to lead to the sort of open, friendly society we want. The way forward, then, is to tackle excessive consumerism and its associated ills by various reforms, such as greater control of advertising, and to strengthen measures to keep global warming and resource depletion within reasonable limits, while the world economy carries on growing.

Which writer

has a different view to the others about continuing to aim for economic growth?

`37`

expresses a different opinion from the others on the link between continued economic growth and happiness?

`38`

takes a similar view to writer B's opinion about economic growth and the use of technology?

`39`

shares writer A's opinion about what the consequences of economic growth imply for advertising?

`40`

Essential tips

▶ Remember that you need to decide whether four different writers have similar or different views on the same subject.

▶ Go through each text carefully in turn, highlighting the sections relating to each question. Write the question numbers next to the parts you highlight.

▶ Starting with Question 37, compare the views expressed in all four texts.

Question 37: The key words in this question are *different view from the others* and *about continuing to aim for economic growth*. Writer A says: *There is no alternative but to opt out of further growth.* Writer B says *it is tragic that growth has such a bad name* and calls for *more resources and better technology rather than less*, so B appears to be in favour of continued economic growth. Look carefully at texts C and D, and decide whether they share A or B's view.

Question 39: The key words here are: *similar view to writer B's* and *economic growth and the use of technology*. Writer B says: *we need more resources and technology rather than less. We should invest in high–tech energy production, sea walls to resist flooding and other engineering-based solutions.*

Writer A says we need *to fundamentally rethink the uses to which we put our technological expertise,* and talks about *superfluous consumption* so writer A's view on this issue seems different from B's. What about writers C and D?

PAPER 1 Reading and ▶
         Use of English

PAPER 2 Writing

PAPER 3 Listening

PAPER 4 Speaking

Part 1
Part 2
Part 3
Part 4
Part 5
Part 6
Part 7
Part 8

You are going to read a magazine article. Six paragraphs have been removed from the article. Choose from the paragraphs **A–G** the one which fits each gap (**41–46**). There is one extra paragraph which you do not need to use.

Mark your answers **on the separate answer sheet**.

The lost civilisations of Peru

An expedition in the mountainous regions of southern Peru has found some important remains from the Inca civilisation. Their discovery came when the expedition stumbled across a small, flat area cut into a forested mountainside. At first, it looked like nothing in particular, but then the explorers realised it could have been a platform where Inca priests stood and watched the path of the sun.

41

Qoriwayrachina, as the site they discovered is known, is of outstanding importance. In fact, it became clear that this was one of the most significant historical finds in South America since the unearthing of Machu Picchu, the fabulous lost city of the Incas, in the 20th century.

42

For example, recent archaeological work near the Peruvian capital has revealed another ancient city, dating back to well before the Incas. This has reinforced the feelings of many archaeologists that there are many more hidden remains buried for hundreds (or even thousands) of years, still waiting to be found.

43

But it is the mountains of the Vilcabamba range that perhaps hold the most promise. Vilcabamba, which means 'sacred valley', was the hub of the vast Inca civilisation. In the 16th century, when the Spanish conquest led to the demise of this ancient way of life, this area was the last part of the Inca empire to fall. Hundreds of years later, it slowly began to yield its secrets to archaeologists, Macchu Picchu perhaps being the most notable of a series of impressive finds. By no means everything there has been unearthed, however.

44

Knowing that there is more to be found is important, because although many valuable Inca sites have been discovered and researched, we still know surprisingly little about the Inca way of life. What's more, studying remains will be of great value, as many are in danger of being ruined forever, either by thieves on the hunt for ancient treasure, or by modern developments such as the building of roads or new towns.

45

It is not all action-man excitement, however. The best explorers spend time reading the accounts of the Spanish conquerors, studying maps and talking to local people who know their own area and are often willing to reveal the whereabouts of previously unidentified remains. Raising funds to pay for the work is also part of the challenge.

46

Peter Frost, one of the group which discovered Qoriwayrachina, knows this. As a tour guide, photographer, and travel writer working in the region for 30 years (though not an archaeologist), he has become an expert on the Incas. Since his initial work at Qoriwayrachina, he has led two lengthy expeditions to the area, and has uncovered the ruins of 200 structures and storehouses, an intricately engineered aqueduct, colourful pottery and several tombs, all valuable evidence for the study of the region's past.

A Far from it. Archaeologists know from having found traces of homes and infrastructure, that there are several potentially major sites still waiting for proper investigation.

B The importance of this kind of preparation is underlined by Hugh Thompson in his recent book about exploring for Inca ruins, *The White Rock*. According to him, anyone can go into the jungle and look for ancient remains. However, they may cause a great deal of damage in the process and indeed, the history of Peruvian exploration is littered with failures.

C According to these experts, what we now know as Peru has hosted advanced civilisations for as long as almost anywhere else in the world. The likelihood, therefore, of making further discoveries almost anywhere in the country, is high.

D These worries mean it is fortunate that the urge to discover ruins swallowed by the jungle is still as strong as ever. Many archaeologists feel a keen sense of adventure, seeing themselves in an Indiana Jones fantasy, hunting for lost

civilisations. The thought of finding a lost city, hidden by the jungle for hundreds of years, and containing unimaginable treasures from a mysterious people is, for some, difficult to resist.

E The previous year, 1989, saw a number of expeditions to the region in search of the mythical lost city, but the end result was similarly disappointing. Undeterred, the courageous explorer refuses to abandon his attempts to raise money for one last try.

F But that staggering discovery took place over 100 years ago, and so many explorers, archaeologists and tourists have been in the region since then that one might assume all its secrets have been surrendered. But the mountains of Peru are still full of hidden ruins, as are other parts of the country.

G So, a decision was made to battle on through the thick jungle. Their reward was to uncover significant evidence of the civilisation that once lived there: tombs, a water system, and traces of many other buildings.

Essential tips

Question 42: The last sentence of the previous paragraph mentions a discovery made in a particular period. Which gapped paragraph has a time reference which might relate to this?

Question 44: The last sentence of the previous paragraph contains a negative structure which emphasises that not all the ancient remains have been discovered (*By no means everything*

has been unearthed, however.) Which gapped paragraph starts by agreeing with this idea?

Question 46: The previous paragraph describes things explorers do before they go on expeditions. Which gapped paragraph refers to this?

PAPER 1 Reading and ▸
          Use of English

PAPER 2 Writing

PAPER 3 Listening

PAPER 4 Speaking

Part 1
Part 2
Part 3
Part 4
Part 5
Part 6
Part 7
Part 8

You are going to read an article in which four people talk about volunteering in science laboratories. For questions **47–56**, choose from the people (**A–D**).

Mark your answers **on the separate answer sheet**.

Which student

gained an awareness of how frustrating scientific work can be?	**47**
gained in confidence as a result of the work experience?	**48**
particularly valued the opportunity to discuss ideas with professional scientists?	**49**
experienced difficulties in understanding scientific ideas?	**50**
was impressed by the way their volunteer work resembled a real job?	**51**
realised the importance of choosing an area of personal interest for voluntary work?	**52**
discovered something of immediate practical benefit in their research?	**53**
believes it is wise to volunteer in areas of science that are well-publicised?	**54**
made the most of a personal misfortune?	**55**
made a discovery that contradicted expectations?	**56**

Essential tips

Question 47: When people say that work is 'frustrating', they mean that they are not making the progress they had hoped for. Which student describes a situation like this?

Question 51: All four students volunteered in order to gain experience of work, but which of the four specifically mentions the similarities with 'a real job'?

Question 53: All four students carried out research that would probably be of benefit in some way. But which research led to a discovery with 'immediate' and 'practical' consequences?

Volunteering in science laboratories

A Eric Martens

A talented athlete, Eric Martens trained so hard in his final year at school that he sustained knee injuries, which kept him off the track for months. Rather than becoming discouraged, however, Eric turned to science and landed a voluntary stint in a sports research unit in his summer holidays. 'There are people there who are particularly interested in how human joints develop and function,' says Eric. 'It was brilliant being able to ask them about their work – and challenge it sometimes.' Eric assisted on a number of projects, and eventually was allowed to conduct an experiment himself. Barefoot jogging has become fashionable among some amateur runners. Eric observed a number of experienced joggers running barefoot on treadmills and found that that they still ran as if they were wearing shoes, landing heel-first rather than on the balls of their feet. The impact sustained could easily lead to injury. The implications for runners were obvious and the findings were soon made known more widely. 'It was a great experience,' says Eric. 'I'm definitely thinking of going into research when I finish university.'

B Angela Michaelis

In her final year at school, Angela Michaelis had become fascinated by human behaviour. So, she emailed various people involved in brain research and was eventually offered a placement with a well-known psychologist called Carmen Gago. With Dr Gago's help, Angela wound up investigating trust and turned to a group of people for whom trust is crucial – skydiving instructors. Angela assumed that learners would base the degree of trust they placed in an instructor on levels of experience and perhaps appearance. What novices reported, though, was that it mainly related to the way the instructors talked. 'Dr Gago was impressed,' says Angela. 'And I was pleased because the whole thing was a real challenge. We made several false starts. One skydiving group agreed to take part and then pulled out. Then we had trouble recording the interviews and organising the data. At one stage I wasn't sure it would ever happen. I suppose it's good to know that research can be like this, and I'm glad I was working on something I was curious about. If I hadn't been, I wouldn't have got nearly so much out of it.'

C Katie Oldham

Katie Oldham is also very interested in the human brain. She spent two months helping a neuroscientist, Frank Hebble, explore how the brain reacts to sudden changes in the environment, such as sounds or touches. She mapped how brain activity shifts when these changes occur, using a technique that measures electrical pulses in the brain. Such maps may help doctors who study children with certain medical conditions. 'It was intimidating at first,' Katie says. 'This is quite advanced science and the people working on it are seriously clever. I did eventually feel part of the team, though. It was good to know they valued my contribution and respected me. They didn't pay me but I was expected to show up on time and do an eight-hour day, just like everyone else.' There is no resentment in Katie's comments, however. She believes she has a head start on some of her fellow students in having had an authentic taste of life as a scientist.

D Tariq Bashir

Tariq Bashir won a placement with medical scientists working on new ways to treat malaria. 'It's such an important thing,' says Tariq. 'So many people around the world are affected by malaria, and if we could come up with solutions, it would make such a difference.' Tariq regards himself as fortunate to be interested in a subject that attracts a lot of attention in the media at large, as well as scientific circles. It means the research is well-funded, and scientists involved have the money and time to dedicate to students like Tariq. It also means the competition for student places tends to be stiff, however. 'I did lots of preparation before I applied', Tariq says. 'I read all the research I could. Some of it went over my head, of course, but I asked a friend of my dad's, who's a doctor, to simplify some of it. But I think the malaria team were impressed that I invested time finding out about what they're doing.'

PAPER 1 Reading and
         Use of English

PAPER 2 Writing ▶ Part 1
                      Part 2

PAPER 3 Listening

PAPER 4 Speaking

You **must** answer this question. Write your answer in **220–260** words in an appropriate style on the separate answer sheet.

1   Your class has attended a lecture by a careers tutor about the advantages of joining a company whose employees work online from home. You have made the notes below.

> **The advantages of working from home:**
>
> • no travelling
> • flexibility
> • comfort

> **Some opinions expressed after the lecture:**
>
> 'There are too many distractions.'
>
> 'I could work whatever part of the day I wanted.'
>
> 'You would miss the company of fellow workers.'

Essential tips

▶ You don't need to have had experience of working from home to be able to answer this question well. Think of times from your own experience (e.g. when you were at school or university) of the advantages and disadvantages of being able to stay at home.

Write an **essay** for your tutor discussing **two** of the advantages in your notes. You should **explain which advantage you think is more important**, and **provide reasons** to support your opinion.

You may, if you wish, make use of the opinions expressed after the lecture, but you should use your own words as far as possible.

PAPER 1 Reading and
Use of English

PAPER 2 Writing ▶ Part 1 / Part 2

PAPER 3 Listening

PAPER 4 Speaking

Write an answer to **one** of the questions **2–4** in this part. Write your answer in **220–260** words in an appropriate style on the separate answer sheet. Put the question number in the box at the top of the page.

2 You are on a planning committee. You hope to bring a music festival to your town. Write to the mayor explaining why a music festival would be good for your town, where it would be held, and what kinds of events there would be. Acknowledge that there may be some disadvantages. Outline what these might be, and how you would try to avoid them.

Write your **proposal.**

3 You work for a hotel chain and have been sent to a holiday resort where your company plans to open a new hotel. You have been asked to report on the leisure facilities of the resort. Write your report, giving information on:

- sports and recreational opportunities
- cinemas and theatres
- cafés and restaurants

Write your **report.**

4 You recently witnessed a car accident. Nobody was seriously hurt, but there was a disagreement about who caused the accident and you had to make a statement to the police, which was an interesting experience. Write a letter to a friend describing:

- the events leading up to the accident
- the accident itself
- the reaction of the drivers and passers-by
- your experience with the police

Write your **letter.**

Essential tips

Question 2

▶ What style would be appropriate for this report? Bear in mind that the report is written for the mayor, and needs to be formal as well as persuasive.

▶ Remember to give a balanced set of ideas in the proposal. Mention problems as well as benefits, before arriving at a set of recommendations that considers both sides of the argument.

Question 3

▶ Remember the overall purpose of this report is to comment on the resort's facilities, with the view of setting up a new hotel there. Bear this in mind throughout your report, as this will help you focus your argument, and avoid making any unnecessary points.

Question 4

▶ Begin by giving a general description of the event. We usually start with general overviews, explaining the situation, before moving to smaller, specific descriptions. Bear in mind the reader is a personal friend, so this should not be a formal-sounding report. Try to make it interesting by adding your own comments on what happened.

Essential tips

Question 2: Does the woman list possible future benefits of the job for Keith's career?

Question 4: Read the wording of the options in this question carefully. What does Rusty say about the purpose of having a samba referee?

Question 6: All the options may appear possible, but listen carefully to what both speakers actually agree on.

🎧 **Track 9**

You will hear three different extracts. For questions **1–6**, choose the answer (**A**, **B** or **C**) which fits best according to what you hear. There are two questions for each extract.

Extract One

You hear two people talking about a job that the man may apply for.

1   What does Keith think is the main disadvantage of the job?
    A   It involves working at weekends.
    B   He will have to use his own car.
    C   The basic pay is not very good.

2   Annie is enthusiastic about the job because
    A   it should lead to a good career for Keith.
    B   Keith is particularly well qualified for it.
    C   it will enable Keith to work from home.

Extract Two

You hear part of an interview with Rusty Upshaw, a bossaball referee.

3   According to Rusty, bossaball is played
    A   on trampolines and sand.
    B   on inflatables.
    C   on trampolines and inflatables.

4   Rusty believes that the samba referee
    A   enhances the attraction of the sport.
    B   distracts the crowd from the game.
    C   keeps the crowd under control.

Extract Three

You hear two people talking about cooking.

5   What does Ricky say about his work as a chef?
    A   Being well organised is the key to success in this profession.
    B   It pays for a chef to specialise in one kind of cooking.
    C   Good chefs have an interest in food from an early age.

6   Both people say they enjoy cooking because it
    A   gives pleasure to friends.
    B   requires total concentration.
    C   helps them maintain good health.

Track 10

You will hear an archaeologist talking about a recent find. For questions **7–14**, complete the sentences with a word or a short phrase.

AN ANCIENT CHARIOT

The chariot was found at a site where (**7**) ....

is being built.

It was buried in a limestone chamber with a man's (**8**) ....

inside it.

The chariot's wheels don't match, suggesting it had a

(**9**) .... function.

The remains of a large number of (**10**) .... were also

discovered near the chariot.

The chamber was probably the tomb of the (**11**) ....

of a tribe.

The Parisii came to Britain from (**12**) ....

Until the discovery of the chariot, it was not known that the Parisii had lived

so far (**13**) ....

It is hoped that the chariot can be moved to (**14**) ....

Essential tips

Question 7: What kinds of constructions are built these days? Do you need to include an article in your answer? Is an adjective necessary?

Question 9: From the structure of the sentence you can see that an adjective is needed here. If the wheels of a vehicle don't match so that it can't be used for practical purposes, what sort of function might the vehicle have?

Question 12: What kind of word might complete the phrase: 'The Parisii came to Britain from . . .'? It could be the name of a place: a city, country etc. Remember that you will hear the word or words you want, but not in the same context as in the question.

PAPER 1 Reading and Use of English

PAPER 2 Writing

PAPER 3 Listening ▶ | Part 1
| Part 2
| **Part 3**
PAPER 4 Speaking | Part 4

Essential tips

Question 15: The question refers to Reilly's main concern. Listen out for a phrase which has a similar meaning to, my 'main concern'.

Question 17: To prepare for this question, think how you would explain the situations in the options. In the recording you will hear one of these situations expressed in different words.

Question 20: Think about what would motivate you to buy a product, and then think of other ways that the speakers could express the different options.

Track 11

You will hear part of an interview with Fergus Reilly, a marine scientist, about the non-profit organisation he works for: Sustainable Fishing. For questions **15–20**, choose the answer (**A, B, C** or **D**) which fits best according to what you hear.

15 Fergus Reilly says he is mainly concerned about
   A the size of the industries involved in processing the fish.
   B the number of stages the fish pass through before being sold.
   C the methods used by the fishing industry to maximise their catches.
   D the financial motivation for the industry to continue over-fishing.

16 According to Reilly, how is Sustainable Fishing going about its campaign?
   A It is increasing the amount of publicity in the media for the work it does.
   B It is improving consumers' knowledge about the fish they are buying.
   C It is persuading supermarkets to offer less endangered species for sale.
   D It is encouraging suppliers to research into the sustainability of fish stocks.

17 What does Reilly say about the situation for the more popular fish species?
   A It has proved impossible to convince people of the rate of their depletion.
   B Scientists are under increasing pressure to rescue them from final collapse.
   C The growing number of people in the world is adding to their vulnerability.
   D Their survival depends on the fishing industry agreeing to unpopular controls.

18 The condition of fish sold in supermarkets is in question because
   A customers are not reliably informed about when it was caught.
   B it often has to travel a long distance after it has been landed.
   C it may be sold as fresh when it has been previously frozen.
   D retailers fail to check the word of salesmen about its age.

19 How does Sustainable Fishing find out what happens to fish after they are caught?
   A It puts pressure on fishing companies to supply the information.
   B It funds retailers to trace the supply chain and send back reports.
   C It receives updates from environmental groups around the world.
   D It makes use of technology to follow the fish's progress at all stages.

20 In order to motivate consumers to buy sustainably caught fish, retailers can
   A display advertisements about the need to maintain healthy oceans.
   B go into schools to give talks about the serious threat to fish stocks.
   C bring down the price by preparing fish for sale without waste.
   D employ chefs to create affordable dishes that are easy to cook.

PAPER 1 Reading and
Use of English

PAPER 2 Writing

PAPER 3 Listening ▶

PAPER 4 Speaking

Part 1
Part 2
Part 3
Part 4

Track 12

You will hear five short extracts in which people talk about children's free-time activities.

While you listen, you must complete both tasks.

TASK ONE

For questions **21–25**, choose from the list **A–H**, the explanation each speaker gives about how his or her child became interested in an activity.

A	Our child began this activity at school.	Speaker 1 [ ] **21**
B	A relative was indirectly responsible for our child taking up this activity.	Speaker 2 [ ] **22**
C	A newspaper article sparked off interest in this activity.	Speaker 3 [ ] **23**
D	We encouraged our child to take up this activity.	Speaker 4 [ ] **24**
E	Our child began this activity as a result of a medical condition.	Speaker 5 [ ] **25**
F	A television programme inspired our child to take up this activity.	
G	Our child became interested in this activity while staying with friends.	
H	The idea for this activity came from reading about it.	

Essential tips

Questions 21–25: Since you will probably not hear most of the key words in the options, you need to be prepared for words and expressions with a similar meaning. For example, instead of saying 'at school' (option A), the speaker might refer to a type of school, a certain class at school, the name of a school etc. Similarly, a speaker may use a word for a certain relative (option B), such as 'aunt', or even a description of who that person is, such as 'my sister's husband'.

Questions 26–30: Think about how someone might describe an activity to convey the idea that it is 'very dangerous' (option A), perhaps by saying what sort of accident might happen. What kind of language could be used to express this? And consider different ways of expressing the idea of 'spirit of cooperation' (option F): what would we call a 'group' in a sport?

TASK TWO

For questions **26–30**, choose from the list **A–H**, what each speaker expresses about these activities.

A	This activity is very dangerous.	Speaker 1 [ ] **26**
B	Our child's physical condition has improved.	Speaker 2 [ ] **27**
C	We were opposed to this activity at first.	Speaker 3 [ ] **28**
D	Our child takes this activity too seriously.	Speaker 4 [ ] **29**
E	We didn't understand what the activity entailed at first.	Speaker 5 [ ] **30**
F	This activity develops a spirit of co-operation.	
G	This activity has become fashionable recently.	
H	Our child has benefited socially.	

PAPER 1 Reading and
Use of English

PAPER 2 Writing

PAPER 3 Listening

PAPER 4 Speaking

Essential tips

Part 1: Think about the vocabulary you need for this topic. You should also consider which tenses are appropriate. For instance, you might say that your father *comes from* a certain city, using the present tense. But, if you want to say when he left that city, you could use a past tense. When you describe how long he has been living in that city, you will probably need to use the present perfect continuous.

Part 2: To describe how people might feel in a certain situation, or what might have happened, you need expressions that express possibility. For example, *he might be feeling*. However, to describe something that has happened, you will need to use appropriate past tenses.

Part 3: An emotion or an abstract concept can be interpreted in different ways. The concept of 'pride' can be positive or negative, for example, so you should be prepared to consider different aspects of the idea you have to talk about. Remember that the point here is not to convince the examiner or the other candidate of your opinion, but to show you can express your views convincingly, and reach a conclusion in an appropriate manner.

Part 4: In this part, you are asked to talk about actual events, or situations and to give your opinion. After answering the question, you may go on to talk more generally about the subject, but you should always show that you have understood the question, first.

Part 1 (2 minutes)

The examiner will ask you a few questions about yourself and about a general topic. For example, the examiner may ask you:

• Would you tell me something about the members of your family?
• Where are the members of your family from?
• Which people from your extended family do you have most contact with?

Part 2 (4 minutes)

You will each be asked to talk on your own for about a minute. You will each be given three different pictures to talk about. After your partner has finished speaking, you will be asked a brief question connected with your partner's photographs.

> **Departing** (compare, contrast and speculate)

Turn to pictures 1–3 on page 175 which show people departing.

(*Candidate A*), it's your turn first. Here are your pictures. They show **people departing**.

I'd like you to compare and contrast **two** of the pictures and say **why you think the people are leaving, and how they might be feeling.**

(*Candidate B*), **in which picture does the departure seem most exciting? Why?**

> **Exhaustion** (compare, contrast and speculate)

Turn to pictures 1–3 on page **176** which show people feeling tired.

Now, (*Candidate B*), here are your pictures. **They show tired people.**

I'd like you to compare and contrast **two** of these situations, and say **why the people might be tired. What kind of exhaustion – mental or physical – do they feel, and why?**

(*Candidate A*), **which type of exhaustion do you find most difficult to get over? Why?**

Part 3 (4 minutes)

Look at page 177 which gives some examples of things people are proud about.

> **Pride** (discuss, evaluate and select)

Here are some different things people are proud about and a question for you to discuss.

First, you have some time to look at the task.

(*Pause 15 seconds*)

Now talk to each other about **why people feel proud about these things.**

Now you have about a minute to decide **which situation gives the most pride.**

Part 4 (5 minutes)

The examiner will encourage you to develop the topic of your discussion in Part 3 by asking questions such as:

• When was the last time you felt proud of something you had achieved?
• Do you think there are forms of pride that can be harmful?
• Would someone who never felt proud of himself or herself be unhappy?
• Are there times when you feel proud of other people? Can you give an example?

For questions **1–8**, read the text below and decide which answer (**A, B, C** or **D**) best fits each gap. There is an example at the beginning (**0**).

Mark your answers **on the separate answer sheet**.

Example:

0	**A** band	**B** range	**C** scale	**D** scope

0	A	B	C	D

Raising awareness

In cities around the world, a wide (**0**) .... of schemes is being instigated to promote environmental awareness. 'It's just as easy to (**1**) .... of litter properly as it is to drop it on the streets,' says city councillor Mike Edwards. 'It's a question of encouraging people to do so as a (**2**) .... of course. Once the habit is ingrained, they won't even (**3**) .... they are doing it. After all, think what we've achieved with recycling in the home. People have become accustomed to it, so it doesn't (**4**) .... to them that they're spending any additional time in the process. Only if they have to carry this waste for some appreciable distance to find a suitable container do they feel they are (**5**) ....

A quirky, (**6**) .... gimmick might be enough to change behaviour. With this in (**7**) ...., the city of Berlin is introducing rubbish bins that say *danke*, *thank you* and *merci* when someone drops an item of rubbish into them. It might just (**8**) .... the trick in this city, too.

1	**A** dispose	**B** discard	**C** dump	**D** dispense
2	**A** principle	**B** system	**C** matter	**D** duty
3	**A** notice	**B** remark	**C** comprehend	**D** appreciate
4	**A** concern	**B** occur	**C** impress	**D** strike
5	**A** inconvenienced	**B** sacrificed	**C** complicated	**D** imposed
6	**A** light-hearted	**B** mundane	**C** subjective	**D** intense
7	**A** context	**B** thought	**C** spirit	**D** mind
8	**A** serve	**B** do	**C** make	**D** play

PAPER 1	Reading and Use of English ▸	Part 1
		Part 2
PAPER 2	Writing	Part 3
		Part 4
PAPER 3	Listening	Part 5
PAPER 4	Speaking	Part 6
		Part 7
		Part 8

For questions **9–16**, read the text below and think of the word which best fits each gap. Use only **one** word in each gap. There is an example at the beginning (**0**).

Write your answers **IN CAPITAL LETTERS on the separate answer sheet.**

Example: 0 | H | A | V | E | | | | | | | | | | | | | | | | | | |

Emotion in books

Something appears to (**0**) …….. happened to the emotional content of books published in the UK. Researchers from the University of Bristol analysed the frequency with (**9**) …….. 'mood' words – those reflecting anger, disgust, fear, joy, sadness and surprise – were used in as (**10**) …….. as 5 million books between 1900 and 2000. (**11**) …….. to one of the researchers, Dr Alberto Acerbi, 'the average book published in 1900 has 14% more emotional content than the average book in 2000.' In (**12**) …….. words, 'a book with 1,000 emotional words in 1900 would have 877 in 2000.'

In (**13**) …….. to this decline in emotional content, the research team found that some interesting differences between British books and those published in the USA have developed since the 1960s. (**14**) …….. having more emotional content than their British counterparts, American books now contain more content-free words. These are words that carry (**15**) …….. or no meaning on their (**16**) …….., such as *and* or *but*, and articles like *the*.

What is the significance of these changes? The researchers say that further work is needed to deal with this question adequately.

PAPER 1 Reading and ▶
Use of English

PAPER 2 Writing

PAPER 3 Listening

PAPER 4 Speaking

Part 1
Part 2
Part 3
Part 4
Part 5
Part 6
Part 7
Part 8

For questions **17–24**, read the text below. Use the word given in capitals at the end of some of the lines to form a word that fits in the gap **in the same line**. There is an example at the beginning (**0**).

Write your answers **IN CAPITAL LETTERS on the separate answer sheet**.

Example: | 0 | N | O | T | O | R | I | E | T | Y | | | | | | | | | | | |

The black widow spider

The black widow spider's (**0**) …….. is not without
foundation. However, an element of exaggeration
has led to certain (**17**) …….. regarding its evil nature.

NOTORIOUS

CONCEPT

Firstly, while it is indeed one of the most venomous
species of spider, its venom being 15 times stronger
than that of the prairie rattlesnake, its bite injects such
a small amount of venom in (**18**) …….. that it is unlikely
to kill humans. In fact (**19**), …….. are rare.

COMPARE

FATAL

Black widows bite only if they are touched or their
web is threatened, and only the adult female is poisonous.
The female is (**20**) …….. by nature, and has been known to
kill and eat the male after mating. Such (**21**) …….. are rare,
but they explain how the spider got its name – and its
reputation.

SOLITUDE

OCCUR

Nevertheless, the (**22**) …….. effects of this spider's bite
should not be (**23**) …….., and if you live in a certain climate
and have a fireplace in your home, it is advisable to take
(**24**) …….. . Black widow spiders often inhabit wood piles,
so you should wear gloves when handling firewood.

PLEASE

ESTIMATE

CAUTION

PAPER 1 Reading and ▶ Part 1
      Use of English   Part 2

PAPER 2 Writing   Part 3

PAPER 3 Listening   **Part 4**

PAPER 4 Speaking   Part 5

                       Part 6

                       Part 7

                       Part 8

For questions **25–30**, complete the second sentence so that it has a similar meaning to the first sentence, using the word given. **Do not change the word given.** You must use between **three** and **six** words, including the word given. Here is an example (**0**).

Example:

0   Jane regretted speaking so rudely to the old lady.

    MORE

    Jane .... politely to the old lady.

Example: | **0** |WISHED SHE HAD SPOKEN MORE|

Write **only** the missing words **IN CAPITAL LETTERS on the separate answer sheet.**

---

25   This novel stands a very good chance of winning the book prize.

    HIGHLY

    It is .... win the book prize.

26   'You really must stay and have dinner with us!' Laura said to us.

    STAYING

    Laura .... for dinner.

27   If you need me, call me any time, night or day.

    MATTER

    Call me if you need me, ... be.

28   I don't want to be disturbed at all this morning!

    ACCOUNT

    On .... disturbed this morning!

29   If Mark hadn't told Bella about that letter, we wouldn't have argued.

    FOR

    Had .... telling Bella about that letter, we wouldn't have argued.

30   We're going to miss the start of the film if we don't hurry.

    TIME

    Unless we hurry, the film .... we get there.

PAPER 1 Reading and ▶   Part 1
        Use of English   Part 2
                           Part 3
PAPER 2 Writing   Part 4
PAPER 3 Listening   **Part 5**
                          Part 6
PAPER 4 Speaking   Part 7
                          Part 8

You are going to read a magazine article. For questions **31–36**, choose the answer (**A, B, C** or **D**) which you think fits best according to the text.

Mark your answers **on the separate answer sheet**.

Are you a 'slumper'?

Amanda Stevens cured her bad posture – and her chronic back pain – with the Alexander technique.

Many people will have heard of the Alexander technique but have only a vague idea what it is about. Until earlier this year, I didn't have the faintest idea about it – and saw no reason to think I should. But, hunched over a computer screen one day, I noticed that the neck and backache I regularly suffered were more painful than usual. I was brought up to think that the preferred way of dealing with aches and pains is to do nothing and hope they'll go away, but I eventually allowed myself to be dragged along by a friend of mine to talk to an osteopath who had performed wonders on her. After examining me, the osteopath said: 'I can treat the symptoms by massaging your neck and upper back. But you actually have bad posture. That is what you need to get sorted out. Go off and learn the Alexander technique.'

I had regularly been told by friends and family that I tend to slouch in chairs but had been under the impression that bad posture was something one was born with and could do nothing about. With hindsight, it's hard to believe just how far off the mark I was. Dentists and car mechanics, among others, tend to develop bad posture from leaning over patients or engine bays. Those of us who are mothers often stress and strain their necks and backs lifting and carrying children, and those who sit in front of computers all day are almost certainly not doing our bodies any favours.

After a little searching online, I found an Alexander technique teacher, Teresa Stirling, in my area of town and booked a first appointment. Three months later I am walking straighter and sitting better, while my neck and back pain are things of the past. I feel taller, too, which I may be imagining, but the technique can increase your height by up to five centimetres if you were badly slumped beforehand.

The teaching focuses on the neck, head and back. It trains you to use your body less harshly and to carry out the sorts of movements and actions that we do all the time with less effort. There is very little effort in the lessons themselves, which sets apart the Alexander technique from pilates or yoga, which are exercise-based. A typical lesson involves standing in front of a chair and learning to sit and stand with minimal effort. You spend some time lying on a bench with your knees bent to straighten the spine and relax your body while the teacher moves your arms and legs to train you to move them correctly.

The key is learning to break the bad habits accumulated over years. Try, for example, folding your arms the opposite way to normal. It feels odd, doesn't it? This is an example of a habit the body has formed which can be hard to break. Many of us carry our heads too far back and tilted skywards. The technique teaches you to let go of the muscles holding the head back, allowing it to resume its natural place on the summit of our spines. The head weighs four to six kilos, so any misalignment can cause problems for the neck and body.

The Alexander technique teaches you to observe how you use your body and how others use theirs – usually badly. Look how a colleague slumps back in a chair with his or her legs crossed. That puts all sorts of stresses and strains on the body. Even swimming can harm the neck. The Alexander technique can teach you to swim better, concentrating on technique rather than clocking up lengths.

So who was Alexander and how did he come up with the technique? Frederick Matthias Alexander, an Australian theatrical orator born in 1869, found in his youth that his voice was failing during performances. He analysed himself and realised his posture was bad. He worked on improving it, with dramatic results. He brought his technique to London 100 years ago and quickly gathered a following that included some very famous people. He died in 1955, having established a teacher-training school in London, which is thriving today.

So if you are slouching along the road one day, feeling weighed down by your troubles, give a thought to the Alexander technique. It could help you walk tall again.

31 What does the writer suggest in the first paragraph?
- **A** She had been reluctant to seek treatment for her back problems.
- **B** She was initially sceptical about the Alexander technique.
- **C** She had little faith in the osteopath's methods.
- **D** She was wrong to follow her friend's advice.

32 What does the writer say about bad posture in the second paragraph?
- **A** She had thought that it only affected people in certain occupations.
- **B** She had been told that she would inevitably suffer as a result of it.
- **C** She had misunderstood what the causes of it were.
- **D** She had developed it after having children.

33 What principle of the Alexander technique does the writer identify in the fourth paragraph?
- **A** A person's natural movements shouldn't be altered.
- **B** The Alexander technique shouldn't be attempted without supervision.
- **C** Familiar physical actions shouldn't be performed in a strenuous manner.
- **D** The Alexander technique shouldn't be combined with other types of exercise.

34 What does the writer say about bad habits in the fifth paragraph?
- **A** They are a consequence of actions we perform.
- **B** They inevitably cause physical pain.
- **C** They develop in early childhood.
- **D** They can be difficult to change.

35 What does the writer suggest about Frederick Alexander?
- **A** He was keen to make a name for himself.
- **B** He managed to recover his vocal powers.
- **C** He developed a form of exercise for actors.
- **D** He needed to leave home to develop his technique.

36 What is the writer's main purpose in the article?
- **A** To explain the widespread occurrence of back pain.
- **B** To suggest that back problems can be remedied.
- **C** To explain how debilitating backache can be.
- **D** To challenge common ideas about back pain.

You are going to read four writers' contributions to a debate about hosting the Olympic Games. For questions **37–40**, choose from the contributions **A–D**. The contributions may be chosen more than once.

Mark your answers **on the separate answer sheet**.

Hosting the Olympics – is it a good idea?

Four writers give their views about what an Olympic Games can do for the host country.

A

The Olympics are undoubtedly expensive to stage and none of the Games in recent times have made an immediate profit, but they should be considered a long-term investment. The large infrastructure projects like new roads and transport systems, the new sports venues and cultural facilities, the regeneration of rundown urban areas and the increase in tourism all end up stimulating the economy eventually. The international media focus on the Games can also lift the host country's profile to another level. This has a knock-on effect on attitudes within the host country. International attention and proof of a capacity to rise to the challenge can pull the country together, make it feel good about itself and put it in a position to compete in the modern world.

B

Weighing up the pros and cons of hosting an Olympics is a complex business. Research suggests that few former hosts have experienced long-term economic gains. Indeed, certain cities like Montreal and Los Angeles have taken decades to pay off the debts incurred in preparing for and running the two-week-long event, and in cases like these, an unwelcome PR effect of international dimensions seems to come attached. The real benefits are less tangible in that they inspire a local feel-good factor, enhancing a sense of pride in belonging to a city and country that can pull off such a massive and awkward enterprise. There is also the chance for everyone, the younger generations in particular, to observe elite athletes, and therefore sporting excellence, exercise and fitness become cool things to aspire to.

C

For a host city, the Olympic Games are all about 'legacy'. They present an opportunity to showcase, domestically and to the world at large, the notion that the city possesses the know-how and manpower to manage a hugely complex international event, plus an impressive new infrastructure of sports facilities, accommodation and public transport, a vibrant, competent, friendly local population, and historic sites and places of natural beauty for tourists to visit. There is the sporting legacy too, with the greatest athletes from around the world inspiring mass participation, a crucial development when modern lifestyles tend to have a significantly detrimental effect on fitness and health. Critics of the notion of hosting the Olympics often focus on the more easily measurable economic implications which suggest that the Games are not a viable proposition, but the Olympics are not just about money; they are about other aspects of legacy which are at least as significant.

D

Most positive developments that might be associated with hosting the Olympics would happen anyway. The infrastructural investments could be made, incentives for tourists to visit could be offered and trade delegations could be energised. Past experience suggests the financial costs tend to outweigh the benefits anyway, when variables like the absurd bidding process, security and mismanagement are factored in. What of the more intangible spinoffs? First, there is no hard evidence that hosting the Olympics leads to greater public involvement in sports. In fact, studies show sporting activity actually fell in certain Olympic cities once the 'after-party enthusiasm' had worn off. Genuine long-term participation in sports comes from grassroots investment in schools and community facilities rather than glitzy shows. Most Olympic Games are concentrated in one city, usually the capital, and have little impact, economic or otherwise, on other parts of the country. In fact, in some cases, research reveals significant regional resentment about all the attention from government, the media and other organisations being directed at one city. So much for pride in one's country.

Which writer

has a different opinion to the others regarding the economic impact of hosting the Olympics?

37 [ ]

shares writer B's opinion about the implications for sport in the host country?

38 [ ]

expresses a different view to the others about the effect that hosting the Olympics can have on a national sense of identity?

39 [ ]

takes a similar view to writer A about the likely consequence for the host country's international reputation?

40 [ ]

PAPER 1	Reading and ▶	Part 1
	Use of English	Part 2
PAPER 2	Writing	Part 3
		Part 4
PAPER 3	Listening	Part 5
		Part 6
PAPER 4	Speaking	**Part 7**
		Part 8

You are going to read a magazine article. Six paragraphs have been removed from the article. Choose from the paragraphs **A–G** the one which fits each gap (**41–46**). There is one extra paragraph which you do not need to use.

Mark your answers **on the separate answer sheet**.

Close encounters of the wild kind

The rise of wildlife-watching experiences.

Wildlife observation has always proved inspirational for humans. It led Charles Darwin to provide us with a better understanding of how we evolved and it has inspired such everyday innovations as Velcro. US author Peter Matthiessen wrote: 'The variety of life in nature can be compared to a vast library of unread books, and the plundering of nature is comparable to the random discarding of whole volumes without having opened them and learned from them.'

41

'What is interesting is how much people are willing to pay to be in a wilderness environment,' says Julian Matthews, director of Discovery Initiatives, a company which takes people on small–group trips to more than 35 countries. 'It's still a small part of the tourism industry but it's undoubtedly expanding. There are definitely more and more people seeking wildlife experiences now.'

42

Matthews recognises the contribution that television has made to our knowledge of nature, but he says 'there's no way to compare seeing an animal in the wild with watching one on TV. While a filmmaker may spend six months shooting an animal and will get closer to it than you ever will, there's no greater pleasure than seeing an animal in its own environment. On film, you're only getting the visuals and the sound. As impressive as they may be, it's not the real thing.' And the good thing is that tourists can now watch wildlife 'live' while helping to protect it – a concept that comes under the broad label of 'ecotourism'.

43

In practice, this means that many tour operators, guided by ethical policies, now use the services of local communities, train local guides and have close ties to conservation projects. Tour operator Rekero, for example, has established its own school – the Koyiaki Guide School and Wilderness Camp – for Maasai people in Kenya.

44

Conservation organisations have also realised that tourism can help educate people and provide a valuable source of revenue and even manpower. The World Wildlife Fund, for example, runs trips that give donors the chance to see for themselves how their financial aid is assisting conservation projects in the field, and some organisations even allow tourists to take part in research and conservation.

45

Similarly, Biosphere Expeditions takes about 200 people every year on what its field operations director, Dr Matthias Hammer, calls an 'adventure with a conscience'. Volunteers can visit six destinations around the world and take part in various activities including snow leopard, wolf and bear surveys and whale and dolphin research.

46

Of course, going in search of wildlife doesn't always mean you will find it. That sightings of animals in large wild areas don't come automatically is a fact of life. Although potentially frustrating, it makes sightings all the more rewarding when they are made. And the opportunity to do something to help both the environment and local people can only add to the experience.

A He is confident that, if done properly, this combination of tourism and conservation can be 'a win–win situation'. 'People have a unique experience while contributing to conservation directly. Local people and habitats benefit through job creation, research and an alternative income. Local wildlife benefits from our work.'

B While there is indeed much to learn from many species not yet known to science, it's the already opened texts that attract the majority of us, however. And we are attracted in ever increasing numbers.

C As people are able to travel to more extreme places in search of the ultimate wildlife experience, it's worth remembering that you don't have to go to the ends of the earth to catch rewarding glimpses of animals. Indeed, some of the best wildlife-watching opportunities are on our doorstep.

D This growth has been stimulated by the efforts of conservation groups and natural history documentaries. Greater awareness of the planet has led to an increased demand for wildlife tours or the addition of a wildlife-watching component to traditional holidays. People want to discover nature at first-hand for themselves – not just on a screen.

E Despite being an important part of the population there, they have largely been excluded from the benefits brought to the region by tourism. This initiative is a concerted effort to enable them to take up jobs and run programmes themselves.

F Earthwatch is a non-profit international environmental group that does just that. 'Participation in an Earthwatch project is a positive alternative to wildlife-watching expeditions, as we offer members of the public the opportunity to be on the front line of conservation,' says Claudia Eckardt, Earthwatch programme manager.

G It is a term which is overused, but the principle behind it undoubtedly offers hope for the future of many endangered species, as money from tourism directly funds conservation work. It also extends to the consideration of the interests of people living in the places that tourists visit.

You are going to read reviews of four psychology books. For questions **47–56**, choose from the books (**A–D**).

Mark your answers **on the separate answer sheet**.

About which book is each following point made?

It is likely to put certain kinds of people off.	47
It has aims which resemble those in other recently published books.	48
It offers unnecessary advice to readers.	49
It makes seemingly original but convincing observations.	50
It avoids obvious answers to an issue which is familiar to many people.	51
It may prompt the publication of other books exploring the same subject matter.	52
It is organised differently from other writing by the same author.	53
It lacks a clear structure.	54
It challenges a modern trend in psychology.	55
It is difficult to understand in places.	56

Reviews of psychology books

A *Missing Out: In Praise of the Unlived Life* by Adam Phillips

In *Missing Out*, a slim volume peppered with insights that may never have been expressed quite like this before but which make you want to scrawl 'yes' in the margins on almost every page, the psychoanalyst and writer Adam Phillips asserts that we all 'learn to live somewhere between the lives we have and the lives we would like'. For 'modern' people, 'the good life is ... filled to the full'; we seek complete satisfaction. But what we need, argues Phillips, isn't satisfaction but frustration. You can't get instant satisfaction because you can't control people or the world. You can't 'get' other people because no one can be fully understood and neither, of course, can you. But a capacity for tolerating frustration allows us to develop. Appropriately, given the subject matter, this book can be a frustrating read – sometimes you think you're just getting to grips with an idea, only for it to slip away. But, as is often true of Phillips's books, what you do feel when you've finished it is that it offers glimpses of the real, messy and never fully knowable human heart.

B *Together* by Richard Sennett

Together is the second book in a planned trilogy about the skills modern humans need for a happy co-existence. The first addressed the joys of making things with your hands, and the third will be about cities. This one looks at how we can all get along together. Sennett explores the importance of equality and how, in unequal societies, people are less willing to co-operate. He argues that our society is becoming atomised, 'deskilling people in practising co-operation'. The trouble is it all feels atomised itself. Sennett's argument seems to bounce from place to place, and he relies on anecdotes and experience more than data. It aims to be a practical, how-to guide for maximising co-operation, but ends up a sort of unsystematic self-help book: listening is as important a skill as the presentation of your own ideas; discussion need not reach agreement but can teach us new things; assertiveness is valuable, but so is politeness and diffidence. All true, but don't we know it already?

C *Teach Us To Sit Still* by Tim Parks

A few years ago, a number of writers dealt movingly about what it's like to have a serious illness. If *Teach Us to Sit Still* does well, we could be in for a glut of writing by people who don't have much wrong with them, yet still write about it at length. But if they are anything like as good as this, it might not be such a gloomy prospect. A few years ago, Tim Parks couldn't sleep and had serious pains in his side. Medical tests all came back negative, but the pain persisted. So, he embarked on a sceptical exploration of the possible causes of and cures for his woes. He tried out an array of theories and therapies. The intensity of Park's search makes for a less than relaxing read, and, in all probability, there will be readers who fail to make it past the first couple of chapters. Parks, an innovative and prolific novelist, writes wonderfully however, and despite the subject matter, a layer of wit runs through it. Parks eventually achieves some relief through special breathing exercises and meditation, but uncovers no magic formulas.

D *The Antidote* by Oliver Burkeman

Should we all be striving for happiness? Should we think positively? Should we try to ignore any difficult thoughts, feelings, or situations that arise? Many self-help books these days would shout 'Yes!' Oliver Burkeman isn't so sure. A leading writer in what could be called the 'anti-self-help self-help' genre – which happily seems to be swelling – Burkeman's work, as represented in *The Antidote*, is not about positive thinking, finding partners, and getting promotions at work and doesn't offer facile instructions for living a happy, easy life. Rather, it uses research to suggest that we reconsider our assumptions and find new ways of thinking and being. *Help! How to Become Slightly Happier*, his previous book, comprised a series of short sections, each a page or two long, which presented an idea fairly quickly. *The Antidote* has just eight chapters and each one explores a subject like success and failure in detail. So what are his conclusions? Well, one is that we have to stop searching for firm answers and quick fixes.

You **must** answer this question. Write your answer in **220–260** words in an appropriate style on the separate answer sheet.

---

1 Your principal has suggested a project in which groups of students spend three days on a survival exercise, living in a remote place where they have to organise their own shelter, food and heat. You have made the notes below.

> **The reasoning behind this proposal:**
>
> - self-sufficiency
> - insight into different living conditions
> - teamwork

> **Some opinions expressed by students:**
>
> 'It could be dangerous.'
>
> 'Three days is too short to gain any new insight.'
>
> 'Participants would need considerable preparation.'

Write an **essay** discussing **two** of the arguments in your notes. You should **explain which argument you think is more important** and **provide reasons** to support your opinion.

You may, if you wish, make use of the opinions expressed in the discussion, but you should use your own words as far as possible.

PAPER 1 Reading and Use of English

PAPER 2 Writing ▶   Part 1   Part 2

PAPER 3 Listening

PAPER 4 Speaking

Write an answer to **one** of the questions **2–4** in this part. Write your answer in **220–260** words in an appropriate style on the separate answer sheet. Put the question number in the box at the top of the page.

---

2   You are a regular contributor to an online magazine called *Film Scene.* You have been asked to write a review of two films which you saw recently, and of which most people had great expectations. You enjoyed one of the films, but found the other one very disappointing.

    Write your **review.**

3   You have been in your first job for a few months. A friend is about to start work and is feeling nervous about it. She wants your advice about how to prepare for the world of work, what to expect and how to behave. Write an email telling her about your experiences and giving her tips on how to cope.

    Write your **email.**

4   Your class is doing a project on endangered species, and you have recently visited a zoo where green spaces have been created for rearing rare animals in captivity. Write a report on green spaces for wildlife in the area where you live, and describe what could be done to create more green spaces.

    Write your **report.**

Track 13

You will hear three different extracts. For questions **1–6**, choose the answer (**A**, **B** or **C**) which fits best according to what you hear. There are two questions for each extract.

___

Extract One

You hear part of an interview with a woman who has changed her lifestyle.

1 The idea for buying an olive farm came from
    A a contact in Greece.
    B Kathy's husband.
    C a site on the internet.

2 Kathy says she had expected to
    A miss her home and family in Britain.
    B find life in Greece more difficult.
    C feel nostalgic about her old job.

Extract Two

You hear part of a radio discussion in which two teachers are talking about teaching poetry.

3 The man feels that generally poetry
    A is not taken seriously by teachers.
    B is not a popular subject to teach.
    C makes for an uninspiring lesson.

4 The woman's main argument is that
    A teachers should encourage students to respond to poetry in their own way.
    B students need guidance if they are to understand and appreciate poetry.
    C only the poet can give us a valid interpretation of his or her work.

Extract Three

You hear two people talking about an unusual kind of competition.

5 According to Jake, he stopped at the pub
    A out of curiosity.
    B to eat something.
    C to meet someone.

6 The object of the competition is to
    A tell the most convincing lie.
    B tell the funniest anecdote.
    C tell the most obvious tall story.

PAPER 1 Reading and
         Use of English

PAPER 2 Writing

PAPER 3 Listening   Part 1
                             Part 2
PAPER 4 Speaking   Part 3
                             Part 4

🎧 **Track 14**

You will hear part of a talk by the director of a sports academy. For questions **7–14**, complete the sentences with a word or a short phrase.

THE WATERMAN SPORTS ACADEMY

The Waterman Sports Academy offers training in several sports, including

swimming and (**7**) ....

Helen coached a girl who wanted to compete in the

(**8**) ....

Her interest in sports medicine dates back to the time when her

(**9**) .... suffered a back injury.

To be successful in a particular sport, an athlete must have

the right (**10**) ....

Helen says that fitness is important, even in sports like

(**11**) ....

She stresses that a (**12**) .... is vital in physical

development.

Athletes who do not have the latest (**13**) ....

are handicapped in competitions.

In Helen's opinion, the most important factor for success is having the

right (**14**) ....

PAPER 1 Reading and
          Use of English

PAPER 2 Writing

PAPER 3 Listening ►
          Part 1
          Part 2
          Part 3
          Part 4

PAPER 4 Speaking

Track 15

You will hear part an interview with Jon Kennedy, who works on oil rigs.
For questions **15–20**, choose the answer (**A**, **B**, **C** or **D**) which fits best according
to what you hear.

15 What does Jon Kennedy say about his present job?
   A His work on accident prevention is the most interesting part of it.
   B He would prefer to spend less time doing paper work in the office.
   C He is annoyed at the level of confidentiality his company demands.
   D The location of the rig is inconvenient for workers taking shore leave.

16 Where oil workers are concerned, Jon feels
   A the industry could make an effort to attract a wider range of recruits.
   B college graduates should be more open-minded about a career in the
          industry.
   C it is regrettable that some engineers feel discouraged about entering the
          industry.
   D the industry is important because of the opportunities offered to unskilled
          workers.

17 Jon expresses pride in the drill ship because
   A it is able to withstand extreme weather.
   B it drills wells at maximum subsea depths.
   C it is the newest ship to have been constructed.
   D it cost more to build than other ships of its type.

18 What does Jon say about arriving on the ship?
   A He enjoys meeting up with his co-workers again.
   B He looks forward to getting down to work.
   C He always finds the flight out very exciting.
   D He listens carefully to the safety briefing.

19 Jon says the workers on the rig
   A come to him when they need advice on any problem.
   B are polite to him because he has a high-ranking position.
   C have little time to relax because their jobs are very demanding.
   D don't know each other well because they belong to different companies.

20 What does Jon say gives him particular enjoyment in his current job?
   A developing systems that increase safety for the rig's personnel
   B dealing with emergencies that could be expensive for his company
   C saving money by identifying potential failure in the rig's equipment
   D devising technology to improve the efficiency of the drilling gear

PAPER 1 Reading and
Use of English

PAPER 2 Writing

PAPER 3 Listening   ▶

PAPER 4 Speaking

Part 1
Part 2
Part 3
Part 4

Track 16

You will hear five short extracts in which people talk about their experiences at the theatre.

While you listen, you must complete both tasks.

TASK ONE

For questions **21–25**, choose from list **A–H**, what each speaker says about the show he or she enjoyed most.

A	The atmosphere was intimate.	Speaker 1	21
B	I loved the period costumes.	Speaker 2	22
C	The play was very moving.	Speaker 3	23
D	I saw the play a couple of times.	Speaker 4	24
E	The play had a large cast.	Speaker 5	25
F	I went along reluctantly.		
G	The star of the show was very talented.		
H	The show was performed by a foreign company.		

TASK TWO

For questions **26–30**, choose from list **A–H** the view each speaker has about why theatre is an interesting medium.

A	The thrill of watching big stars is unforgettable.	Speaker 1	26
B	You can get carried away by the performance.	Speaker 2	27
C	The theatre can be a communal experience.	Speaker 3	28
D	It is interesting to learn from the cast.	Speaker 4	29
E	Ideas can be conveyed with stunning force.	Speaker 5	30
F	Each performance is a unique experience.		
G	You sometimes feel transported to a different era.		
H	The theatre can surprise and stimulate the audience.		

Part 1 (2 minutes)

The examiner will ask you a few questions about yourself and about a general topic. For example, the examiner may ask you:

- What do you enjoy doing when you go away for a holiday?
- How would you describe the best holiday you have ever had?
- What sorts of things can spoil a holiday for you?

Part 2 (4 minutes)

You will each be asked to talk on your own for about a minute. You will each be given three different pictures to talk about. After your partner has finished speaking, you will be asked a brief question connected with your partner's photographs.

Sports (compare, contrast and speculate)

Turn to pictures 1–3 on page 178 which show people taking part in different sports.

(*Candidate A*), it's your turn first. Here are your pictures. They show **people taking part in different sports.**

I'd like you to compare and contrast **two** of the pictures and say **what kind of training each of these sports requires. What are the advantages and disadvantages of taking part in a team sport, as opposed to an individual sport?**

(*Candidate B*), **which of these sports would you find most enjoyable? Why?**

Accommodation (compare, contrast and speculate)

Turn to pictures 1–3 on page 179 which show different homes.

Now, (*Candidate B*), here are your pictures. **They show places where people live.**

I'd like you to compare and contrast **two** of these homes, and say **what you think would be the advantages and disadvantages of living in each one, and what might be the impractical aspects of living there.**

(*Candidate A*), **which of these homes do you think is the most practical? Why?**

Part 3 (4 minutes)

Look at page 180 which gives some examples for reducing the use of cars in a city.

Transport (discuss, evaluate and select)

Here are some different ideas for reducing the use of cars in a city and a question for you to discuss.

First, you have some time to look at the task.

(*Pause 15 seconds*)

Now talk to each other about **how practical each idea is.**

Now you have about a minute to decide **which idea is most likely to improve a city.**

Part 4 (5 minutes)

The examiner will encourage you to develop the topic of your discussion in Part 3 by asking questions such as:

- Should private cars be banned from city centres? (Why? / Why not?)
- What do you think could be done in your area to encourage people to use public transport?
- Some cities encourage people to take passengers in their cars to reduce congestion. Do you think this is a good idea, and would it work in your area? (Why? / Why not?)

For questions **1–8**, read the text below and decide which answer (**A, B, C** or **D**) best fits each gap. There is an example at the beginning (**0**).

Mark your answers **on the separate answer sheet**.

Example:

0	**A** rises	**B** strikes	**C** arrives	**D** hits

0	A	**B**	C	D

Mountain rescue in Scotland

Last year, over 200 climbers were rescued from the mountains of Scotland by local teams, who go out in all weathers whenever disaster (**0**) .... Many of these people are volunteers, giving their time and energy freely and, on (**1**) ...., putting themselves in danger. They will risk life and (**2**) .... in an emergency when they are (**3**) .... upon to rescue foolhardy or unlucky climbers. A whole (**4**) .... of things can go wrong up in the mountains, from sudden, violent storms with virtually zero visibility to unforeseen accidents, and many walkers and climbers owe a huge (**5**) .... of gratitude to the rescue teams!

While rescue teams often work for little or no pay, there are still considerable costs (**6**) .... in maintaining an efficient service. Equipment such as ropes and stretchers is of (**7**) .... importance, as are vehicles and radio communications devices. Although some of the costs are borne by the government, the rescue teams couldn't operate without (**8**) .... from the public. Fortunately, these tend to be very generous.

1	**A** situation	**B** event	**C** moment	**D** occasion
2	**A** limb	**B** blood	**C** bone	**D** flesh
3	**A** pulled	**B** called	**C** summoned	**D** required
4	**A** scope	**B** extent	**C** host	**D** scale
5	**A** recognition	**B** liability	**C** debt	**D** claim
6	**A** implied	**B** involved	**C** featured	**D** connected
7	**A** lively	**B** main	**C** essential	**D** vital
8	**A** grants	**B** allowances	**C** donations	**D** aids

For questions **9–16**, read the text below and think of the word which best fits each gap. Use only **one** word in each gap. There is an example at the beginning (**0**).

Write your answers **IN CAPITAL LETTERS on the separate answer sheet**.

Example: | 0 | A | S | | | | | | | | | | | | | | | | | | | | |

The ubiquitous shopping mall

It started, (**0**) ...., many modern trends have, in the United States, but it has now spread to many parts of the world. Many towns and cities no (**9**) .... have a genuine centre. Instead, a shopping mall somewhere on the outskirts serves some of the functions of an urban centre. Here, shops and banks are all crowded together, (**10**) ...., especially for those who use a car, is very convenient. After (**11**) .... parked in the basement car park, people can do all their shopping inside the mall, and then load up the car and drive home. (**12**) .... is no need even to go outside, so it doesn't matter what the weather's (**13**) ....

So why should anyone possibly object (**14**) .... the growing number of shopping malls springing up in and around our cities? (**15**) .... of the main reasons is that when most shops are concentrated in malls, it leaves city and town centres deserted and lifeless. Another is that malls all tend to look very similar, (**16**) .... the result that many towns and cities are losing their individual characters.

For questions **17–24**, read the text below. Use the word given in capitals at the end of some of the lines to form a word that fits in the gap **in the same line**. There is an example at the beginning (**0**).

Write your answers **IN CAPITAL LETTERS on the separate answer sheet**.

Example: | 0 | D | A | I | L | Y | | | | | | | | | | | | | | | |

Blogging in the modern day

The earliest blogs tended to be personal accounts of
(**0**) .... events. Very soon, however, many types emerged   **DAY**
including critical news commentaries, often well-informed
and (**17**) .... expressed. With many millions of bloggers   **ELOQUENCE**
now writing on almost every (**18**) .... subject each day,   **CONCEIVE**
the traditional media cannot afford to ignore them or
treat them with (**19**) .... Their ubiquity means they have   **RESPECT**
become increasingly (**20**) ...., as can be seen in the number   **INFLUENCE**
of 'official' news stories that are (**21**) .... or called into   **CREDIT**
question by bloggers, and also the numerous stories
initiated through blogs.

Most large media organisations have now (**22**) ....   **CORPORATE**
some form of blogging into their news services, but
independent bloggers still have a freedom unavailable
to mainstream journalists. They bypass editors and
publishers, who tend to distort stories. The material
on blogs is raw, (**23**) .... by editors, and often harsh and   **MODIFY**
direct in its criticism of the way news is reported by the
traditional media. Thus, bloggers act as a kind of media
watchdog, able to check facts and verify or, alternatively,
(**24**) .... information in a way that mainstream journalists   **PROOF**
are often unable to.

For questions **25–30**, complete the second sentence so that it has a similar meaning to the first sentence, using the word given. **Do not change the word given**. You must use between **three** and **six** words, including the word given. Here is an example (**0**).

Example:

0 Jane regretted speaking so rudely to the old lady.

MORE

Jane .... politely to the old lady.

Example: | 0 | WISHED SHE HAD SPOKEN MORE

Write **only** the missing words **IN CAPITAL LETTERS on the separate answer sheet**.

---

25 'Mr Brown, a holiday would do you good,' said Dr Mansley.

FROM

'Mr Brown, you .... a holiday,' said Dr Mansley.

26 We were never aware at any moment that something was wrong.

TIME

At .... that something was wrong.

27 If Gary hadn't had that accident, he would have become a professional football player.

FOR

If it .... , Gary would have become a professional football player.

28 We get on very well with Laura's parents.

TERMS

We .... Laura's parents.

29 This wardrobe is so big that I don't believe only one person assembled it.

HAVE

This wardrobe is so big that it .... together by only one person.

30 Someone snatched Sue's bag at the concert.

HAD

Sue .... at the concert.

PAPER 1 Reading and ▶ | Part 1
Use of English | Part 2

PAPER 2 Writing | Part 3
| Part 4
PAPER 3 Listening | Part 5
| Part 6
PAPER 4 Speaking | Part 7
| Part 8

You are going to read a newspaper article. For questions **31–36**, choose the answer (**A**, **B**, **C** or **D**) which you think fits best according to the text.

Mark your answers **on the separate answer sheet**.

The land under the sea

Underwater maps reveal a hidden history

Ten thousand years ago, as the last ice age drew to a close, sea levels around the world were far lower than they are today. Much of the land under both the North Sea to the east of Britain and the English Channel which now separates France and Britain was part of a huge region of forests and grassy plains, where herds of horses and reindeer roamed free and people lived in villages by the lakes and rivers. Then the climate gradually became warmer (a phenomenon certainly not confined to our own age!) and the water trapped in glaciers and ice caps was released. This ancient land was submerged in the resulting deluge and all that remains to tell us that it was once lush and verdant – and inhabited – is the occasional stone tool, harpoon or mammoth tusk brought up from the seabed by fishing boats.

Now the development of advanced sonar technology, known as *bathymetry*, is making it possible to study this flooded landscape in extraordinary detail. A special echo sounder is fixed to the bottom of a survey vessel, and it makes wide sweeps across the seabed. While previous technology has only been able to produce two-dimensional images, bathymetry can now deploy computers, satellite-positioning equipment and special software to create accurate and remarkably detailed maps. For the first time, an ancient riverbed leaps out of the three-dimensional image, complete with rocky ledges rising up from the bottom of the valley. The sites of pre-historic settlements can now be pinpointed, and it is also possible to see in stunning detail the sunken shipwrecks that litter this part of the seabed.

According to archaeologist Dr Linda Andrews, this technological development is of huge significance. 'We now have the ability to map the seabed as accurately as we can map dry land,' she says. She is, however, scathing about the scale of financial support for such projects. 'We have better images of Mars and Venus than of two-thirds of our own planet! Britain is an interesting case. It's been a a maritime nation for much of its history, and the sea has had such a massive influence on it, and in view of this, it's an absolute scandal that we know so little about the area just off the country's shores!'

Once bathymetric techniques have identified sites where people might have built their homes and villages, such as sheltered bays, cliffs with caves and the shores of freshwater lakes, divers can be sent down to investigate further. Robot submarines can also be used, and researchers hope they will find stone tools and wood from houses (which survives far longer in water than on dry land) as proof of human activity. The idea shared by many people in Britain of their country as a natural island kingdom will be challenged by these findings: Britain has been inhabited for about 500,000 years, and for much of this time, it has been linked on and off to continental Europe. It remains to be seen how far this new awareness is taken on board, however.

In fact, the use of bathymetry scanners will not be limited to the study of lost landscapes and ancient settlements. It will also be vital in finding shipwrecks. Records show that there are about 44,000 shipwrecks off the shores of Britain, but there is good reason to believe that the real figure is much higher. In addition, commercial applications are a real possibility. Aggregates for the construction industry are becoming increasingly expensive, and bathymetry scanners can be used to identify suitable sites for quarrying this material. However, mapping the seabed will also identify places where rare plants and shellfish are living. Government legislation could prevent digging at such sites, either to extract material for a profit or to make the water deeper. This is significant in view of the plans to dredge parts of the English Channel to provide deeper waterways for massive container ships.

31 What point is made in the first paragraph about the area now under the sea?

A The fact that it was populated has only recently been discovered.

B It was created by the last ice age.

C Ancient man-made objects have been found there.

D It was flooded, drowning the inhabitants.

32 How does the new sonar technology work?

A It has an echo sounder placed on the seabed.

B It produces two-dimensional images of the sea floor.

C It makes use of a number of different devices.

D It bases its calculations on the location of archaeological sites.

33 How does Dr Andrews feel about the lack of accurate maps of the waters around Britain?

A outraged

B resigned

C astonished

D amused

34 In the fourth paragraph, the writer suggests that a better understanding of the settlements on the seabed may

A inspire more people to take an interest in archaeology.

B modify the attitudes of the British to their country's history.

C provide confirmation about the need to deal with climate change.

D alter the perception people in other countries have about Britain.

35 Quarrying is mentioned in the final paragraph to show that

A there are ways of obtaining funds for research.

B underwater surveys should be completed as soon as possible.

C damage to the seabed has not been recorded accurately so far.

D there are potentially practical benefits for industry.

36 The use of bathymetry scanners may help to

A preserve the marine environment.

B promote the clearing of the English Channel.

C identify new species of plants and animals.

D obtain approval to look for shipwrecks.

PAPER 1 Reading and ▶   Part 1
           Use of English   Part 2

PAPER 2 Writing   Part 3
                     Part 4

PAPER 3 Listening   Part 5

PAPER 4 Speaking   **Part 6**
                     Part 7
                     Part 8

You are going to read extracts from four reviews of a book about the way children are brought up. For questions **37–40**, choose from the reviews **A–D**. The reviews may be chosen more than once.

Mark your answers **on the separate answer sheet**.

Kith: the riddle of the childscape by Jay Griffiths

Four reviewers comment on Jay Griffiths' new book.

A

In this new book, Jay Griffiths draws the familiar but erroneous conclusion that traditional societies and tribes treat nature and children better than modern ones. She is no anthropologist, writing more like a romantic poet about nature and people's identification with the place they grow up in. To justify her admiration for tribal practice, she cites a 2007 UNICEF report that ranked the UK lowest among 21 industrialised countries for the well-being of its children. No analysis of this finding is provided, however. Instead, a single idea of lost childhood freedom is dressed up in excessively poetic, at times, absurd language, and applied to various cultures. According to Griffiths, what children in Britain and similar countries lack is access to nature and the freedom to express their true selves in it. The idea of 'kith', an attachment to your 'home territory' is an interesting one, but the claims she makes about children's development are too often illogical and unsupportable.

B

In a 2007 UNICEF report, the UK came last among 21 industrialised countries for the well-being of its children. Jay Griffiths' question is: why do they feel so unhappy? Her main answer, passionately and eloquently expressed, is that they are 'imprisoned' indoors in front of their TV or computer screens and have lost contact with their kith – the woods, mountains, rivers, streams and wilds of their home territory. There's definitely something in this idea, but the trouble is that Griffiths pursues it in ways that simply don't hold up. Part of the problem is that she regards children as originally innocent and good, and that these characteristics are suppressed by the restrictions imposed on them. As parents have known for millennia, however, children are far more complex than that. She is also guilty of selective deployment of evidence. That same UNICEF report found that children in the UK are healthier and safer than ever before, for example.

C

Jay Griffiths is a self-confessed romantic, believing in the innate purity of children and a need for them to be close to nature, mystery and risk and be gloriously free. She warns us, however, that children in the West today are caged indoors and deprived of their 'kith', a natural domain of woodland, play, solitude, animals, adventure and time to daydream. It's a fascinating proposition, fluently and vividly delivered. But this book is also deeply frustrating. Griffiths ignores all the science that shows that children are, in fact, far from being the simple innocents of romantic tradition. She also fails to provide convincing evidence for her assertion that children in Euro-American cultures are less happy than other children. She refers to a UNESCO report on children's well-being in the UK, Spain and Sweden to support her argument about the importance of the outdoors. That report, however, finds that well-being depends on many factors like time with family, good relationships with friends, involvement in creative and sporting activities, as well as being outdoors.

D

In Euro-American culture, argues Griffiths, infants often lack closeness with their parents and wider families, which leaves psychological scars. Simultaneously, older children are controlled, denied access to natural spaces and pushed through a school system designed to produce employees but not psychologically rounded citizens. Parents refuse to let children play outdoors for fear of over-hyped risks, and in so doing, deny children access to the outer worlds of private, unwatched play so vital to their psychological development. The natural playgrounds of childhood, the fields and woods, have been lost to most children. The result, as the UNICEF surveys of well-being that Griffiths, quotes reveal, is a generation of children who are unhappy and unfulfilled. Her warning message is made particularly compelling by the rare vitality and admirable energy in Griffiths' writing.

Which scientist

has a different opinion from the others about
Griffiths' style of writing?

37	

shares reviewer A's view of the way Griffiths
develops her ideas about the treatment of children?

38	

expresses a different view from the others about
the use Griffiths makes of data gathered internationally
about children?

39	

has a similar opinion to reviewer B about Griffiths'
depiction of children's basic nature?

40	

You are going to read a newspaper article in which a zoology student talks about her experience of doing practical research in an area of rainforest. Six paragraphs have been removed from the article. Choose from the paragraphs **A–G** the one which fits each gap (**41–46**). There is one extra paragraph which you do not need to use.

Mark your answers **on the separate answer sheet**.

Fieldwork in the rainforest of Ecuador – the experiences of a zoology student

When I was at school, I was a huge fan of TV wildlife programmes, and at a certain point I realised that somehow the natural world would have to be part of my life. So here I am a few years later, in the tropical rainforest of eastern Ecuador, a novice field scientist. The word scientist evokes various images, typically perhaps ones of laboratories and white coats, test tubes and lab rats. But what does it mean to be a field scientist?

41 [   ]

I am currently spending a year at a small scientific research station in a remote patch of the Ecuadorian rainforest belonging to the Kichwa community of San José de Payamino. It is glorious – everything you would expect a tropical rainforest location to be, and a world away from my university in the UK. The air is hot and thick, the trees are densely packed, and everywhere is teeming with life.

42 [   ]

The local people own the land and govern themselves, but the Ecuadorian government also provides for them: a school complete with computer room and satellite internet, for instance. Each year, they vote for a new president and vice-president, who organise the democratic community meetings. Each family has a *finca* in the forest: a wooden home on stilts.

43 [   ]

But my normal life here as a work experience student revolves mainly around my personal research, which is a biodiversity study of frogs. I am trying to establish exactly which species are here, where and when I can find them, and what condition they are in.

44 [   ]

For most of the time, I am just crawling along looking at leaves. Much of field research is like this. It isn't all finding new species and being transfixed by exotic wildlife behaviour. Have you ever seen the behind-the-scenes footage at the end of many nature documentaries, where it turns out a cameraman has been sitting in a tree for three days waiting for a bird to dance? Research is like this – laborious and monotonous – but it can be rewarding too.

45 [   ]

Being a field scientist basically means being an academic, collecting data and publishing scientific papers. It's interesting but it doesn't pay well, and getting started can be tough. When I was looking for work experience, there were plenty of openings with pharmaceutical companies, but very few matching my desire to explore and investigate wildlife.

46 [   ]

This is one reason I count myself lucky to be involved in this project. It's largely funded by my university, so I can afford it. Then, by the end of this year, I will have acquired valuable skills, and I am hopeful that the experience will facilitate my progression into post-graduate study.

A To do this, I walk slowly along several paths in the forest, accompanied by a local guide, and at night equipped with a torch. When I spot what I'm looking for, I feel an intense adrenaline rush. Will I manage to capture it? Have I collected this particular species yet?

B Because of this, and having experienced fieldwork, I've decided it's definitely something I would like to do as a career. Once this year is over, I will ask my lecturers to advise me what to do next.

C This morning, for example, a half metre square of mushrooms sprouted on the dirt floor of my kitchen. My favourite time here is in the early evenings. It's finally cool enough to be comfortable, and the nocturnal creatures begin their nightly cacophony, while the setting sun paints the trees orange.

D The reality is, however, that to make your way you need to build up a range of contacts and a portfolio of work. Many of the initial work opportunities that do exist are voluntary – in fact, you often have to pay to join a scheme. A student job where you are paid expenses, let alone a basic salary, is quite rare.

E By and large, they work outdoors, and are interested in pretty much everything from discovering new species to the effect of obscure parasites on ecosystems. They explore and investigate, aiming to understand what they observe. Just two years into my undergraduate zoology degree, I don't quite qualify as one yet, but hopefully I'm heading that way.

F They have their own traditions, too. One day, a local lady was bitten by a lethal snake; whilst I administered shots of anti-venom to her, the local traditional healer, was applying plant remedies to the wound and attempting to suck the venom from it. At least one of the treatments must have worked because she recovered.

G And the thing is to imagine being the person that has made a discovery – the person who first questions something, investigates and then contributes to the vast catalogue of information that is science. I find this concept inspirational.

You are going to read an article in which people talk about their experiences of job interviews. For questions **47–56**, choose from the people (**A–D**).

Mark your answers **on the separate answer sheet**.

Which person mentions the following?

establishing how the interview will be conducted	**47**
the importance of keeping to the point	**48**
a relaxed atmosphere in the workplace	**49**
an abrupt ending to an interview	**50**
taking responsibility for past errors	**51**
appearing to have rehearsed responses	**52**
preparing inquiries to put to a prospective employer	**53**
awareness of body language	**54**
revealing what motivates you	**55**
advantages in being honest about your weaknesses	**56**

Tell us something about yourself

Being interviewed for a job can be a stressful experience.
We asked four people what they learnt from being in that situation.

A My first interview for a job taught me a great deal. I was applying for the position of junior account executive in an advertising company, which involves dealing with clients on a face-to-face basis. It follows that you have to be good at interpersonal skills, and unfortunately, that's not the impression I gave. Like a lot of people, I tend to babble when I'm nervous. The interviewer began by asking me to say something about myself, and I started talking about my hobbies. But I got carried away and went off at a tangent, which made a bad impression. The other lesson I learnt was that if you are asked to talk about things you aren't good at, you really shouldn't be evasive. You could mention something that can also be a strength. For example, being pedantic is not always a bad thing in certain circumstances, and you should explain how you cope with that deficiency, but you have to say something.

B In my present job, I have to interview applicants, and I can offer a few general tips. Firstly, a candidate should not learn a speech off by heart; you will come across as insincere. Secondly, it is crucial to understand what the interviewer wants you to talk about. For instance, an interviewer might ask about a situation where your supervisor or manager had a problem with your work. Now, what the interviewer is really after is to see how you react to criticism, and the best thing is to say that you tried to learn from this. Finally, don't try to conceal your real character. Many years ago, an interviewer asked me at the end of our talk if I had any questions. I was very keen to get the job, so I asked what opportunities there were for promotion. I wondered if perhaps I had been too direct, but I later discovered that employers like you to seem eager and ambitious.

C I remember one interview I attended with a company that makes ice cream and other dairy products. I turned up in a smart business suit and tie, only to find that my prospective employers were in jeans! They believed in being casual: no private offices, everyone ate in the same canteen, people all used first names with each other. I realised I should have done more research. Needless to say, I didn't get the job. On another occasion, as the interview was drawing to a close, I was asked if I had anything to say. I was so relieved it was over that I just smiled and blurted out: 'No thanks!' I later realised this was a mistake. A candidate should decide in advance on at least ten things to ask the interviewer: it's not necessary to ask more than two or three questions, but you need to have some in reserve in case the question you wanted to ask is answered in the course of the interview.

D Preparation is of extreme importance; things like finding out what form the interview will take. Will there be any sort of written component, for instance, and will you be talking to one person or a panel? And of course, you need to prepare answers to those awkward questions designed to find out more about your character. For example, you might be asked about your most important achievement so far; don't answer this in a way that makes you seem swollen-headed or complacent, as this will suggest that you don't learn easily. Actually, it's not so much what people say that makes them seem arrogant as the way they sit, how they hold their heads, whether they meet the interviewer's eye, so bear that in mind. Another question interviewers sometimes ask, to find out how well you work in a team, is about mistakes you have made. You should have an example ready and admit that you were at fault, otherwise it looks as though you are the kind of person who shifts the blame onto others. But you should also show that you learnt from the mistake and wouldn't make it again.

You **must** answer this question. Write your answer in **220–260** words in an appropriate style on the separate answer sheet.

---

1 Your class has attended a lecture on ways for the government to boost students' interest in science. You have made the notes below.

> **Methods for encouraging an interest in science:**
>
> - TV programmes
> - improved teaching facilities
> - career opportunities

> **Some opinions expressed in the discussion:**
>
> 'Not many young people watch science programmes on TV.'
>
> 'It is expensive to provide laboratories with new equipment.'
>
> 'The government cannot guarantee career opportunities.'

Write an **essay** for your tutor discussing **two** of the methods in your notes. You should **explain which method you think is more important**, and **provide reasons** to support your opinion.

You may, if you wish, make use of the opinions expressed in the discussion, but you should use your own words as far as possible.

PAPER 1 Reading and
Use of English

PAPER 2 Writing ▶ Part 1

PAPER 3 Listening **Part 2**

PAPER 4 Speaking

Write an answer to **one** of the questions **2–4** in this part. Write your answer in **220–260** words in an appropriate style on the separate answer sheet. Put the question number in the box at the top of the page.

2 You have just spent a weekend with a friend you hadn't seen since you were at school together many years ago. Write to your friend saying what the reunion meant to you, what you particularly enjoyed doing during the weekend, and what plans you have for meeting in the future.

Write your **letter**.

3 Your company requires you to wear formal dress to work. There is a proposal to introduce a 'dress-down' day, that is one day at the end of the working week when employees can wear informal clothes. Your manager has asked you to write a report on the advantages and disadvantages of this proposal.

Write your **report**.

4 Your student magazine has asked you to write a review of the latest film in a popular series. Say what is good and bad about the film, and whether it lives up to the earlier films in the series.

Write your **review**.

PAPER 1 Reading and
          Use of English

PAPER 2 Writing

PAPER 3 Listening   ▶ Part 1

PAPER 4 Speaking   Part 2
                                 Part 3
                                 Part 4

🎧 **Track 17**

You will hear three different extracts. For questions **1–6**, choose the answer (**A, B** or **C**) which fits best according to what you hear. There are two questions for each extract.

___

Extract One

You hear part of a radio programme in which a man is being interviewed about an unusual sport.

1 According to Chris, cheese-rolling takes place
    A at only one venue in the world.
    B on muddy ground.
    C once a year.

2 Which statement best sums up how Chris feels about cheese-rolling?
    A It's too dangerous.
    B It's worth the risks.
    C It requires training.

Extract Two

You hear two students on a business course talking about a book they are studying.

3 Sue found the book worth reading because it included
    A case studies of successful enterprises.
    B advice on how to negotiate a contract.
    C the legal aspects of setting up a company.

4 What criticism of the book do both speakers express?
    A Some important information was omitted.
    B Some of it was badly organised.
    C It used too much jargon.

Extract Three

You hear two people talking about yawning.

5 According to the woman, until recently, yawning was thought to
    A be simply a sign that we were tired.
    B help us breathe more deeply.
    C promote alertness.

6 Research suggests that contagious yawning is a way of
    A maintaining alertness in a group.
    B expressing understanding in a group.
    C communicating with each other.

Track 18

You will hear an astrobiologist talking about her work. For questions **7–14**, complete the sentences with a word or a short phrase.

WHAT IS ASTROBIOLOGY?

It could be claimed that the science of astrobiology has no

(7) ....

However, astrobiologists are also concerned with how life

evolved **(8)** ....

There are some popular misconceptions about what

(9) .... might look like.

For much of the Earth's history, single-celled **(10)** ....

were the only life forms in existence.

Multi-cellular life evolved during the **(11)** ....

known as the Cambrian era.

Then, about **(12)** .... years ago, human-like

creatures evolved.

Life on other planets will probably be **(13)** ....

life on Earth.

Human beings might not have evolved if **(14)** ....

had not become extinct.

PAPER 1   Reading and
              Use of English

PAPER 2   Writing

PAPER 3   Listening   ▶

PAPER 4   Speaking

Part 1
Part 2
Part 3
Part 4

 Track 19

You will hear part of a radio interview with Pete Birtwhistle, a playwright. For questions **15–20**, choose the answer (**A**, **B**, **C** or **D**) which fits best according to what you hear.

15   What was Pete's attitude to the theatre before he started writing?
    A   He felt it had little relevance to his life.
    B   He didn't feel qualified to judge it.
    C   He thought it would be boring to watch a play.
    D   He preferred comedies to tragedies.

16   How did he feel about leaving his previous job?
    A   He felt very relieved.
    B   He was anxious about his health.
    C   He worried how others would see him.
    D   He was very depressed.

17   What was the most difficult aspect of writing his first play?
    A   disciplining himself to write every day
    B   coming up with a suitable story
    C   allowing the characters to develop
    D   finding an appropriate ending

18   What is the biggest impact that writing has had on Pete's life?
    A   It has made people respect him more.
    B   It has enabled him to express himself.
    C   It has opened up new professional opportunities.
    D   It has allowed him to appreciate other plays.

19   How does Pete choose the theme of a new play?
    A   He looks around for a challenging theme.
    B   He looks for a subject that is in the news.
    C   He looks for a theme that he understands.
    D   He thinks about issues that affect society.

20   How does Pete feel about writing for films?
    A   enthusiastic
    B   worried
    C   cautious
    D   intimidated

PAPER 1 Reading and
          Use of English

PAPER 2 Writing

PAPER 3 Listening ►
                        Part 1
                        Part 2
                        Part 3
                        Part 4

PAPER 4 Speaking

Track 20

You will hear five short extracts in which people talk about tracing their ancestors.

While you listen, you must complete both tasks.

TASK ONE

For questions **21–25**, choose from list **A–H**, the person who is speaking.

A	One of my ancestors went abroad to find adventure.	Speaker 1		21
B	A relative ran away from home when he was young.	Speaker 2		22
C	I am descended from immigrants.	Speaker 3		23
D	A family tradition turned out not to be true.	Speaker 4		24
E	At one time the family was wealthy.	Speaker 5		25
F	My great-grandmother came from a rich family.			
G	A relative emigrated to Australia.			
H	My great-great-grandfather changed his name.			

TASK TWO

For questions **26–30**, choose from list **A–H** what view each speaker is expressing.

A	I get angry at the thought of their suffering.	Speaker 1		26
B	Learning the truth caused considerable bitterness.	Speaker 2		27
C	I have become more curious about the story.	Speaker 3		28
D	The whole thing made us feel quite embarrassed.	Speaker 4		29
E	I was delighted to make contact with my relatives.	Speaker 5		30
F	The story saddened me.			
G	I am very proud of my ancestor.			
H	I was disappointed at first.			

Part 1 (2 minutes)

The examiner will ask you a few questions about yourself and about a general topic. For example, the examiner may ask you:

• When and how did you start learning English?
• In what ways is knowing a foreign language useful to you now?
• How do you expect language skills to be important to you in the future?

Part 2 (4 minutes)

You will each be asked to talk on your own for about a minute. You will each be given three different pictures to talk about. After your partner has finished speaking, you will be asked a brief question connected with your partner's photographs.

Groups (compare, contrast and speculate)

Turn to pictures 1–3 on page 181 which show people in groups.

(*Candidate A*), it's your turn first. Here are your pictures. They show **people in groups**.

I'd like you to compare **two** of the pictures and say **what the advantages are of doing these things in groups**.

(*Candidate B*), **do you enjoy doing things in a group? Why? / Why not?**

Experience (compare, contrast and speculate)

Turn to pictures 1–3 on page 182 which show different skills.

Now, (*Candidate B*), here are your pictures. **They show people with different specialist skills.**

I'd like you to compare **two** of these skills, and say **how difficult it might be to acquire these skills.**

(*Candidate A*), **which of these skills would take the longest time to acquire? Why?**

Part 3 (4 minutes)

Look at page 183 which gives some situations where there is a need for time management.

Time management (discuss, evaluate and select)

Here are some different situations where time management is necessary and a question for you to discuss.

First, you have some time to look at the task.

(*Pause 15 seconds*)

Now talk to each other about **why time management is necessary in each situation.**

Now you have about a minute to decide **which situation would benefit most from better time management.**

Part 4 (5 minutes)

The examiner will encourage you to develop the topic of your discussion in Part 3 by asking questions such as:

• Do you think it is a problem if someone is often late for appointments and meetings? (Why? / Why not?)

• Which aspects of modern life, where time is managed badly, do you find most annoying?

• Does modern life make us too anxious about punctuality? (Why? / Why not?)

• When was the last time you were late, and what caused you to be late?

For questions **1–8**, read the text below and decide which answer (**A, B, C** or **D**) best fits each gap. There is an example at the beginning (**0**).

Mark your answers **on the separate answer sheet**.

Example:

| 0 | **A** define | **B** generate | **C** adopt | **D** cause |

```
0  A   B   C   D
   ⎵   ▬   ⎵   ⎵
```

A new look at the Middle Ages

The Institute for Medieval Studies is holding a series of lectures to (**0**) .... interest in a period of European history which is all too often (**1**) .... It is hoped that these lectures will (**2**) .... some of the misconceptions that (**3**) .... to this day about the long and eventful span of time between the sixth and the 15th centuries.

It is true that Europe was (**4**) .... by the plague in the latter part of the 14th century, and that living (**5**) .... for the majority of people were appalling by modern standards, and life (**6**) .... was low. The peasants suffered under a brutal feudal system and the (**7**) .... of learning was open only to a small minority.

However, these negative aspects of medieval life cannot be properly evaluated unless they are viewed in the broader (**8**) .... The Middle Ages were also a period of great achievements in architecture, science, technology, art and trade, and the lectures will explore the more progressive and enlightened features of the age, as well as its darker aspects.

1	**A** neglected	**B** abandoned	**C** subdued	**D** deserted
2	**A** respond	**B** refuse	**C** rectify	**D** revive
3	**A** insist	**B** persist	**C** consist	**D** resist
4	**A** injured	**B** eliminated	**C** wounded	**D** ravaged
5	**A** states	**B** circumstances	**C** conditions	**D** situations
6	**A** estimate	**B** forecast	**C** prediction	**D** expectancy
7	**A** pursuit	**B** chase	**C** desire	**D** quest
8	**A** background	**B** setting	**C** context	**D** environment

For questions **9–16**, read the text below and think of the word which best fits each gap. Use only **one** word in each gap. There is an example at the beginning (**0**).

Write your answers **IN CAPITAL LETTERS on the separate answer sheet**.

Example: | 0 | | I | N | | | | | | | | | | | | | | | | | | | | | | |

Speed limits

Engineers have succeeded (**0**) …….. developing a sophisticated system for limiting the speed that cars and other vehicles can reach. Known (**9**) …….. 'intelligent speed adaptation', or ISA, it is a concept for (**10**) …….. there is considerable support. It also has many opponents, however. ISA involves fitting a vehicle with a communications box that knows (**11**) …….. fast the vehicle is legally permitted to travel on a particular section of road, and automatically regulates the car's speed. It therefore becomes impossible for a vehicle fitted with (**12**) …….. a device to exceed the speed limit.

The communications box could have other uses too. In (**13**) …….. to encourage the reduction of traffic, various cities around the world, Singapore and London (**14**) …….. them, have introduced congestion zones requiring motorists to pay to enter central areas. At present, (**15**) …….. time a vehicle enters the zone, its number plate is photographed and checked against a list, but this system is costly and (**16**) …….. from foolproof. The ISA communications box could be easily adapted for this purpose and would be cheaper.

While ISA has its opponents, eventually governments are likely to require a version of it on all vehicles.

For questions **17–24**, read the text below. Use the word given in capitals at the end of some of the lines to form a word that fits in the gap **in the same line**. There is an example at the beginning (**0**).

Write your answers **IN CAPITAL LETTERS on the separate answer sheet**.

Example: | 0 | C | E | L | E | B | R | A | T | I | O | N | | | | | | |

The origins of Halloween

Nowadays, Halloween is a popular (**0**) .... which   **CELEBRATE**
people enjoy in many parts of the world. It is a time
when young people in particular dress up as witches
or ghosts and have parties.

Halloween (**17**) .... about 2,000 years ago with the   **ORIGIN**
Celts, however. These people were the (**18**) .... of   **INHABIT**
an area that includes Britain, Ireland and Brittany. They
relied on the land for their (**19**) ...., and this meant that **LIVE**
they were at the mercy of (**20**) .... weather conditions,   **PREDICT**
especially during the winter.

The Celtic new year began on 1 November, which
also marked the beginning of winter, a period (**21**) ....   **TRADITION**
associated with death. On the eve of the new year, it was
believed that the barriers between the worlds of the living
and the dead were (**22**) .... withdrawn, and it was possible **TEMPORARY**
to communicate with spirits. The Celts believed that the
spirits offered them (**23**) .... and protection, and their   **GUIDE**
priests were (**24**) .... able to predict the future on this night. **REPUTE**

Halloween is very different now, of course, but it is interesting
to consider what it once was.

For questions **25–30**, complete the second sentence so that it has a similar meaning to the first sentence, using the word given. **Do not change the word given.** You must use between **three** and **six** words, including the word given. Here is an example (**0**).

Example:

0 Jane regretted speaking so rudely to the old lady.

MORE

Jane .... politely to the old lady.

Example: 0 WISHED SHE HAD SPOKEN MORE

Write **only** the missing words **IN CAPITAL LETTERS on the separate answer sheet.**

___

25 They believe that Mario failed his exam because he was nervous.

DOWN

Mario's failure in his exam .... the fact that he was nervous.

26 'Why didn't I ask Linda for her phone number?' thought Sam.

ASKED

'If .... Linda for her phone number!' thought Sam.

27 We didn't think Mr Mason was going to recover, so it was a relief when he did.

PULLED

We were relieved when Mr Mason .... we didn't think he would.

28 'I really don't like what the press are saying about me!' said Tina.

OBJECTED

Tina .... about her by the press.

29 'I don't mind you staying out late, but your father does,' Robbie's mother told him.

RATHER

'It's .... minds you staying out late,' Robbie's mother told him.

30 They think that students vandalised the school last night.

WAS

It is .... by students last night.

PAPER 1 Reading and
         Use of English

PAPER 2 Writing

PAPER 3 Listening

PAPER 4 Speaking

Part 1
Part 2
Part 3
Part 4
Part 5
Part 6
Part 7
Part 8

You are going to read a newspaper article. For questions **31–36**, choose the answer (**A**, **B**, **C** or **D**) which you think fits best according to the text.

Mark your answers **on the separate answer sheet**.

Learning to run

An article published in the prestigious scientific journal *Nature* sheds new light on an important, but hitherto little appreciated, aspect of human evolution. In this article, Professors Dennis Bramble and Daniel Lieberman suggest that being able to run was a crucial element in the development of our species. According to the two scientists, humans possess a number of anatomical features that make them surprisingly good runners. 'We are very confident that strong selection for running – which came at the expense of the historical ability to live in trees – was instrumental in the origin of the modern human body form,' says Bramble, a biology professor at the University of Utah.

Traditional thinking up to now has been that the distinctive, upright body form of modern humans has come about as a result of the ability to walk, and that running is simply a by-product of walking. Furthermore, humans have usually been regarded as poor runners compared to such animals as dogs, horses or antelopes. However, this is only true if we consider running at high speed, especially over short distances. Even an Olympic athlete can hardly run as quickly as a horse can gallop, and can only sprint for 15 seconds or so. Horses, antelopes and greyhounds, on the other hand, can run at top speed for several minutes, clearly outperforming us in this respect. But when it comes to long-distance running, humans do astonishingly well. They can maintain a steady pace for many kilometres, and their overall speed is at least on a par with that of horses or dogs.

Bramble and Lieberman examined 26 anatomical features found in humans. One of the most interesting of these is the nuchal ligament, a band of tissue that extends from a ridge on the base of the skull to the spine. When we run, it is this ligament that prevents our head from pitching back and forth or from side to side. Therefore, we are able to run with steady heads, held high. The nuchal ligament is not found in any other surviving primates, although the fossil record shows that *Homo erectus*, an early human species that walked upright, much as we do, also had one. Then there are our Achilles tendons at the backs of our legs, which connect our calf muscles to our heel bones – and which have nothing to do with walking. When we run, these tendons behave like springs, helping to propel us forward. Furthermore, we have low, wide shoulders, virtually disconnected from our skulls, an anatomical development which allows us to run more efficiently. Add to this our light forearms, which swing out of phase with the movement of our legs to assist balance, and one begins to appreciate the point that Bramble and Lieberman are trying to make.

But what evolutionary advantage is gained from being good long-distance runners? One hypothesis is that this ability may have permitted early humans to obtain food more effectively. 'What these features and fossil facts appear to be telling us is that running evolved in order for our direct ancestors to compete with other carnivores for access to the protein needed to grow the big brains that we enjoy today,' says Lieberman. Some scientists speculate that early humans may have pursued animals for great distances in order to exhaust them before killing them. Running would also have conferred an advantage before weapons were invented: early humans might have been scavengers, eating the meat and marrow left over from a kill by lions or other large predators. They may have been alerted to the existence of a freshly killed carcass by vultures, and the faster they got to the scene of the kill, the better.

'Research on the history of human locomotion has traditionally been contentious,' says Lieberman. 'At the very least, I hope this theory will make many people have second thoughts about how humans learned to run and walk and why we are built the way we are.'

31 What does the writer say in the first paragraph about the human ability to run?

   A It is worse than our body shape might indicate.

   B It developed in combination with other human activities.

   C It has always been more important than being able to climb trees.

   D It was once overlooked as a determining factor in human evolution.

32 What comparison does the writer make in the second paragraph?

   A Humans run as well as horses and dogs at certain distances.

   B Humans are better runners than most other animals.

   C Humans don't need to run as fast as many animals.

   D Humans cannot run for as long as we might think.

33 What does the writer say about the nuchal ligament?

   A It can only be found in modern primates.

   B It enables us to run in the manner that we do.

   C It forces us to look in the direction we're running.

   D It makes us run on two legs rather than four.

34 What does the writer suggest in the third paragraph?

   A We could run better if we had stronger arms.

   B We could walk without using our calf muscles.

   C Our Achilles tendons are an adaptation for running.

   D The shape of our shoulders affects the position of our heads.

35 Which conclusion is drawn about early humans in the fourth paragraph?

   A They followed birds to avoid dangerous situations.

   B They evolved as a result of their hunting skills.

   C They developed big brains for running.

   D They were unable to kill large animals.

36 According to the final paragraph, what does Professor Lieberman hope to do?

   A Dispel any remaining doubts about the nature of the human body.

   B Inform people of the real reason why humans are able to run and walk.

   C Cause people to reconsider previously held ideas about human anatomy.

   D Prove conclusively that humans did not always walk in an upright position.

PAPER 1 Reading and ▶   Part 1
         Use of English   Part 2

PAPER 2 Writing   Part 3

                     Part 4

PAPER 3 Listening   Part 5

                     Part 6

PAPER 4 Speaking

                     Part 7

                     Part 8

You are going to read extracts from four reviews of a film called *The Great Gatsby*. For questions 37–40, choose from the reviews **A–D**. The reviews may be chosen more than once.

Mark your answers **on the separate answer sheet**.

The Great Gatsby

Four reviewers comment on The Great Gatsby *directed by Baz Luhrmann.*
The film is based on a novel by F. Scott Fitzgerald.

A

Four previous film versions of *The Great Gatsby* have fallen short of the book's brilliant portrayal of a society succumbing to greed, and, unfortunately, Baz Luhrmann's attempt fares little better. F. Scott Fitzgerald's short, lean, subtle novel conjures up disillusion, pain and tragedy as the main characters' relationships unfold, but this sense is largely drowned out by the lavish excess, the fancy camerawork and the general superficiality in this film. Surprisingly, the soundtrack mixing 1920s orchestral pieces with hip hop and modern pop works a treat and is likely to appeal to younger audiences, as is the very strong cast of actors who give some excellent performances, almost in spite of the over-the-top direction. Whether this will prompt them to go back and read the novel, as some have suggested, is highly questionable, however.

B

As other commentators have pointed out, F. Scott Fitzgerald's great novel, revealing the emptiness and pain that lies behind the pursuit of power and wealth, is a concise, elegant, almost understated work. There is no reason, however, why a film of the same story shouldn't take on a different style and this is what Baz Luhrmann does, largely to good effect. Creating huge cinematic set pieces out of 1920s upper-class life, he plays up the fake, the superficial and the decadent. The narrative is unchanged but rather squeezed in, but then it is rather slight in the novel anyway; Fitzgerald's lyrical prose and characterisation are what make it compelling. The decision to mix contemporary pop with music from the 1920s, has a certain logic to it, given Luhrmann's visual approach, but for some reason the mix feels uneasy rather than complementary. There may be an element of wanting to attract teenage viewers – nothing wrong with that, of course.

C

F. Scott Fitzgerald's classic 1925 novel, *The Great Gatsby*, tells the story of a man who ruthlessly chases wealth, ultimately in pursuit of love, only to learn that one can't buy the other. In keeping with his previous films, director Baz Luhrmann's version is a loud confection of colour, lights and noise from start to finish. Its musical soundtrack is a mix of period pieces, contemporary rap and dance tunes which somehow hang together and support the excesses of the parties, car chases and general hysteria. The narrative structure of the novel exposes the artificiality and heartlessness of the American dream – that of acquiring great wealth from nothing – but the film's overblown nature drowns this message out. The great hope is that all the noise and visual excitement will persuade younger viewers to try reading the novel – which would be a very positive consequence.

D

Baz Luhrmann used modern pop music to energise William Shakespeare's *Romeo and Juliet* and also 19th-century Paris in his film *Moulin Rouge* to great effect. In his version of *The Great Gatsby,* the same strategy merely serves to distance the audience from the human drama they should be engaged with. With his exaggerated operatic style, Luhrmann is the wrong director to shoot F. Scott Fitzgerald's small but perfectly formed novel. It's not that he makes substantial changes to the narrative of the film; the original has a thin plot anyway, and the film is largely faithful to it. It's more that all the noise, flashing lights and dizzying crowd scenes typical of Luhrmann overwhelm both the tragedy and the subtlety characteristic of the original. Audiences, especially perhaps younger ones, will undoubtedly be attracted by the visual and auditory glamour, but they will miss out on what makes the novel great.

Which reviewer

expresses a different view from the others about
the film's potential impact on younger audiences?

37

takes a similar view to reviewer C on the appropriacy
of the music that goes with the film?

38

shares reviewer B's opinion about the film's storyline?

39

has a different opinion from the others about the way
the film is directed?

40

PAPER 1	Reading and ▶	Part 1
	Use of English	Part 2
PAPER 2	Writing	Part 3
		Part 4
PAPER 3	Listening	Part 5
PAPER 4	Speaking	Part 6
		Part 7
		Part 8

You are going to read a newspaper article. Six paragraphs have been removed from the article. Choose from the paragraphs **A–G** the one which fits each gap (**41–46**). There is one extra paragraph which you do not need to use.

Mark your answers **on the separate answer sheet**.

Energy-efficient design

If you consider yourself to be particularly environmentally friendly, there is a community which may interest you. Here, in a large, multi-home development known as BedZED, you can find architecture which is truly green. Buildings come with thick windows and walls, which regulate the temperature at a comfortable level throughout the year. The south-facing windows collect heat and light from the sun, as do solar panels fitted onto the exterior. Not only that, but BedZED is stylish, and every flat comes with a private garden.

41

As far as countries in the West are concerned, the buildings that people live and work in consume far more energy than transport, for example. However, architecture need not consume so much energy, nor produce so much in the way of CO_2 emissions. The intelligent design of the housing at BedZED housing demonstrates that buildings can be made environmentally friendly, without particularly high costs or advanced technology.

42

And indeed, the BedZED community – which has some 84 homes – is really rather cost-effective because of economies of scale: the more homes you build, the less you pay proportionately for the materials and construction of each individual home. This, as well as all the other benefits, is why BedZED is receiving more and more attention.

43

The technology used in the BedZED design could be implemented far more than it currently is, across different forms of architecture. It is neither a challenge,

nor costly to install solar panels, triple-glazed windows, or to insulate floors and walls better. Indeed, according to some estimates, it would be easy to reduce the energy consumption of most of our buildings by up to 20% if we just used more effective design.

44

In large part, the drive for these changes has come from Europe. Here, governments are becoming more concerned about the dangers of relying too much on our current energy and aware of the need to meet energy-reduction goals. Many governments have given financial incentives for using energy-efficient design in the construction industry, and have also tightened regulations. Moreover, a European Union directive now requires house builders to present evidence of how they are meeting energy-efficiency guidelines.

45

It also seems that governments are becoming more involved in the research and development of environmentally friendly designs. At one laboratory in California, a team has experimented with architectural designs such as windows which become darker on sunny days, thereby reducing the amount of heat coming into the home. This would, in theory, offer significant savings for people who make heavy use of air-conditioning in hot, sunny climates. Interesting initiatives have been taken elsewhere, too.

46

We still have not reached a situation in which the general public fully accepts such measures. From a marketing perspective, it can still be difficult to convince customers that energy efficient products are worthwhile. However, as energy prices rise, this is sure to change.

A Indeed, according to one researcher from the European Commission in Brussels, who works on energy efficiency, it would be possible to achieve a great deal simply by using existing technologies.

B Governments elsewhere in the world are playing their part too. In the US, the Energy Star programme provides standards for the energy efficiency of consumer products, from home construction to computers and kitchen appliances. This has resulted in energy-efficient products becoming commonplace, and indeed, an attractive choice for consumers.

C Both of these regions still make every possible attempt to meet energy consumption guidelines as governments around the world attempt to come to grips with the threat of global warming. There seems every likelihood that this project could lead the way–one can only hope that others will follow.

D In India, for example, a New Delhi-based non-profit organisation has helped to create systems whereby small villages can use waste products from farming, and convert them into power. And in Sweden, there is research into how heat from the ground can be used to provide hot water or heating for homes.

E Although it might seem like a state-of-the-art paradise for the super-rich, it's actually an estate of affordable housing built between 2000 and 2002 in a suburb of London. It can't be said that the people who live here are all eco-warriors, but they are part of a growing tendency to find buildings which use less energy.

F This essentially, means finding out how to increase efficiency in the least complicated manner possible. BedZED, for example, was planned so that even if the homes need more energy, despite their eco-friendly designs, there is still a power plant based on the site. This plant, which uses waste materials, can meet any remaining energy demands from residents.

G Recently, this has been coming from Asia in the form of Indian and Chinese visitors. Also, more zero-energy communities are under construction elsewhere in the UK, as well as in the USA.

You are going to read a newspaper article in which people talk about changes in their careers. For questions **47–56**, choose from the people (**A–D**).

Mark your answers **on the separate answer sheet**.

In which section of the article are the following mentioned?

the unexpected demands of the business	47
a cautious approach to doing business	48
an established network of contacts	49
taking advantage of modern communications	50
realising an ambition	51
the cost of setting up a business	52
plans to branch out	53
the competitive nature of a business	54
the need to update knowledge	55
helping people to fill in official forms	56

A change in direction

It is becoming increasingly common for people to change careers at some point in their lives. Four people describe their experiences of changing direction.

A I used to work in the accounts department of a large engineering company before it was taken over by a bigger corporation. I found the new management style hard to adjust to, so I looked for something else. I'm interested in maths and my wife suggested I try teaching, but I figured I'd better not stray far from what I was familiar with. I knew a change in the way self-employed people complete their tax returns was due to be introduced, and I had an idea for some software showing people how to go about it. So, I teamed up with a programmer I knew, with me writing the content and him doing the technical side. It proved much more successful than I'd anticipated, and we've gone on to produce more software showing people how to manage their finances. I've deliberately kept the operation small-scale. I work from home and the outlay for office equipment was low. People say I should expand, but that brings all sorts of new challenges and I like things as they are.

B Two years ago, I felt like a change. I'd been teaching physical education to secondary school students for eight years. I wanted to continue in something to do with sports, so I became an independent personal trainer. It's worked out well. I have agreements with gyms around the city to use their facilities, and I train adults – individuals and small groups. Luckily, I had a ready-made clientele, in the shape of former colleagues and people they recommended me to. Any personal trainer worth their salt should attend training courses on a regular basis to familiarise themselves with the latest developments in sports science – there's lots of really good research these days about things like running techniques, nutrition and rehabilitation from injury. It interests me but also knowing this stuff is good for my reputation. As long as my clients enjoy and can afford my sessions, I can't ever see myself being short of work. If anything, the number of people wanting help to get fit is only likely to increase.

C I studied sociology at university and when it was over, I didn't know what to do next. Several other people on my course started to work for local government services and it looked as though that was a possibility for me. Then, I heard about a new project to re-landscape a park in the city – there were gardening jobs going. I thought: 'That's it!' I can't say I'd dreamed of becoming a gardener, but I'd always thought that working outdoors would be brilliant. I now run my own landscape gardening company and employ three other people. I still spend most of my time in parks and gardens doing physical work, but I also have to manage the business. At first, I was surprised at how much paperwork I had to deal with. Completing forms and things like that is very time-consuming, and I'm thinking of hiring someone to do it. I've also been invited to write articles about gardening for a couple of magazines and websites, and I definitely want to do more of that in the future.

D I worked for an advertising agency for about ten years, but the sector's very cut-throat, and when we got a new boss he decided to make his mark by getting rid of a few people, myself included. Once I got my breath back, I decided to go freelance rather than join another agency. It occurred to me that a lot of companies need not only an advertising campaign but also a consultant, an independent expert to give them an honest view of their situation. I do almost all my work from home, using email, video conferencing and other online tools. It's satisfying as well as being financially rewarding. One advantage, of course, is that I have control over my own time, which wasn't the case before. For example, if there are forms or other tedious paperwork to deal with, I can usually put it off to another day, or even pay someone to do it for me. Like most self-employed people, I work very hard, but I knew it would be like this, and I don't mind it.

PAPER 1 Reading and
        Use of English
PAPER 2 Writing ▶ | Part 1
                    Part 2
PAPER 3 Listening
PAPER 4 Speaking

You **must** answer this question. Write your answer in **220–260** words in an appropriate style on the separate answer sheet.

1 Your class has attended a seminar discussing the possibility that your school should be sponsored by companies in the neighbourhood. You have made the notes below.

> **Reasons for commercial sponsorship of your school:**
>
> - generous funding
> - professional management
> - local involvement

> **Some opinions expressed in the discussion:**
>
> 'Finance cannot be guaranteed.'
>
> 'The companies will influence the teaching curriculum.'
>
> 'It's good to encourage children to contribute to the local environment.'

Write an **essay** for your tutor discussing **two** of the reasons in your notes. You should **explain which reason you think is more important** for the school to consider, and **provide reasons** to support your opinion.

You may, if you wish, make use of the opinions expressed in the discussion, but you should use your own words as far as possible.

Write an answer to **one** of the questions **2–4** in this part. Write your answer in **220–260** words in an appropriate style on the separate answer sheet. Put the question number in the box at the top of the page.

---

2   Your class has had a discussion on the role of education in preparing young people for work, and you agreed to write a report on the discussion for your teacher.

These are the questions that were discussed:

  • Is it better to specialise with a view to becoming an expert in one field, or should students have as broad an education as possible?
  • What do employers want from someone they hire?

Write your **report**.

3   You are working as an entertainments assistant in a summer camp for children aged 8–15. Write an email to your friend at home who is thinking about doing a similar job about the highs and lows of the experience, describing the work, your relationship with the children and your social life.

Write your **email**.

4   The music section of a national newspaper has announced a competition, and is inviting customers to write a review of a live concert they have been to. Reviews must mention aspects of the concert they enjoyed, and also ones they found disappointing. You have decided to enter the competition, and write about a concert you have been to recently.

Write your **review**.

PAPER 1 Reading and Use of English

PAPER 2 Writing

PAPER 3 Listening ▶ **Part 1**
Part 2
Part 3
Part 4

PAPER 4 Speaking

 Track 21

You will hear three different extracts. For questions **1–6**, choose the answer (**A**, **B** or **C**) which fits best according to what you hear. There are two questions for each extract.

Extract One

You hear an interview with a head teacher about the environmental policy at her school.

1 Some students are currently helping to
  A source organic food for the school canteen.
  B reduce the school's fossil-fuel consumption.
  C develop a system for recycling rubbish.

2 According to the teacher, one positive outcome of the program is that
  A the school gets valuable publicity for its environmental projects.
  B the students are motivated to work for the future of the environment.
  C the parents have become concerned about the environment.

Extract Two

You hear an interview with a man talking about his first day at work.

3 What did Colin find most difficult about his first day at work?
  A remembering people's names
  B following his supervisor's instructions
  C finding his way around the company

4 Who should listeners contact first if they want personal advice?
  A Colin
  B the interviewer
  C the programme producer

Extract Three

You hear part of an interview with a film maker, Tony Dupois.

5 Tony believes that the film school he went to
  A did not cater for people with backgrounds in video and television.
  B offered a broad curriculum that inspired him to be creative.
  C gave him the opportunity to make valuable contacts.

6 The interviewer mentions a character from one of Tony's films in order to
  A illustrate the importance of guilt as a theme in Tony's work.
  B exemplify the complexity of the characters Tony creates.
  C highlight the problem of stereotyping villains in films.

Track 22

You will hear an archaeologist talking about an experience he had in South America. For questions **7–14**, complete the sentences with a word or a short phrase.

AN UNPLEASANT ADVENTURE

The archaeologist's original task was to (**7**) ....
the ruined city and the area around it.

He was then asked to suggest ways to (**8**) ....

It appears that the (**9**) .... air exhaled by visitors is
damaging the walls.

The archaeologist wanted to survey a tomb near the site of a proposed
(**10**) ....

Unfortunately, the tomb had been damaged by flood water from
(**11**) ....

The archaeologist lost his footing on some (**12**) ....

As he fell, he broke his (**13**) ....

He was found when a (**14**) .... heard his shouts for help.

Track 23

You will hear part of a radio interview with Professor Hector Williams, a linguist. For questions **15–20**, choose the answer (**A**, **B**, **C** or **D**) which fits best according to what you hear.

15 What was the assumption behind medieval interest in an artificial language?
   A   It would be easy to learn a logical language.
   B   The language would be more suited to classification.
   C   The universe was constructed on linguistic principles.
   D   The language would be a key to understanding the universe.

16 The artificial language based on the names of the notes in the scale
   A   had a vocabulary of single-syllable words.
   B   could be understood by people in the west.
   C   simplified the task of reading music.
   D   was intended to be easy to learn and understand.

17 How did Professor Williams feel when he first heard Esperanto spoken?
   A   He thought it was a dialect of Italian.
   B   He felt it had a pleasant sound.
   C   He considered it was successful in its aims.
   D   He wanted to know the logic behind it.

18 According to Professor Williams, what is the main objection to an artificial language?
   A   It is not very expressive.
   B   It cannot be used to talk about the past.
   C   It does not have any native speakers.
   D   It has a limited vocabulary.

19 What characteristic of Esperanto speakers does Professor Williams find most striking?
   A   their optimism
   B   their naivety
   C   their dedication
   D   their elitism

20 Professor Williams considers that no artificial language will ever become universal because
   A   the language instinct is fundamental in all human beings.
   B   identity and language are strongly linked for most people.
   C   it is impossible to invent a completely artificial language.
   D   too few people would ever consider learning one.

PAPER 1 Reading and
         Use of English

PAPER 2 Writing

PAPER 3 Listening   Part 1

PAPER 4 Speaking   Part 2
                               Part 3
                               Part 4

Track 24

You will hear five short extracts in which people whose jobs involve travelling talk about their work.

While you listen, you must complete both tasks.

TASK ONE

For questions **21–25**, choose from list **A–H**, what job each person has.

A a musician

B a journalist

C a sports person

D a technical trouble shooter

E an ecologist

F a sales representative

G a translator

H an airline pilot

Speaker 1	21
Speaker 2	22
Speaker 3	23
Speaker 4	24
Speaker 5	25

TASK TWO

For questions **26–30**, choose from list **A–H** what view each speaker is expressing.

A I'm pleased if I can settle misunderstandings.

B I'm glad to get a break from the office.

C I worry about having a negative impact.

D I wouldn't be able to tolerate a desk job.

E I get bored if I'm not constantly travelling.

F I'm happy that I can make friends easily.

G I'm excited to go on overseas assignments.

H I enjoy communicating when I'm abroad.

Speaker 1	26
Speaker 2	27
Speaker 3	28
Speaker 4	29
Speaker 5	30

Part 1 (2 minutes)

The examiner will ask you a few questions about yourself and about a general topic. For example, the examiner may ask you:

- What means of transport did you use to get here today?
- What sort of public transport is available in this area?
- Which forms of transport do you prefer, and which do you dislike?

Part 2 (4 minutes)

You will each be asked to talk on your own for about a minute. You will each be given three different pictures to talk about. After your partner has finished speaking, you will be asked a brief question connected with your partner's photographs.

Anxiety (compare, contrast and speculate)

Turn to pictures 1–3 on page 184 which show people feeling anxious.

(*Candidate A*), it's your turn first. Here are your pictures. They show **people in stressful situations.**

I'd like you to compare **two** of the pictures and say **what might be making the people anxious.**

(*Candidate B*), **which situation would you least like to be in? Why?**

Achievement (compare, contrast and speculate)

Turn to pictures 1–3 on page 185 which show different skills.

Now, (*Candidate B*), here are your pictures. **They show people who have achieved something.**

I'd like you to compare **two** of the pictures, and say **what you think these people have achieved and what difficulties they might have had in reaching their goals.**

(*Candidate A*), **which person do you think might be most proud of their achievement? Why?**

Part 3 (4 minutes)

Look at page 186, which shows situations where you need to consider appearance.

Appearance (discuss, evaluate and select)

Here are some different situations where your appearance is important and a question for you to discuss.

First, you have some time to look at the task.

(*Pause 15 seconds*)

Now talk to each other about **why your appearance is important in each situation.**

Now you have about a minute to decide in **which situation it's most important to have a good appearance.**

Part 4 (5 minutes)

The examiner will encourage you to develop the topic of your discussion in Part 3 by asking questions such as:

- In what sort of situations do you think someone's appearance is most important?
- Do you think it is possible to ignore fashion? (Why? / Why not?)
- To what extent do you judge a person by his or her appearance?
- How important is appearance to someone who cares what other people think?

For questions **1–8**, read the text below and decide which answer (**A**, **B**, **C** or **D**) best fits each gap. There is an example at the beginning (**0**).

Mark your answers **on the separate answer sheet**.

Example:

0 **A** frequent   **B** common   **C** general   **D** normal

0	A	B	C	D
	⎵	**▬**	⎵	⎵

Vanilla surprise

Vanilla is such a (**0**) …….. flavour that it comes as a surprise to learn that it is also one of the world's most expensive crops. The vanilla plant is (**1**) …….. to the Americas. Its flowers grow in (**2**) …….. , and in nature they are pollinated by hummingbirds and bees. The (**3**) …….. seed pods resemble oversized French beans, and develop their (**4**) …….. flavour and fragrance during the curing process. After harvesting, the beans are treated with heat or hot water and are placed in the sun every day for many weeks. When they have (**5**) …….. to a fifth of their original size, they are divided according to size and quality.

Like other spices that we (**6**) …….. for granted today, vanilla has a fascinating history. In the 16th century, the Spanish imported the spice to Europe. However, attempts to grow vanilla in other locations (**7**) …….. with failure: the plants would not produce pods, and it was only when a way was found to pollinate the flowers artificially that the commercial exploitation of this valuable crop (**8**) …….. under way.

1	**A** resident	**B** local	**C** native	**D** inhabitant
2	**A** series	**B** bouquets	**C** bands	**D** bunches
3	**A** deriving	**B** resulting	**C** producing	**D** arising
4	**A** distinctive	**B** appetising	**C** tasteful	**D** potential
5	**A** concentrated	**B** shrunk	**C** sunk	**D** lessened
6	**A** give	**B** make	**C** do	**D** take
7	**A** resulted	**B** hit	**C** met	**D** finished
8	**A** got	**B** started	**C** came	**D** began

For questions **9–16**, read the text below and think of the word which best fits each gap. Use only **one** word in each gap. There is an example at the beginning (**0**).

Write your answers **IN CAPITAL LETTERS on the separate answer sheet.**

Example: 0 O F

Ancient cartoons

The technique of telling a story through a sequence (**0**) …….. pictures, though associated with modern cartoons, was in fact in use about 500 years ago. The British Library in London has some wonderful examples of these early cartoons, all of (**9**) …….. were produced to order for wealthy clients. (**10**) …….. makes this art form so interesting is that it flourished in one small part of Europe – Flanders, today a region of northern Belgium – (**11**) …….. to die out as printing was developed.

Many of the tiny pictures were (**12**) …….. larger than a postage stamp. They were painted by hand in books about the size of a modern paperback. The artists, (**13**) …….. skills were rewarded by high salaries, worked slowly, and the buyers sometimes had to wait years for the work to be completed. In the (**14**) …….. of one four-volume example, the buyer waited for well (**15**) …….. a decade.

The cartoons show a variety of subjects, but episodes from history were popular, (**16**) …….. were fairy tales.

PAPER 1 Reading and ▶ Part 1
Use of English Part 2
Part 3
PAPER 2 Writing Part 4
PAPER 3 Listening Part 5
PAPER 4 Speaking Part 6
Part 7
Part 8

For questions **17–24**, read the text below. Use the word given in capitals at the end of some of the lines to form a word that fits in the gap **in the same line**. There is an example at the beginning (**0**).

Write your answers **IN CAPITAL LETTERS on the separate answer sheet.**

Example: | 0 | C | R | E | A | T | O | R | | | | | | | | | | | | |

Sir Arthur Conan Doyle

Famous the world over as the (**0**) …….. of Sherlock Holmes,   **CREATE**
Sir Arthur Conan Doyle was born in Edinburgh in 1859
into an Irish family who were (**17**) …….. in the art world.   **INFLUENCE**
Arthur probably inherited the ability to tell stories from
his mother, who was a source of (**18**) …….. to him.   **INSPIRE**

Thanks to the (**19**) …….. of some relatives, Arthur was   **GENEROUS**
able to study medicine at Edinburgh University. He
was a bright student, but (**20**) …….., and his zest for   **REST**
adventure led him to accept a contract as ship's
surgeon. Returning home, he completed his (**21**) ……..   **MEDICINE**
studies in 1881, and eventually settled in the south
of England.

It is believed that Doyle based Holmes' character on
one of his university tutors, Dr Joseph Bell, whom
he regarded with (**22**) …….. for his powers of logic.   **ADMIRE**
The first Sherlock Holmes story was received with
such (**23**) …….. that Doyle was encouraged to write more.   **ENTHUSE**
In 1893 he killed off his hero in order to concentrate on
writing what he saw as more serious work, but this
caused a public (**24**) …….., and he was forced to bring   **CRY**
Holmes back to life.

For questions **25–30**, complete the second sentence so that it has a similar meaning to the first sentence, using the word given. **Do not change the word given.** You must use between **three** and **six** words, including the word given. Here is an example (**0**).

Example:

0   Jane regretted speaking so rudely to the old lady.

  MORE

  Jane .... politely to the old lady.

Example: | **0** | WISHED SHE HAD SPOKEN MORE |

Write **only** the missing words **IN CAPITAL LETTERS on the separate answer sheet**.

---

25   Sally showed absolutely no fear when climbing the wall.

  DISREGARD

  Sally showed .... own safety when climbing the wall.

26   The identity of the murderer was never discovered.

  NEVER

  The police .... was.

27   'It's not a good idea to call Leo just yet,' Valerie told me.

  AGAINST

  Valerie advised .... for a while.

28   It was only after I left the office that I realised I had forgotten the file.

  DID

  Only after .... I had forgotten the file.

29   If I lose this match, people will never let me forget it!

  LIVE

  If I lose this match, I .... down!

30   Internal Affairs are investigating allegations of police fraud.

  INTO

  Allegations of police fraud .... Internal Affairs.

PAPER 1	Reading and Use of English ▶	Part 1
		Part 2
		Part 3
		Part 4
		Part 5
PAPER 2	Writing	Part 6
PAPER 3	Listening	Part 7
PAPER 4	Speaking	Part 8

You are going to read a newspaper article. For questions **31–36**, choose the answer (**A**, **B**, **C** or **D**) which you think fits best according to the text.

Mark your answers **on the separate answer sheet**.

Saving the big birds

At first glance, why anyone would want to save California condors is not entirely clear. Unlike the closely related Andean condors with their white neck fluff or king vultures with their brilliant black-and-white colouring, California condors are not much to see. Their dull black colour – even when contrasted with white underwings – featherless head and neck, oversized feet and blunt talons are hardly signs of beauty or strength. Their appeal begins to become evident when they take flight. With a nine-and-a-half-feet wingspan and a weight of up to 28 pounds, California condors are North America's largest fully flighted birds. In the Americas, only Andean condors are bigger. California condors can soar almost effortlessly for hours, often covering hundreds of miles a day – far more than other birds. Only occasionally do they need to flap their wings – to take off, change direction or find a band of warm air known as a thermal to carry them higher.

When it was discovered that the condor population was becoming dangerously small, scientists and zookeepers sought to increase condor numbers quickly to preserve as much of the species' genetic diversity as possible. From studying wild condors, they already knew that if a pair lost an egg, the birds would often yield another. So the first and sometimes second eggs laid by each female in captivity were removed, artificially incubated, and the chicks raised using hand-held puppets made to look like adult condors. Such techniques quickly proved effective.

Despite these achievements, the effort to save California condors continues to have problems. Survival rates of captive-hatched condors released to the wild are, for some people, too low, and some have had to be recaptured after they acted foolishly or became ill. As a result, the scientists, zookeepers and conservationists who are concerned about condors have bickered among themselves over the best ways to rear and release the birds.

Some of the odd behaviour on the part of these released birds is hard to explain. At times they landed on people's houses and garages, walked across roads and airport runways, sauntered into park visitor centres and takeaway restaurants, and took food offered by picnickers and fishermen. None are known to have perished by doing so, though. More seriously, one condor died from drinking what was probably antifreeze. Others died in collisions with overhead electrical transmission wires, drowned in natural pools of water, or were killed by golden eagles and coyotes. Still others were shot by hunters and killed or made seriously ill from lead poisoning. Some just disappeared. Most recently, some of the first chicks hatched in the wild died after their parents fed them bottle caps, glass shards, pieces of plastic and other man-made objects that fatally perforated or blocked their intestines. These deaths may be due to the chicks' parents mistaking man-made objects for bone chips eaten for their calcium content.

Mike Wallace, a wildlife specialist at the San Diego Zoo, has suggested that some of the condors' problems represent natural behaviour that helps them survive as carrion eaters. The real key to successful condor reintroduction, he believes, lies in properly socialising the young birds as members of a group that follow and learn from older, preferably adult birds. That, he argues, was missing from earlier condor releases to the wild. Typically, condors hatched in the spring were released to the wild that autumn or winter, when they were still less than a year old. Especially in the early releases, the young condors had no adults or even older juveniles to learn from and keep them in their place. Instead, the only other condors they saw in captivity and the wild were ones their own age. Now, condor chicks at several zoos are raised in cave-like nest boxes. The chicks can see older condors in a large flight pen outside their box but cannot interact with them until they are about five months old. Then the chicks are gradually released into the pen and the company of the social group. The group includes adult and older juvenile condors that act as mentors for younger ones. It is hoped that this socialisation programme will help the birds adapt to the wild when they are released.

31 What does the writer say is the Californian condor's most impressive feature?

    A The height at which it can fly.

    B The range of colours it displays.

    C The way it glides through the air.

    D The similarity it has to the Andean condor.

32 In the initial stage of the conservation programme,

    A eggs were taken from the nests of wild condors.

    B female condors were captured and studied carefully.

    C scientists and zookeepers tried to create genetic diversity.

    D condors were encouraged to produce more eggs.

33 What does the writer say in the third paragraph about the attempts to save Californian condors from extinction?

    A Freed condors have tried to return to the places where they were born.

    B There is disagreement about the breeding methods employed.

    C The majority of birds reintroduced into the wild have died.

    D Attempts to breed condors in captivity have failed.

34 In the fourth paragraph, the writer says that some of the condors released into the wild

    A adapted surprisingly quickly to their new surroundings.

    B displayed a tendency to seek out human contact.

    C died from ingesting too much fast food.

    D kept altering their eating habits.

35 According to Mike Wallace, there will be fewer problems

    A if young condors are taught appropriate behaviour by mature birds.

    B if the chicks are surrounded by older birds when they hatch.

    C if young condors are trained not to eat so much carrion.

    D if the chicks are kept in special boxes for five months.

36 The main purpose of the article appears to be

    A to evaluate the need to preserve the California condor.

    B to gain support for the California condor conservation project.

    C to examine developments in the California condor conservation programme.

    D to analyse factors surrounding the California condors' failure to adapt to the wild.

PAPER 1 Reading and ▶   Part 1
         Use of English   Part 2

PAPER 2 Writing   Part 3
                          Part 4
PAPER 3 Listening   Part 5
PAPER 4 Speaking   **Part 6**
                          Part 7
                          Part 8

You are going to read extracts from four reviews of a book about memory. For questions **37–40**, choose from the reviews **A–D**. The reviews may be chosen more than once.

Mark your answers **on the separate answer sheet**.

Moonwalking with Einstein: the art and science of remembering everything by Joshua Foer

Joshua Foer spent a year training his memory. Four reviewers comment on the book he wrote about his experiences.

A

Brain-training, particularly memory-training, is a large industry and Joshua Foer consults some of its best-known gurus in his quest to become a 'warrior of the mind'. While not a self-improvement manual from that stable, this book details various time-honoured memorisation techniques largely derived from the ancient Greeks and Romans, and presents some intriguing portraits of memory champions able to perform apparently supernatural feats of recall. After a year's hard training, Foer himself becomes an elite memoriser, winning the US Memory Championships. He also supplies a useful, reader-friendly guide to 'memory' in history and an introduction to psychological and neuroscientific research on memory. At times, it feels a little too friendly, with the science in particular deserving a linguistically more formal and detached approach. It is good, however, to be reminded of what we are all capable of if we only put our minds to it.

B

Joshua Foer describes the year he spent training to compete in the US Memory Championships, and of what he learned about memory – how it works, its historical role in society and in education, and how techniques can be acquired to transform someone with an average memory into an outstanding mental athlete. It's a delight to travel with Foer into the geeky, largely male subculture of the competitive memorisers, and his account of the neurological functions of memory, delivered in clear, lively prose, is generally sound and up-to-date, with one notable exception. The idea that all our past experiences are stored in the brain, waiting to be retrieved, is now largely disputed by scientists. Foer's book is a reminder of how extraordinary our minds can be.

C

Joshua Foer admits his normal recall is no better than average. After a year of dedicated training, however, he won the US Memory Championships, and broke the speed record for memorising the order of a shuffled pack of cards. It's an entertaining story, which Foer combines with lucid, accessible explanations of a complex subject – the function and operation of memory in the human brain. Foer is not a neuroscientist, but his treatment of the subject is balanced and faithful to the science, apart, that is, from suggesting that all memories are permanently retained, though not always re-activated; studies now suggest that memory is very much subject to change. If a self-help, brain-training guide is what you are after, look elsewhere, but there are interesting accounts here of ancient memorisation methods, some of which have been in use for thousands of years.

D

As Joshua Foer rightly points out, the 'art of memory' has a long and noble history. In fact, until recently, memorisation was central to education, learning and authority. Now, it is largely disdained as a waste of time, and we externalise our memories into books and digital records. In training for the US Memory Championships, Foer employed techniques that have been known and used for thousands of years, and he developed his skills to the point that he became national champion. Sadly, what these competitive memorisers have to memorise is utterly trivial – sequences of playing cards, long lists of unfamiliar words, random numbers. In the sections of the book that deal with the history and science of memory, Foer proves he has a gift for communicating quite complex ideas in a manner that is palatable without being patronising. It's a pity that so much of the book is taken up with the dreary world of mental athletes, who perform tricks to store pointless information.

Which reviewer

expresses a different attitude to the others regarding
Foer's descriptions of memory?

37

takes a similar view to reviewer B about the accuracy
of Foer's account of how memory works?

38

expresses a different view from the others about
Foer's writing style?

39

shares reviewer C's opinion of how useful Foer's book
is for people who want to acquire better memory skills?

40

PAPER 1 Reading and ▶ Part 1
Use of English   Part 2
PAPER 2 Writing   Part 3
                      Part 4
PAPER 3 Listening   Part 5
                      Part 6
PAPER 4 Speaking   **Part 7**
                      Part 8

You are going to read a magazine article. Six paragraphs have been removed from the article. Choose from the paragraphs **A–G** the one which fits each gap (**41–46**). There is one extra paragraph which you do not need to use.

Mark your answers **on the separate answer sheet**.

All this jazz

What makes someone give up a stable career for the uncertainy of playing the saxophone in a jazz band? Walter Williams finds out.

I'm sitting backstage with Marjorie Anderson in a small theatre in the French town of Villeneuf. In a few minutes she will walk on stage with the jazz band she plays with, Les Jazzistes. They have been together for two years now, slowly but steadily building up a loyal following, and there is little doubt that tonight's gig will be a success.

41

Yet she is clutching her saxophone like a petrified child. 'I'm scared of the audience,' she says. 'You've got to be kidding,' I tell her. 'No,' she says with a snort. 'I freeze up when I look at them.'

42

Marjorie lives in France and plays the sax professionally. She has a distinctive technique, honed to perfection by hours of practice and, some would claim, plays with added passion by virtue of the fact that she has made huge sacrifices in order to devote herself to jazz. In addition to being a fine musician, she's a vet by training: two careers not normally associated with each other.

43

It was probably something in her childhood. She grew up in Sydney, Australia, and was something of a child prodigy – as a flautist. She played with a youth orchestra, but then abruptly decided that music was not for her. 'I auditioned for a prestigious orchestra, but nothing came of it.' Her sense of rejection at the time was overwhelming. 'I was very thin-skinned in

those days,' Marjorie admits. 'I felt threatened every time someone commented on my playing or my technique.'

44

However, it emerged a decade later that contentment of this sort was not what Marjorie really yearned for. Her brother treated her to a week in Paris for her 35th birthday, and they went to a club whose lively jazz scene has been attracting a demanding clientele for over 70 years. The effect on Marjorie was immediate; it was as if she was hearing music for the first time.

45

'I moved here because it hit me that for 35 years, I'd never been in touch with my inner self, with my needs and desires,' she told me. 'Oddly enough, I didn't consider taking up the flute again. It was the saxophone that grabbed my attention. It was so much more expressive in terms of my own essential being.'

46

I ask her if she has any regrets about dropping out to follow her dreams. She says no, but that she feels a bit guilty. 'I realise playing the sax in a band isn't saving the world. Sometimes I feel I ought to be doing something more useful.' Being a musician leaves Marjorie little time for much else. Nevertheless, she has decided to reinvent herself yet again – as a writer this time. In fact, she has just finished her autobiography, entitled *Why Not Try It?* It's a question many readers, envious of her courage, will find uncomfortable.

A To help her with this, she reaches for her sunglasses. Wearing them throughout her appearance in front of this small crowd – maybe 250 people – is one of the methods she uses to control her nerves.

B Marjorie refused to let such a minor problem daunt her. Soon she was playing music again, this time with renewed determination to be one of the best sax players in the world. Then, without any warning, she developed a fear of performing in public that nearly paralysed her. It was time to take action.

C 'I thought I'd gone to heaven,' she says. 'It was a turning point. The experience told me I had to hear and play more music, and really live before it was too late.' This was the moment when she decided to make a radical change in her life.

D As if this combination wasn't unusual enough, five years ago, she suddenly decided to sell her thriving vet practice in Australia and moved to France – without knowing a word of French. What would make someone abandon her entire life and take up playing music at the age of 35?

E Her new-found stagefright was the other curious factor about this return to public performance. Marjorie believes her terror is related to the sense that she is baring her soul when she performs. 'The other thing I do to make myself less scared is stand completely still on stage,' she explains.

F So she went to college instead, and trained as a vet. She threw herself into her profession, channelling her energy into building up a practice. 'I became stronger psychologically because I was successful in my career,' she says. 'I see it as a positive thing. I was satisfied with my life.'

G It is an enviable position to be in, especially for someone who, like Marjorie, has managed to make a living in a notoriously precarious profession. What is more, she has done it in a country a long way from her place of origin.

You are going to read an article in which four scientists talk about the emotional side of their work. For questions **47–56**, choose from the people (**A–D**).

Mark your answers **on the separate answer sheet**.

Which scientist

acknowledges the role another scientist has had in the development of their career?

47

draws a parallel between significant and less well-known scientific findings?

48

points out how unimpressed by reputation scientists tend to be?

49

mentions the desire scientists have to achieve a major breakthrough?

50

says that certain aspects of their work can be tedious?

51

comments on the impact discussion can have on the generation of new ideas?

52

draws attention to a common misconception?

53

mentions the satisfaction derived from thinking about the value of their work?

54

mentions a reconciliation with a colleague?

55

describes the anxiety involved in switching from one field of study to another?

56

Scientists and their emotions

A Steven Greene, biologist

Not long ago, I had a long argument with a fellow biologist about a particular set of experiments. Things got pretty loud and heated, and harsh words were said. A week later, we sent mutually apologetic texts and made up.

This sort of thing doesn't find its way into scientific papers. We have to present our data, analysis and interpretation in a way that allows another scientist to understand each step. I am sometimes jealous of artists for whom sharing and explaining the emotional journey of a piece of work is celebrated. The absence of a natural forum for scientists to describe their emotions in their work can lead to the erroneous view that we don't have any. In fact, we usually make a huge emotional investment in our work.

Science is not for the faint-hearted. I remember attending a talk years ago, at which the speaker, a distinguished biologist, was continually challenged by the audience. At one point, a fierce debate broke out at which the speaker was a mute bystander. This lack of deference is by no means exceptional.

B Catherine Edwards, oceanographer

Writing a proposal is where most new science begins these days and it's set out like a business case. After all, your fabulous new idea needs money: equipment, salaries, overheads. The funding bodies are tough to impress. So the excitement of having a big new idea is only the first step.

The first proposal I ever wrote was for a three-year project. Initially, writing about why my research topic mattered cheered me up no end. It's easy to forget the bigger picture when you're working on details, and it was reassuring to be reminded of the importance of my research subject.

Working out the project details was fiddly and time-consuming. Then it slowed down even more, to a dull plod, as I checked and rechecked things. This was my idea and I desperately wanted it to be good, to deserve funding. Months after the deadline, an email told me my project would be funded. My idea wasn't rubbish! Others wanted it too!

C Dominika Gajewska, neuroscientist

While doing my postgraduate studies in psychology, I got temporarily side-tracked by the question of why certain serious psychological problems that afflict some people always seem to emerge at the end of adolescence. You can make it through childhood and adolescence and then suddenly become affected. Does something happen in brain development during adolescence that acts as a trigger? As I read the existing literature, I became increasingly frustrated that there didn't seem to be many answers.

I talked to my psychology professor, an expert on child development, and she said: 'Why don't you fill the gap yourself? Apply for funding and start some new research in developmental neuroscience focusing on human adolescence?'

As she said those words, I remember feeling excited and slightly apprehensive. It wasn't until then that I realised it was exactly what I wanted to do – move into a subject that was rather unknown territory to me. I was taking a risk by moving into developmental work with so little experience, but my mentor's encouragement made all the difference. Ten years later, I'm pleased with the outcome.

D Arif Shah, chemist

In a lab recently, a student of mine excitedly showed me a flask containing a dark solution. She shone a torch and it lit up, in a vivid bright green. 'Fluorescence,' I said. The glow attracted a small crowd. Although not a research-changing observation, it sparked off excited speculation. What was the structure? How was the light being generated? What spectrums and measurements should be recorded to understand the observation?

That buzz was a faint echo of the moment, over 200 years ago, when the pioneering chemist Humphry Davy first electrolysed molten potash and was rewarded with a spray of brilliant flashing droplets of potassium. Davy apparently danced round the room in delight.

Few of us are likely to come close to a discovery of that importance, though it's something many yearn for. There is, however, something profoundly pleasurable in going over results and observations with students and colleagues. The unexpected turns up in little ways in day-to-day research and each time a miniature brainstorming session ensues, where adjustments are made to the way research is going.

You **must** answer this question. Write your answer in **220–260** words in an appropriate style on the separate answer sheet.

---

1 The government wants to economise on local library services. Your class has attended a seminar held by a government representative. You have made the notes below.

> **Methods of economising:**
>
> - reduced hours
> - library closures
> - voluntary assistants

> **Some opinions expressed in the discussion:**
>
> 'Most libraries already have inconvenient opening hours.'
>
> 'Libraries are an important educational resource.'
>
> 'It's important to have trained librarians.'

Write an **essay** discussing **two** of the methods in your notes. You should **explain which method you think is more important** for the local government to consider and **provide reasons** to support your opinion.

You may, if you wish, make use of the opinions expressed in the discussion, but you should use your own words as far as possible.

Write an answer to **one** of the questions **2–4** in this part. Write your answer in **220–260** words in an appropriate style on the separate answer sheet. Put the question number in the box at the top of the page.

2   There has been a fire in your home. No one was hurt, but there was a lot of damage. Write to your insurance company describing what happened, the reason for the fire, and asking about payment for your temporary accommodation.

    Write your **letter.**

3   You would like to promote healthy eating in your college, and believe one way to do this is to get students interested in cookery. You write to your principal proposing a weekend *Festival of Cookery* in the college. Explain how this could be organised and suggest ideas for making the festival exciting and fun.

    Write your **proposal.**

4   Your class has just returned from a two-week visit to a school in another country. You stayed with host families and took part in classes and activities at the school. Each participant has been asked to write a report on the experience for the school magazine, saying what was interesting and enjoyable, and if there were any difficulties.

    Write your **report.**

Track 25

You will hear three different extracts. For questions **1–6**, choose the answer (**A**, **B** or **C**) which fits best according to what you hear. There are two questions for each extract.

Extract One

You hear two people talking about the sport of karting (racing small vehicles).

1   When the man goes to an event, he
    A   drives a kart.
    B   maintains machines.
    C   helps manage the races.

2   The woman thinks that karting
    A   is a good way to learn driving skills.
    B   is a growth area for sports companies.
    C   is too expensive for most people to afford.

Extract Two

You hear an interview in which an interior designer is giving advice on colour in the home.

3   According to Eugene, orange
    A   calms and reassures you.
    B   stimulates and inspires you.
    C   is a natural cure for insomnia.

4   The interviewer believes that the living room is difficult to decorate because of
    A   the need to consider several other factors.
    B   the paintings on the wall.
    C   the need to be sociable.

Extract Three

You hear a conversation between a man and a woman about something that has happened.

5   What experience is the man describing?
    A   He knocked down an old man with his car.
    B   He was involved in a head-on collision with a lorry.
    C   He hit another car while trying to avert an accident.

6   The man thinks the police
    A   may prosecute the lorry driver.
    B   are unlikely to take action against the old man.
    C   will hold the old man responsible for the accident.

Track 26

You will hear part of a talk by a writer who has written a book about bread. For questions **7–14,** complete the sentences with a word or short phrase.

OUR DAILY BREAD

Supermarket (**7**) .... believe that baking bread on the

premises attracts customers.

About (**8**) .... of bread in Britain is no longer baked in

the old-fashioned way.

In the past, it took (**9**) .... for the yeast to ferment.

Nowadays, the fermentation process is faster, and less

(**10**) .... is used.

Unless salt is added, bread baked in the modern way is

(**11**) ....

Calcium propionate can be sprayed on the bread to prevent it from going

(**12**) ....

The speaker believes certain (**13**) .... may be caused

by modern bread-making methods.

Supermarkets (**14**) .... on the sale of bread.

🎧 **Track 27**

You will hear part of a discussion between Velma Andrews, a lawyer, and Sergeant William Bailey, a police officer. For questions **15–20**, choose the answer (**A**, **B**, **C** or **D**) which fits best according to what you hear.

---

15 How did William feel the first time he gave evidence in court?

    A   humiliated

    B   nervous

    C   furious

    D   indifferent

16 Velma suggests that police officers giving evidence should

    A   study the evidence more carefully.

    B   ignore the lawyer for the defence.

    C   not take comments personally.

    D   demonstrate that they are honest and reliable.

17 Velma compares a police officer's evidence to a piece in a jigsaw puzzle because

    A   it is unimportant unless it is part of a bigger picture.

    B   it may not fit in with the rest of the evidence.

    C   the defence lawyer will try to destroy it.

    D   the police officer should only talk about his or her evidence.

18 William suggests that lawyers

    A   adopt a special manner in the courtroom.

    B   can be detached about a case.

    C   might actually be close friends.

    D   do not take their work seriously.

19 Velma's advice suggests that police officers should

    A   never volunteer a personal opinion.

    B   not answer a question unless they are sure of the answer.

    C   remember they are not really addressing the lawyer.

    D   not get into an argument with the judge.

20 William's main concern is that

    A   a criminal could get away with his or her crime.

    B   a court case could be confusing.

    C   young police officers find courts terrifying.

    D   police officers might argue with the lawyer.

PAPER 1 Reading and
         Use of English

PAPER 2 Writing

PAPER 3 Listening ▶
                          Part 1
                          Part 2
                          Part 3
                          Part 4

PAPER 4 Speaking

🎧 **Track 28**

You will hear five short extracts in which people talk about wind power.

While you listen, you must complete both tasks.

TASK ONE

For questions **21–25**, choose from list **A–H**, the attitude each speaker has towards wind power.

A	Placing wind turbines out at sea is acceptable.	
		Speaker 1 [21]
B	We should exploit wind power.	
		Speaker 2 [22]
C	Wind turbines are a threat to birds.	
		Speaker 3 [23]
D	Wind power has created attractive business opportunities for some people.	
		Speaker 4 [24]
E	Wind turbines are an unpleasant sight.	
		Speaker 5 [25]
F	There are valid objections to situating wind turbines offshore.	
G	Wind power is grossly inadequate.	
H	Wind power is a practical way to generate electricity.	

TASK TWO

For questions **26–30**, choose from list **A–H** what each speaker says about the alternatives to wind power.

A	We should consider nuclear power, if it is safe.	
		Speaker 1 [26]
B	Hydroelectric power cannot create enough energy.	
		Speaker 2 [27]
C	Other renewable energy-generating schemes would be expensive to set up.	
		Speaker 3 [28]
D	Only if various renewable sources are exploited collectively will they produce enough energy.	
		Speaker 4 [29]
E	Hydroelectric power is a feasible way of generating enough electricity for our needs.	
		Speaker 5 [30]
F	Wind power cannot completely replace fossil fuels.	
G	Nuclear power is the safest alternative to fossil fuels.	
H	The best way is to use fossil fuels efficiently.	

Part 1 (2 minutes)

The examiner will ask you a few questions about yourself and about a general topic. For example, the examiner may ask you:

• What job do you do, or would you like to do?
• What kind of working environment would suit you best?
• What sort of job would you dislike, and what working conditions would not appeal to you?

Part 2 (4 minutes)

You will each be asked to talk on your own for about a minute. You will each be given three different pictures to talk about. After your partner has finished speaking, you will be asked a brief question connected with your partner's photographs.

Respect (compare, contrast and speculate)

Turn to pictures 1–3 on page 187 which show people showing respect.

(*Candidate A*), it's your turn first. Here are your pictures. They show **people showing respect**.

I'd like you to compare **two** of the pictures and say **what could be prompting the people to show respect, and how the people receiving the show of respect might feel.**

(*Candidate B*), **are the old and the young in your country respectful towards each other?**

Partnership (compare, contrast and speculate)

Turn to pictures 1–3 on page 188 which show different partnerships.

Now, (*Candidate B*), here are your pictures. **They show people in partnerships**.

I'd like you to compare **two** of the pictures, and say **what kind of partnerships they illustrate and say how you think the partners feel about each other.**

(*Candidate A*), **do you prefer to work with a partner or on your own? Why?**

Part 3 (4 minutes)

Look at page 189 which shows some recreational activities.

Recreation (discuss, evaluate and select)

Here are some different things that people do in their spare time and a question for you to discuss.

First, you have some time to look at the task.

(*Pause 15 seconds*)

Now talk to each other about **why people want to do these things.**

Now you have about a minute to decide **which activity is the most enjoyable for most people.**

Part 4 (5 minutes)

The examiner will encourage you to develop the topic of your discussion in Part 3 by asking questions such as:

• Why do you think some people choose to do dangerous recreational activities like mountain climbing?

• Do you think everyone needs some sort of recreational activity? (Why? / Why not?)

• Would it be possible to encourage more children to take up recreational activities other than sports (hobbies, such as collecting stamps, or gardening)?

For questions **1–8**, read the text below and decide which answer (**A, B, C** or **D**) best fits each gap. There is an example at the beginning (**0**).

Mark your answers **on the separate answer sheet**.

Example:

0 **A** long   **B** wide   **C** far   **D** high

0	A	B	C	D
	⏝	▬	⏝	⏝

Mushrooms

In order to maintain a healthy diet, we are encouraged to eat a (**0**) .... range of fruit, vegetables and other natural foodstuffs. The nutritional (**1**) .... of such things as carrots, fish and beans are often praised, but mushrooms tend to be (**2**) .... Research, however, suggests that they may well be qualified to join the (**3**) .... of so-called superfoods like broccoli and blueberries.

'They may seem plain,' says dietician Dr Sarah Schenker, but studies have (**4**) .... that they help reduce the risk of serious illnesses. They contain (**5**) .... no fat, sugar or salt, and they're a valuable (**6**) .... of dietary fibre. They also contain many essential vitamins and minerals, and they're good, too, for people wanting to (**7**) .... down on their calorie intake – adding them to dishes like stews can make you feel fuller, but they're 90% water.

More than 2,500 (**8**) .... of mushrooms grow in the wild, but, so far, most research has focused on a few types like *shitake*, *maitake* and white button mushrooms. There is clearly much more to discover about this intriguing food.

	A	**B**	**C**	**D**
1	profits	aids	favours	benefits
2	overdrawn	overlooked	overgrown	overseen
3	ranks	grades	rows	files
4	presented	displayed	revealed	exposed
5	virtually	fairly	closely	utterly
6	outset	base	root	source
7	break	cut	pull	let
8	breeds	classes	varieties	bands

For questions **9–16**, read the text below and think of the word which best fits each gap. Use only **one** word in each gap. There is an example at the beginning (**0**).

Write your answers **IN CAPITAL LETTERS on the separate answer sheet**.

Example: | 0 | A | L | L | | | | | | | | | | | | | | | | | | |

Independent television

People going to the UK for the first time are often surprised that there are no advertisements at (**0**) …….. on the BBC television channels. Their absence is (**9**) …….. to the fact that the constitution of the BBC forbids it to accept advertising. So, (**10**) …….. does the BBC get the money it needs to keep it going? The answer is that, (**11**) …….. selling BBC programmes to other broadcasters around the world, the BBC is financed from revenue raised by the sale of television licences. The fee for the licences is set by the government, but (**12**) …….. this, the BBC is not state run, and it retains an independence of (**13**) …….. it is very proud. It can be said that the viewers themselves pay for the BBC, since (**14**) …….. single household that owns a television in Britain has to purchase a licence. Some viewers prefer other channels, but a valid licence is obligatory, (**15**) …….. or not you watch the BBC. Failure to buy one is (**16**) …….. the law.

PAPER 1 Reading and
         Use of English

PAPER 2 Writing

PAPER 3 Listening

PAPER 4 Speaking

Part 1
Part 2
Part 3
Part 4
Part 5
Part 6
Part 7
Part 8

For questions **17–24**, read the text below. Use the word given in capitals at the end of some of the lines to form a word that fits in the gap **in the same line**. There is an example at the beginning (**0**).

Write your answers **IN CAPITAL LETTERS on the separate answer sheet**.

Example: | 0 | H | E | I | G | H | T | | | | | | | | | | | | | |

From coin to paper

In 9th-century China, at the (**0**) …….. of the Tang dynasty,	**HIGH**
the government became concerned about the serious	
(**17**) …….. of carrying around large amounts of coins in	**CONVENIENT**
order to conduct business (**18**) …….. . Consequently, they	**TRANSACT**
devised a method of paying merchants with money	
certificates, which could be exchanged for coin money	
on demand at the capital. These certificates had an	
unfortunate (**19**) …….. to blow away if there was any wind,	**TEND**
but they were (**20**) …….., so merchants began exchanging	**TRANSFER**
them with each other instead of using coins.	

It was not until the Song dynasty that actual paper	
money was created. Initially introduced by a group	
of merchants and (**21**) …….., each banknote had images	**FINANCE**
of houses, trees and people printed on it. These were	
(**22**) …….. by various intricate markings, the identification	**COMPANY**
of which could be made only by the issuing banks. Then,	
in 1023, the government decided to (**23**) …….. the banknotes	**DRAW**
and issue government notes in their place. These could be	
exchanged for government-issued coins, and so could be	
used to buy simple groceries. As a result, the use of paper	
money soon became (**24**) …….. .	**SPREAD**

For questions **25–30**, complete the second sentence so that it has a similar meaning to the first sentence, using the word given. **Do not change the word given.** You must use between **three** and **six** words, including the word given. Here is an example (**0**).

Example:

0   Jane regretted speaking so rudely to the old lady.

   MORE

   Jane .... politely to the old lady.

Example: | **0** | WISHED SHE HAD SPOKEN MORE |

Write **only** the missing words **IN CAPITAL LETTERS on the separate answer sheet**.

___

25   Fatima's warm welcome surprised me.

   ABACK

   I .... of Fatima's welcome.

26   Tom hates parties, so don't try to persuade him to go.

   WORTH

   It .... Tom into going to parties because he hates them.

27   'You will have to travel a lot in this job,' the manager told Sofia.

   INVOLVE

   The manager informed Sofia .... a lot.

28   We would have arrived here late if Ravi's father hadn't taken us to the bus stop.

   FOR

   Had .... Ravi's father taking us to the bus stop, we would have arrived here late.

29   It is possible that Theresa took your car keys this morning by mistake.

   ACCIDENTALLY

   Theresa .... your car keys this morning.

30   I didn't recognise Sara until she took off her sunglasses.

   ONLY

   It .... her sunglasses that I recognised her.

PAPER 1 Reading and ▶
        Use of English
PAPER 2 Writing
PAPER 3 Listening
PAPER 4 Speaking

Part 1
Part 2
Part 3
Part 4
Part 5
Part 6
Part 7
Part 8

You are going to read a newspaper article. For questions **31–36**, choose the answer (**A**, **B**, **C** or **D**) which you think fits best according to the text.

Mark your answers **on the separate answer sheet**.

Senses that work together

A few years ago, on work experience at Oxford University, I had the privilege of being roped in for an experiment by a research team led by Professor Charles Spence. Sitting in a tiny room in a warren of labs and offices, I was shown a rack of bottles of scent and a computer program that let me play the sound of musical instruments at different pitches. My task was to sniff all the scents, and pick the sound that fitted each one best. Puzzled, I inhaled my first sample – sweet and slightly sickly, like bubble gum. Deep blaring brass seemed instinctively wrong, so I tried out higher, purer sounds and eventually settled on a high piano note. I left not much the wiser about what was going on. But the team was covering new ground in a field known as cross-modal perception.

When we think about how our senses work, we imagine them operating individually: you sniff a flower, and the smell is delivered uninterrupted from nose to brain. However, it's more complicated than that. Our senses mingle more often than we realise, collaborating to help us make sense of the world more easily. We call dull thuds 'heavy' and associate them with large objects, even though the sound itself has no size or weight. This would have helped our ancestors decide whether to run away from predators based on how big they sounded, without stopping to look them over. Most evidence for cross-modal perception comes from studies into sound and vision – not surprising considering how often we use them together. But research that shows other senses crossing over is emerging all the time, and it seems that even sound and smell sometimes form an unlikely pairing.

When two New York researchers, Daniel Wesson and Donald Wilson, began investigating an 'enigmatic' area of the brain called the olfactory tubercle, they were confronted with **this fact**. Originally, they only intended to measure how olfactory tubercle cells in anesthetised mice responded to smell. But during testing, Wesson noticed that every time he clunked his coffee mug down next to the experiment, the mouse cells jumped in activity. In fact, the olfactory tubercle is physiologically well-placed to receive both smell and sound information from the outside world; and so Wesson and Wilson broadened their investigation.

They found that among individual cells, most responded to odour but a significant number were also active when a tone was played. Some cells even behaved differently when smell and sound were presented together, by increasing or suppressing their activity. There may be some evolutionary sense behind the phenomenon – a sound accompanied by an unfamiliar smell could alert you to the presence of a predator.

Of course, mice aren't people, and a handful of firing cells don't always add up to a conscious experience. But Charles Spence's team have been carrying out experiments like the one in which I participated at Oxford University, which seem to show that sounds and smells cross over in human perception, too. Recently, they pulled together a group of people and gave them various drinks to smell. Participants were asked to sniff different samples, and then match them to an appropriate musical instrument and pitch. The results were interesting: piano was regularly paired with fruity scents; musky smells sounded like brass.

Further research found that listening to different sounds can alter your perceptions. Studying taste this time, the team ordered some special toffee and put together 'soundscapes' corresponding to bitterness and sweetness. Participants tasted identical pieces of toffee while listening to each soundscape, and found the toffee more bitter or sweeter, depending on which soundtrack they were listening to.

Studies like this are helping scientists redefine our understanding of the senses, and how the brain integrates them to its advantage. The consequences are worth considering. Could we see collaborations between musicians and chefs to produce sound-enhanced food and drink? Will you be ordering a coffee with a soundtrack to bring out your favourite aromas? Come to think of it, that could be one notion you hope coffee shops chains *don't* get round to.

31 What does the writer suggest about the experiment she was involved in?
- **A** The findings that came out of it were disappointing.
- **B** Those running it treated her with kindness.
- **C** It was conducted in a light-hearted manner.
- **D** She had little understanding of its purpose.

32 In the second paragraph the writer is
- **A** introducing a new idea into her report.
- **B** illustrating a point she has made previously.
- **C** making her reservations about something clear.
- **D** explaining the background to a particular issue.

33 What point does *this fact* in the third paragraph refer to?
- **A** Evidence about the way senses work is hard to obtain.
- **B** Sound and vision are relatively easy to study.
- **C** There can be a link between sound and smell.
- **D** A lot of research focuses on the senses.

34 In Wesson and Wilson's research,
- **A** the link between sound and smell in mice was discovered by chance.
- **B** the mice were affected in the same way by both sound and smell.
- **C** the results confirmed what the researchers had suspected.
- **D** the mice used seemed to be afraid of certain sounds.

35 What does the writer say about the experiment described in the fifth paragraph?
- **A** The participants were initially reluctant to be involved in it.
- **B** Its outcomes failed to support what was found in other experiments.
- **C** The associations made between sounds and smells were consistent.
- **D** Its purpose was different from that of the experiment she'd taken part in.

36 How does the writer feel about wider implications of the research she reports on?
- **A** convinced the findings will have a major impact in the near future
- **B** uneasy about how the knowledge acquired might be applied
- **C** surprised by developments that have already taken place
- **D** excited about forthcoming creative opportunities

PAPER 1 Reading and ▶
           Use of English

PAPER 2 Writing

PAPER 3 Listening

PAPER 4 Speaking

Part 1
Part 2
Part 3
Part 4
Part 5
Part 6
Part 7
Part 8

You are going to read extracts from four articles written by scientists about the idea of bringing extinct animals back to life. For questions **37–40**, choose from the extracts **A–D**. The extracts may be chosen more than once.

Mark your answers **on the separate answer sheet**.

De-extinction

*Developments in genetic science mean that scientists
may be able to bring extinct species back to life. Four scientists give
their views on this topic.*

A

Thanks to advances in genetic technology, scientists may eventually be able to revive species we thought were gone forever. The idea is stunning and would revolutionise the way we think about science. Having destroyed countless species over the last 10,000 years, humans could, through science, begin to reverse the damage we have caused. It would deliver a profoundly hopeful message. Knowledge and techniques developed for de-extinction would also be directly applicable to living species that are endangered, so conservation would benefit. Revived species would also help to restore a great deal of ecological richness. Returning certain birds to the forests of North America would bring much greater plant diversity to these areas that are so important for humans, as well as for other wildlife. De-extinction may be difficult to achieve but it would undoubtedly be worth it.

B

Major breakthroughs, such as species revival, would have various consequences, one being that they can restore our faith in science, progress and even in ourselves. Species revival would show that science can be used for good, not simply to feed our lower appetites. We could also apply what we learn from it to efforts to conserve living species. Achieving de-extinction would require considerable time and effort, of course, but the idea that it would divert resources from conservation rests on a false assumption. The truth is that money invested in high-tech solutions would not otherwise be available for the protection of wild environments and species; it would probably go into such activities as plant research for commercial use. What we do need to think through carefully, however, is how we would re-introduce species into nature. The ecosystem of a vanished species will have changed since it last inhabited it, and anyway, its extinction almost certainly resulted from the deterioration of its natural habitat. But we have time to consider this, and it doesn't mean de-extinction isn't worth pursuing.

C

Work on genetic techniques that may help restore species will happen whether we approve of it or not, and the funds required would not alternatively be available for conservation but would instead be directed at some other cutting edge field like medical science. So scientists and the general public alike may as well go along with it. The fact is, it is likely to be widely welcomed and will help create a favourable climate for science. What does concern me is how animals that have been brought back to life could be put into the wild once again. Besides the challenge of recreating conditions within which they might survive – which in many cases would require changing the biodiversity of huge geographical areas, for example – there is the thought that they might pose a serious threat to existing species, either because they could carry diseases or because they invade and destroy habitats for other creatures.

D

Just suppose we managed to bring a species back to life and that it was able to reproduce. What then? It's hard enough introducing zoo-raised species into the wild, let alone ones that are no longer with us and whose disappearance was due to changes in the environments they depended on. Our endeavours to conserve living species and the ecosystems they rely on are already starved of resources. Diverting funds to work on de-extinction would only deprive them further. But the most dangerous aspect of the de-extinction notion is that it reinforces the idea that advanced science can solve all our problems. If we can reclaim extinct species in a laboratory, then why bother protecting forests, wetlands, rivers and oceans? Why worry about endangered species if we can simply keep their DNA and revive them some time later? De-extinction only distracts us from safeguarding out planet's biodiversity for future generations.

Which scientist

has a similar opinion to scientist B about the
financial implications of investing in de-extinction?

37 [ ]

has a different opinion from the others about how
attitudes towards science would be influenced by
working on de-extinction?

38 [ ]

expresses a different view from the others about
environmental issues associated with de-extinction?

39 [ ]

shares scientist A's view of how de-extinction research
would contribute to other areas of science?

40 [ ]

You are going to read a newspaper article about an extraordinary archaeological discovery in Orkney, an island in the north of Scotland. Six paragraphs have been removed from the article. Choose from the paragraph **A–G** the one which fits each gap (**41–46**). There is one extra paragraph which you do not need to use.

Mark your answers **on the separate answer sheet**.

5,000 year-old temples discovered on the Scottish island of Orkney

North-west of Kirkwall, the capital of Orkney, lies the Ness of Brodgar, a narrow strip of land which separates the island's two largest freshwater lakes. At their edges, the water laps against a green, hilly landscape, peppered with giant stone rings, ancient villages and other archaeological riches.

41

What had escaped their attention was the temple complex of the Ness of Brodgar. Its size and complexity have since left archaeologists searching for superlatives to describe the wonders unearthed there. 'It's a Neolithic site without parallel in western Europe. Yet we previously thought it was just a hill,' says archaeologist Nick Card. 'It's actually entirely man-made, although it covers more than six acres of land.'

42

The people responsible for this architectural marvel arrived on Orkney about 6,000 years ago in the Neolithic (or New Stone) Age. They were the first farmers in Britain, and on Orkney rapidly established a vibrant culture with their giant stone circles, communal tombs, and the buildings at the Ness of Brodgar. The beliefs that underpinned the temple complex are unknown, however, as is the purpose of its great structures.

43

What is clear is that the cultural energy of the farming folk of Orkney dwarfed that of other civilisations at that time. In size and sophistication, the temple complex of Brodgar is comparable with the wonders of ancient Egypt, for example, though much older. The fact that it was built on a small island to the north of

Scotland, makes it all the more remarkable. For many archaeologists, its discovery has revolutionised our understanding of the period.

44

We know that these innovators first reached Orkney on boats from mainland Scotland. They brought cattle, pigs and sheep with them, as well as grain to plant. These early farmers were clearly successful, though life would still have been precarious, with hunting and fishing providing precious supplies of extra protein.

45

Discarded stone tools and pieces of elegant pottery tell us, however, that they lived long and well enough for an increasingly sophisticated society to emerge. Over centuries, small communities coalesced into larger tribal units, and sizeable constructions went up. Many of these – like the huge circles of standing stones and a 5,000-year-old village – have long been acknowledged as highly significant monuments. Eventually, in 1999, they were given World Heritage status by UNESCO, an act that led directly to the discovery of the Brodgar temple complex.

46

The assumption had been that it was a natural feature of the landscape. However, the new investigations indicated quite the opposite. 'The density and extent of what we detected below the surface stunned us,' says Card. Initially, archaeologists thought they had stumbled upon a general site that had been in continuous use for a few thousand years after those early settlers, but it all dated back to Neolithic times. What is more, the quality of workmanship evident in the buildings, carvings and pottery unearthed 'wouldn't be seen again on Orkney almost until modern times'.

A One thing archaeologists are sure of, nevertheless, is that it wasn't a settlement to live in. 'It was a huge ceremonial centre,' says Card, 'but the ideas and views of its builders remain a mystery.'

B The fate of the complex remains a puzzle, on the other hand. About 4,000 years ago, roughly 1,000 years after construction began, it was abruptly abandoned. Whatever the cause, the great temple complex was deserted and forgotten for the next four millennia.

C Evidence for this has been discovered at the site of a Neolithic village: the bones of domesticated animals alongside those of wild deer, whales and seals. Analysis of human bones from the period suggest that few people reached the age of 50 and those who survived childhood usually died in their 30s.

D For decades, researchers have been drawn to this remote place. It was extensively scrutinised until a recent chance discovery revealed that, for all their thoroughness, archaeologists had completely overlooked a Neolithic treasure eclipsing all others on Orkney – and further afield too.

E 'This recognition prompted us to think about the land surrounding the sites we knew,' says Card. 'We decided to survey it to see what else might be found.' Technology, like ground-penetrating radar for pinpointing man-made artefacts hidden underground was used. And the first location selected for this was the Ness of Brodgar.

F And when all the buildings were intact, it must have looked extremely impressive. Two giant walls protected more than a dozen large temples – one measuring almost 25 m square – all linked to outhouses and kitchens by carefully constructed stone pavements.

G 'We need to turn the map upside down when we consider the Neolithic era,' says Card. 'London may be the cultural hub of Britain today, but 5,000 years ago, Orkney was the centre for new ideas. The first grooved pottery, so distinctive of the era, was made here, for example, and then spread southwards.'

You are going to read an article in which four people talk about works of art they admire and the artists who created them. For questions **47–56**, choose from the people (**A–D**).

Mark your answers **on the separate answer sheet**.

Which writer

claims they are indifferent to a lot of art?	**47**
refers to artists being associated with a particular subject?	**48**
describes how a work of art gives an insight into a particular period of time?	**49**
points out the widespread impact an artist has had on other artists?	**50**
is impressed by how the style of an artwork suits its subject matter?	**51**
mentions the influence artists have had on their own work?	**52**
admits to ignorance of certain types of art?	**53**
talks about a work of art stimulating a variety of feelings?	**54**
refers to the universality of the subject matter of a particular work of art?	**55**
compares the significance of artists from different times in history?	**56**

Works of art we admire

A **The author Philip Pullman talks about Claude Monet's *The Four Trees* painted in 1891**

What does it mean for a work of art to be great? I think it must signify influence as well as a self-contained perfection of form. I can only talk about western art because, while I can see beauty in, say, a bronze sculpture from the Benin kingdom of West Africa, I have no idea whether it was influential in its own culture, or typical, or what.

So I've chosen a painting by Monet, who changed the way painters in the west saw and depicted light, and light is the subject of every representational painting: light falling on flesh, on stone, on cloth, on water. *The Four Trees*, one of a series of paintings of a stretch of the river Epte in France, is great because it conveys the sense of a bright morning with freshness and brilliance (the delicious golden light on the curve of trees in the distance); and because it's thrilling–I pity anyone who didn't feel a shock of delight at seeing that grid of dark lavenders over pale blue and gold.

B **The actor Kristin Scott Thomas talks about Gustave Caillebotte's *Paris Street: Rainy Day* painted in 1877**

As the title of the painting suggest, it shows a street scene in Paris on a wet day. The brilliant thing about it is its composition. A lamp post in the middle of the painting creates a sharp division, which makes it like a scene from a film. It throws you into the 19th century city with its wide boulevards and grand buildings. On the right, a couple walk towards us. His coat flaps open as if he'd just enjoyed a good lunch. Her arm is linked through his as they watch something beyond the lamp post that surprises him and amuses her but that we cannot see. On the other side of the black post, life is slower, lonelier and wet. The slippery shining cobblestones in the road give me cold toes, and I can smell the damp wool from all those coats. It isn't a cold day, but a miserable, rainy late autumn afternoon. I experience a twinge of envy as I think about this comfortable, affectionate couple going home to tea and a warm fire.

C **The sculptor Cornelia Parker talks about the photographs of Bernd and Hilla Becher from 1988**

Great artists can make you look at the world differently. Think of Monet with his haystacks at the end of the 19th century, or Turner with his sunsets several decades before: once you've seen their paintings, you never look at those things in the same way. That's exactly what Bernd and Hilla Becher have done for industrial architecture in the last 50 years. The German artists spent decades travelling around, obsessively cataloguing those grim, ubiquitous structures – gas-cooling towers, pitheads, pylons – that most of us think of as ugly. In the Bechers' work, they become like people, each with their own character.

I can't look at any such structures in real life without thinking of their photographs. I have several pinned to the walls of my studio. As a sculptor, I'm fascinated by their shape and form. The best works of art allow space for the viewer to bring their own interpretation and the Bechers' photographs always do this.

D **The artist David Hockney talks about Picasso's *Mother and Child (First Steps)* painted in 1943**

There's not much art I don't like, although nowadays a great deal of art doesn't generate strong feelings in me one way or another. I could say the paintings of Fra Angelico in Florence in Italy are my favourite works, or Rembrandt's great drawing, in the British Museum, of a family teaching a child to walk. But why not Picasso's treatment of this theme? It's something that absolutely everybody has experienced and witnessed. Today, thousands of depictions will be made of this all over the world, most with a camera: Uncle Charlie, for example, teaching little Edna to walk, photographed by mum. But most will not be able to show us what Picasso does: the child, both thrilled and frightened; the anxious mother, whose supple hands clasp the child's still awkward fingers. The way Picasso uses Cubist techniques to break up their bodies and present different perspectives allows him to give us that detail. It's abstract but at the same time manages to convey the humanity of the moment in a wonderfully touching manner.

You **must** answer this question. Write your answer in **220–260** words in an appropriate style on the separate answer sheet.

1   Your class has attended a discussion on the methods governments should use to encourage people to take more exercise. You have made the notes below.

> **Methods governments could use to encourage people to exercise more:**
>
> - more sports facilities
> - education
> - media campaigns

> **Some opinions expressed in the discussion:**
>
> 'Sports facilities are expensive to create.'
>
> 'Schools already do their best.'
>
> 'You cannot guarantee results from media publicity.'

Write an **essay** for your tutor discussing **two** of the methods in your notes. You should **explain which method you think is more important**, and **provide reasons** to support your opinion.

You may, if you wish, make use of the opinions expressed in the discussion, but you should use your own words as far as possible.

Write an answer to **one** of the questions **2–4** in this part. Write your answer in **220–260** words in an appropriate style on the separate answer sheet. Put the question number in the box at the top of the page.

2 You belong to a sports club and recently led a trip, funded by the club, for a group of fellow members to watch a major sports event in your capital city. Write a report on the trip for the club committee, saying why you thought the club's money was well spent.

Write your **report**.

3 Your local tourist office is planning to produce a tourist guidebook. It will give the contract for writing the guidebook to someone who is familiar with the local area. You are interested.

Write to the tourist office, saying why you would be suitable for the job. Outline your familiarity with the area, including your knowledge of:

• places of historical interest
• areas of natural beauty
• theme parks and amusement parks.

Write your **letter**.

4 You work on a student newspaper. You have been asked by the editor to write a review of an enduringly popular novel, outlining its most successful features, its shortcomings and the reasons it has remained popular.

Write your **review**.

Track 29

You will hear three different extracts. For questions **1–6**, choose the answer (**A, B** or **C**) which fits best according to what you hear. There are two questions for each extract.

Extract One

You hear two college friends discussing a lecture they have just attended.

1   What was the subject of the talk?
   A   starting a business
   B   preparing for a job interview
   C   working abroad

2   They liked the talk because the speaker
   A   gave plenty of opportunity for questions.
   B   handed out useful information.
   C   had a friendly and humorous style.

Extract Two

You hear part of a radio programme in which two people are discussing growing herbs.

3   According to Jerry, herbs are particularly useful
   A   in a corner of the garden.
   B   when they grow on windowsills.
   C   if grown among vegetables.

4   Which of the following is not true about growing herbs?
   A   Annual herbs are not used in cooking.
   B   Herbs are easy to cultivate.
   C   Perennial herbs add flavour to food.

Extract Three

You hear two friends talking about job interviews they recently attended.

5   What did James feel about the experience?
   A   He was surprised that only one person interviewed him.
   B   He was relieved that the interviewer asked easy questions.
   C   He was worried about the number of people being interviewed.

6   Susan thinks she was well prepared for her interview because
   A   she had a presentation to show.
   B   she did a lot of research on the company.
   C   she planned the journey there carefully.

Track 30

You will hear an anthropologist talking about a recent find. For questions **7–14**, complete the sentences with a word or short phrase.

A SIGNIFICANT FIND

Several fossil skulls were dug up in Ethiopia last

(**7**) ....

There were at least (**8**) .... adult skulls and one that

belonged to a child.

It appears that the people these skulls belong to were our

(**9**) .... ancestors.

Anthropologists now believe that *Homo sapiens* is

(**10**) .... from Neanderthals.

The reason why the Neanderthals (**11**) ....

is not known.

The people whose skulls have been found probably used

(**12**) ....

They also lived in (**13**) ...., a factor which probably

helped them to survive.

The early days of human evolution are still (**14**) ....

to modern scientists.

PAPER 1 Reading and
Use of English

PAPER 2 Writing

PAPER 3 Listening ▶
Part 1
Part 2
Part 3
Part 4

PAPER 4 Speaking

🎧 **Track 31**

You will hear an interview with Marianne Nolan, a surfing champion. For questions **15–20**, choose the answer (**A**, **B**, **C** or **D**) which fits best according to what you hear.

15 What does Marianne Nolan say about entering the senior surfing championships?
  A She is pleased to have the chance to learn from experienced surfers.
  B She is realistic about the amount of training that will be involved.
  C She has confidence that she will succeed in the early rounds.
  D She has mixed feelings about competing at such a high level.

16 According to Marianne, women surfers today
  A are prepared to take more risks than they did in the past.
  B are mainly concerned with having a beautiful surfing style.
  C are more likely to think in terms of becoming professional surfers.
  D are determined to achieve the same recognition for their skill as men.

17 In Marianne's opinion, young girls who surf should
  A find creative ways to promote surfing as a sport in top international events.
  B thank previous generations for pioneering surfing as a serious sport for women.
  C push their friends to take up surfing as a way of staying fit and healthy.
  D join surfing clubs that encourage boys and girls to compete with each other.

18 What does Marianne say about being considered a good surfer?
  A She thinks it could lead to sponsorship in the future.
  B It gives her hope that she will win the same title.
  C She feels it is both a burden and a compliment.
  D It surprised her to receive so much publicity.

19 When asked about her future, Marianne says she
  A has been too busy with her sport to make decisions about a job.
  B expects that a career will develop naturally out of her sport.
  C wonders how well she will adjust to having a routine job.
  D has changed the idea she previously had for a career.

20 What lesson does Marianne say she has learned from competitive surfing?
  A Prepare for the unexpected.
  B Be generous to people you defeat.
  C Know when you have reached your limit.
  D Do not let victory make you too confident.

PAPER 1 Reading and
Use of English

PAPER 2 Writing

PAPER 3 Listening ▶

PAPER 4 Speaking

Part 1
Part 2
Part 3
Part 4

🎧 **Track 32**

You will hear five short extracts in which people talk about holidays that went wrong.

While you listen, you must complete both tasks.

Task One

For questions **21–25**, choose from list **A–H**, the person who is speaking.

A a working holiday	
	Speaker 1 ☐ 21
B a student exchange trip	
	Speaker 2 ☐ 22
C a sailing holiday	
	Speaker 3 ☐ 23
D a city weekend break	
	Speaker 4 ☐ 24
E a guided walking tour	
	Speaker 5 ☐ 25
F a music course	
G a gastronomic tour	
H a camping holiday	

Task Two

For questions **26–30**, choose from list **A–H** what view each speaker is expressing.

A shame at the way they behaved	
	Speaker 1 ☐ 26
B shock at the cost of the holiday	
	Speaker 2 ☐ 27
C unhappiness with their companions	
	Speaker 3 ☐ 28
D disappointment about the food	
	Speaker 4 ☐ 29
E anger at the condition of their hotel room	
	Speaker 5 ☐ 30
F frustration at the amount of time wasted	
G dissatisfaction with the way the holiday was organised	
H dismay that they had spoilt the holiday for their friends	

Part 1 (2 minutes)

The examiner will ask you a few questions about yourself and about a general topic. For example, the examiner may ask you:

- How popular are the cinema and the theatre in your town or region?
- Which do you prefer: going to the cinema, or watching films on television?
- What was the last film that you enjoyed?

Part 2 (4 minutes)

You will each be asked to talk on your own for about a minute. You will each be given three different pictures to talk about. After your partner has finished speaking, you will be asked a brief question connected with your partner's photographs.

Stress (compare, contrast and speculate)

Turn to pictures 1–3 on page 190 which show stressful situations.

(*Candidate A*), it's your turn first. Here are your pictures. They show **people in stressful situations**.

I'd like you to compare **two** of the pictures and say **what is stressful about these situations, which is the more stressful, and why.**

(*Candidate B*), **what sort of situation do you find stressful?**

Struggling against the elements (compare, contrast and speculate)

Turn to pictures 1–3 on page 191 which show people struggling against the weather.

Now, (*Candidate B*), here are your pictures. **They show people who have to struggle against the elements.**

I'd like you to compare **two** of the pictures, and say **what kind of problems the people face and how they might be feeling.**

(*Candidate A*), **what sort of struggle against the elements would you find most difficult? Why?**

Part 3 (4 minutes)

Look at page 192 which gives some situations where people are being creative.

Creativity (discuss, evaluate and select)

Here are some different situations where people are engaged in creative activities and a question for you to discuss.

First, you have some time to look at the task.

(*Pause 15 seconds*)

Now talk to each other about **what rewards people get when they do these things.**

Now you have about a minute to decide **which creative activity is the most rewarding.**

Part 4 (5 minutes)

The examiner will encourage you to develop the topic of your discussion in Part 3 by asking questions such as:

- How important is it for people to feel creative in some way?
- Do you feel people get a similar sense of satisfaction from other activities?
- It is sometimes said that everyone has the potential to be creative in some way. Do you agree? (Why? / Why not?)

CAMBRIDGE ENGLISH
Language Assessment
Part of the University of Cambridge

Do not write in this box

Candidate Name
If not already printed, write name
in CAPITALS and complete the
Candidate No. grid (in pencil).

Candidate Signature

SAMPLE

Examination Title

Centre

Supervisor:

If the candidate is ABSENT or has WITHDRAWN shade here ▭

Centre No.

Candidate No.

Examination
Details

Candidate Answer Sheet

Instructions
Use a PENCIL (B or HB). Rub out any answer you wish to change using an eraser.

Parts 1 and 5-8: Mark ONE letter for each question.

For example, if you think **B** is the right
answer to the question, mark your
answer sheet like this:

0 | A | B | C | D

Parts 2, 3 and **4:** Write your answer clearly
in CAPITAL LETTERS.

For Parts 2 and 3 write one letter
in each box. For example:

0 | EXAMPLE

Part 1

1	A	B	C	D
2	A	B	C	D
3	A	B	C	D
4	A	B	C	D
5	A	B	C	D
6	A	B	C	D
7	A	B	C	D
8	A	B	C	D

Part 2

Do not write
below here

9
10
11
12
13
14
15
16

Continues over ➡

Part 3

		Do not write below here
17		17 1 0 u
18		18 1 0 u
19		19 1 0 u
20		20 1 0 u
21		21 1 0 u
22		22 1 0 u
23		23 1 0 u
24		24 1 0 u

Part 4

		Do not write below here
25		25 1 0 u
26		26 1 0 u
27		27 1 0 u
28		28 1 0 u
29		29 1 0 u
30		30 1 0 u

Part 5

31 A B C D
32 A B C D
33 A B C D
34 A B C D
35 A B C D
36 A B C D

Part 6

37 A B C D
38 A B C D
39 A B C D
40 A B C D

Part 7

41 A B C D E F G
42 A B C D E F G
43 A B C D E F G
44 A B C D E F G
45 A B C D E F G
46 A B C D E F G

Part 8

47 A B C D E
48 A B C D E
49 A B C D E
50 A B C D E
51 A B C D E
52 A B C D E
53 A B C D E
54 A B C D E
55 A B C D E
56 A B C D E

▸▸ **PART 2**

Candidate A

- Why are the people dressed in this way?
- How do you think they are feeling?

Language bank

These people could be ...

He/She seems to be ...

I imagine ...

I suppose ...

I'm fairly sure ...

I'd say they are probably ...

Apparently, ...

Judging by the fact that ...

Similarly, ...

I can't tell who/where/what ...

actors
annual tradition
audience
carnival
clown in a circus
costume
masks
on stage
professional
put on a performance
street party
take part (in festival, play, etc.)
theatre

▸ 1

▸ 2

▸ 3

▶▶ **PART 2**

Candidate B

Language bank

This picture shows …

They must be …

It might/could be …

He/She seems to be …

In contrast to …

As in the previous picture …

There are a number of advantages/
disadvantages to working …

One advantage/disadvantage
would be that …

I imagine it's very …

agricultural workers
cheap labour
craft
create something with your hands
executive
exhausting
highly paid/badly paid
indoors/outdoors
job satisfaction
manual labour
mentally/physically exhausting
potter
sophisticated modern office
stressful
suffer from heat/stress
tea plantation
well-equipped office

• **What are the advantages and disadvantages of working in these environments?**

▶ **1**

▶ **2**

▶ **3**

▸▸ **PART 3**
Candidates A and B

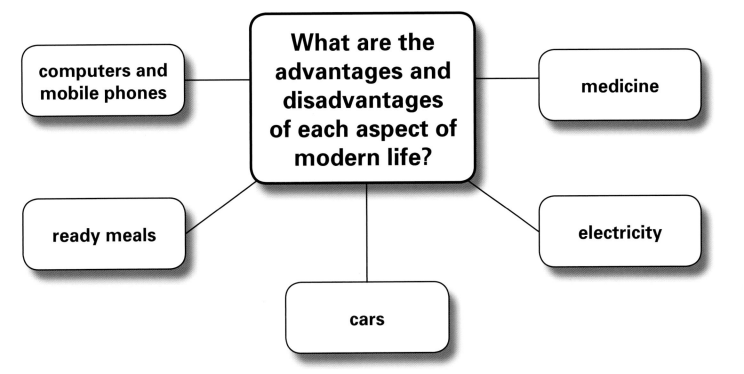

Language bank

The benefits/drawbacks of ... are obvious, I think.

What about the advantages/disadvantages, in your view?

Do the disadvantages outweigh the advantages in your opinion?

It's easy to see the benefits of computers and mobile phones, don't you think?

Mobile phones certainly make it easier to keep in touch, wouldn't you say?

I'm not sure whether there are any health risks associated with heating food in a microwave oven. What do you think?

It's usually more convenient to drive somewhere than to take public transport, but surely the pollution caused by cars is too high a price to pay?

I'd find it difficult to think of any disadvantages connected with electricity.

Perhaps we have to distinguish between electricity itself and the means of generating it.

▶▶ **PART 2**

Candidate A

Language bank

I guess/I imagine ...

He/She appears to be ...

He/She may be ...

He/She looks as though ...

On the other hand, he/she might be ...

To judge from the clothes he/she's wearing, ...

To judge from his/her posture, ...

about to dive
apprehensive
bathing trunks
business suit
concentrate on what you are about to do
diving board
have your arms outstretched
interview for a job
nervous
overcome your fears
wait in the wings
waiting area

• What could the people be anticipating?
• How do you think they are feeling?

▸▸ **PART 2**

Candidate B

Language bank

I can't tell whether the person is a man or a woman. It looks as if/though …

I can't see the expression on his/her face, but I think he/she must be …

Perhaps he/she feels …

It's also possible that he/she …

If I were him/her, I'd probably feel …

The landscape/room might make me feel …

The man looks like he is dressed for cold weather.

The person is dwarfed by the landscape.

Perhaps she's waiting …

She might simply be looking at something outside.

alone

depressing atmosphere

elderly lady

insignificant

inspiring

lonely

peer through the curtains

remote

rugged

spectacular

suffer from loneliness

tracksuit

uplifting

- Why are the people alone?
- How do you think they are feeling?

▸ 1

▸ 2

▸ 3

▸▸ **PART 3**
   Candidates A and B

working in a
factory

How
important is
motivation in
these situations?

training for a
marathon

studying for an
exam

climbing a
mountain

working in an
office

Language bank

I'd imagine that anyone who wishes to ... would have to be motivated.

People can be motivated to overcome difficulties.

If you want to ... , I imagine you would need to work very hard.

A powerful sense of motivation could be negative if a person became obsessed with his/her goals.

It's easy to give up.

You don't need a lot of motivation in this situation because ...

depressed
discouraged/encouraged
inspired
jealous
miss out on other aspects of life
overcome physical hardships
personal ambition
push yourself to achieve a goal
ruthless and unfeeling
single-minded
the desire for knowledge
the desire to acquire material possessions
the desire to be admired by your colleagues
the desire to be the first
the desire to excel
the desire to gain the approval of others
the desire to impress others
the desire to overcome hardship/difficulties
the desire to pursue a career

▶▶ **PART 2**

Candidate A

- Why might the people be leaving?
- How might they be feeling?

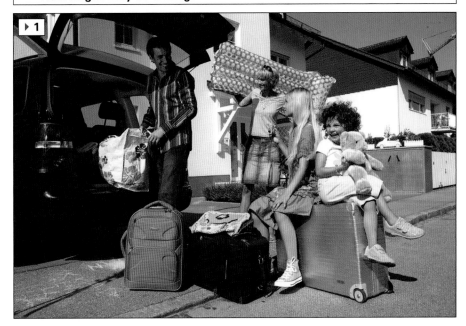

Language bank

It looks as if/though ...

They appear to be ...

They must be ...

I would say he/she's probably ...

Perhaps they're going somewhere on holiday.

They're about to leave on a holiday, not a business trip.

Like the man in the second picture, ...

Unlike the man in the second picture, these people are ...

The mode of transport in this case is very different.

about to board a spaceship
about to set off
boot of the car
briefcase
business trip
casual clothes
crew of a spaceship
embark on a journey/mission
family car
intercity train
load the luggage
members of a family
space mission
spacesuit
station platform
suit and tie
suitcase on wheels

▶▶ PART 2

Candidate B

Language bank

He/She looks very tired.

He/She must be feeling exhausted.

This makes me think he/she's been working ...

In all likelihood, ...

Of course, it's also possible that ...

I suppose they feel satisfied as well as exhausted.

In contrast to the previous two images, this picture shows ...

Judging by his/her expression ...

look after a young child
loosen your tie
mental/physical work
renovate a house
rest your head on your hand
stare at a computer screen
stiff muscles
wear a shirt and tie

- Why might the people be tired?
- What kind of exhaustion – mental or physical – is each person feeling, and why?

▶ 1

▶ 2

▶ 3

▶▶ **PART 3**

Candidates A and B

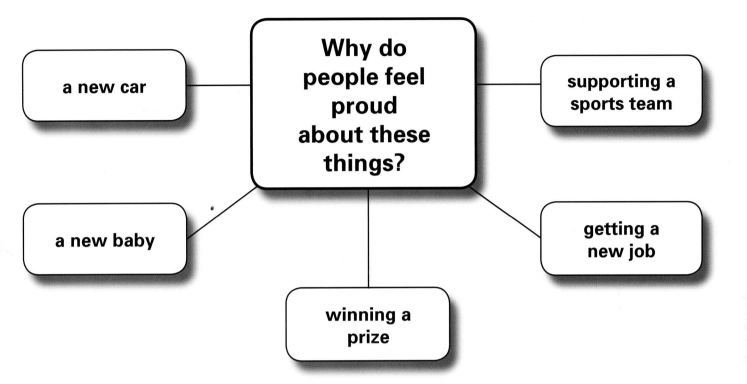

Language bank

achievement
cheer
dedicate yourself to achieving your goal
delighted
feel part of a group
it's natural to be proud of ...
justifiably proud
own an impressive car
parental pride
proud of your child/offspring
public acclaim
satisfied with yourself
trophy
victory
work and save in order to buy something

▶▶ **PART 2**

Candidate A

Language bank

Presumably, this sport appeals to people who ...

It attracts people who are ...

People who are ... are inclined to do this sport.

People who want to excel in this sport must be ...

This sport does not demand the same level of fitness as ...

In contrast to ... , this sport ...

aim
archer
archery
bow and arrow
bull's eye
concentration
co-ordination
head a ball
hit the target
individual/team sport
powerful physique
score a goal
take part in
training and practice
weightlifting

- **What kind of training do these sports require?**
- **What are the advantages and disadvantages of taking part in a team sport, as opposed to an individual sport?**

▶ **1**

▶ **2**

▶ **3**

▶▶ **PART 2**

Candidate B

Language bank

I should think a home like this would be …

In contrast to the other buildings, this home …

The house seems to be made of …

One advantage/disadvantage of a home like this would be …

Its location would be a disadvantage in case of illness or other emergencies.

The building itself would be expensive to keep up because …

It would require a large staff to look after a home like this.

Some people may dislike feeling that their home is just like all the rest.

Privacy might be a problem in a home like this.

cut off from civilisation
flats in an apartment block
high heating and maintenance costs
insulation
isolated
(lack of) privacy
log cabin
mansion
rural/urban environment stately home
unsuitable for domestic purposes

- What are the advantages of living in each place?
- What are the impractical aspects of living in each home?

▶ 1

▶ 2

▶ 3

▶▶ **PART 3**
   Candidates A and B

---

introduce a congestion charge

How practical are these ideas to reduce car use in a city?

ban cars from the city centre

create new cycle paths

introduce a park-and-ride scheme

make public transport cheaper

Language bank

I think this would be very effective, don't you?

I doubt if many people use bikes.

I can't imagine that it would work.

I don't agree with you completely about that.

I think you're absolutely right about that.

I take your point.

I agree with you up to a point, but I think there are other factors to be taken into consideration.

I'm afraid I have to disagree with you on that point.

cause less pollution than other forms of transport
convenient
efficient
extensive transport system
ferry
lane
rush hour
traffic jam
tram
underground train

▸▸ PART 2

Candidate A

Language bank

These people are wearing some kind of uniform ...

They're wearing similar clothes.

It's more effective to be part of a large group.

They look as if they're in the army or some branch of the armed forces.

They look as if they're protesting.

They're musicians in an orchestra.

Clearly, they feel part of a group because ...

As far as I can tell, the orchestra is made up of people of different ages.

Presumably, the sense of belonging to a group comes from their shared interest in music.

They may be amateur musicians, but they might also be professionals.

cello players
holding up a sign
military uniform
officers
protest
sharing a sense of danger
string section of an orchestra
taking action
trying to get their point of view across

• **What are the advantages and disadvantages of doing these activities in a group?**

▸ 1

▸ 2

▸ 3

▸▸ PART 2

Candidate B

• How difficult is it to acquire each skill?

Language bank

The farmer appears to be examining his crops.

He must like working outdoors.

It's not entirely clear from his expression how he feels about ...

He seems to be a teacher.

He may be demonstrating something to his pupils.

Perhaps his experience has led him to conclude that ...

I suppose he's learnt how to use discipline in a class/gain the respect of the children he's teaching.

She seems to be looking after the panda cub.

She must have studied for a long time.

▸ 1

▸ 2

▸ 3

▶▶ **PART 3**
   Candidates A and B

looking after small children

Why is time management necessary in these situations?

training for a marathon

meeting a work deadline

having more than one job

studying for an exam

Language bank

Do we agree that better time management is necessary?

It's difficult to manage your time when …

It's easy to forget thing when …

It's very obvious that …

This illustrates one of the problems connected with bad time management.

It must be frustrating when …

Small children make big demands on your time.

Sometimes, people have no choice but to …

You have to juggle lots of different activities.

It's difficult to concentrate when …

badly organised
demanding
determined
disciplined
have too much time on your hands
inefficient
pressure
stressful

▶▶ PART 2

Candidate A

Language bank

I imagine he/she's anxious about ...

My impression is that he/she ...

My guess would be that he/she ...

Maybe he/she's already ... and is now ...

Whereas, the first picture shows someone worried about ...

This picture depicts someone in a state of anxiety about ...

The person's facial expression shows he/she's anxious or worried.

being told the results
biting her nails
deal with a problem
on board a plane
patient
physician
possible treatment.
take off and landing
waiting nervously

• **What might be making these people anxious?**
• **Which situation would you least like to be in?**

▶ 1

▶ 3

▶ 2

▶▶ PART 2
Candidate B

Language bank

It's obvious that he/she ...

I suppose he/she's pleased/relieved that ...

He/She's probably feeling pleased because ...

He/She's happy because he/she's finally managed (to do something).

I would guess that he/she ... for the first time, and he/she's delighted.

He/She's expressing his/her pleasure at this achievement.

It's not entirely clear what/who ...

academic achievement
congratulate someone on his/her promotion
degree/diploma
doing something for the first time
first feeling of independence
graduate from college/university
shake hands on a deal
successful negotiation

- **What have these people achieved?**
- **What difficulties might they have had in reaching their goal?**

▶ 1

▶ 3

▶ 2

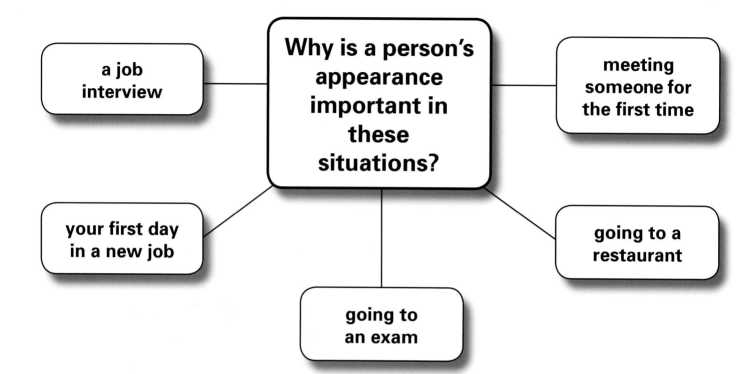

| a job interview | **Why is a person's appearance important in these situations?** | meeting someone for the first time |

- a job interview
- your first day in a new job
- Why is a person's appearance important in these situations?
- going to an exam
- meeting someone for the first time
- going to a restaurant

Language bank

The clothes you wear give the impression that you are ...

First impressions are important because ...

It's normal to judge people by their appearance

Some people don't care about convention/fashion.

You can come across as ...

anti-establishment
arrogant
attractive
capable
confident
conservative
efficient
fashion victim
formal event
scruffy

▶▶ **PART 2**

Candidate A

Language bank

She might be her grandmother.

He/She's looking at ... with a friendly but respectful expression.

He/She may respect ... for several reasons.

She may have been brought up to behave respectfully towards older people.

He appears to have made a speech.

I expect an audience is obliged to applaud a speaker out of politeness, but the facial expressions of these men suggest that their respect is genuine.

I know he's a famous politician, but I can't remember his name.

I think the man in the photo is ..., but I'm not sure.

applaud
bow to someone
express your admiration
honour someone for his/her achievements
(lack of) respect for old people
statesman
make a speech
politeness/courtesy is important
politician

- **What could be prompting people to show respect in these situations?**
- **How might the people receiving the show of respect feel?**

▶ **1**

▶ **2**

▶ **3**

▶▶ PART 2

Candidate B

- • What kind of partnerships are these?
- • How do the partners feel about each other?

Language bank

There's no way of telling whether they're ... or ...

In all likelihood, they're colleagues.

They're wearing ... , so they're probably ...

They must have a great deal of confidence in one another.

Trust would be the basis of their working relationship, I imagine.

In this kind of partnership, I imagine respect for the other person's ability must be crucial.

They obviously have a lot of fun together.

They must enjoy what they do.

building site
buskers
collaboration
colleague
contribution
co-operation
have confidence in someone
intellectual ability
laboratory
lab technician
mutual trust
musician
rely on your colleague
white lab coat

▶ 1

▶ 2

▶ 3

▶▶ PART 3
   Candidates A and B

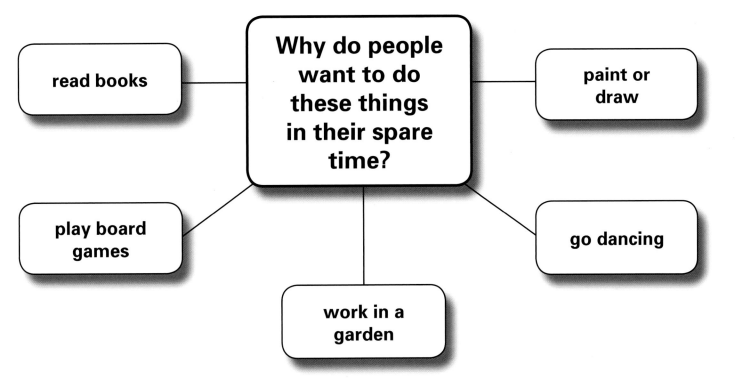

read books

Why do people want to do these things in their spare time?

paint or draw

play board games

go dancing

work in a garden

Language bank

This is a physically demanding activity, but I suppose it's a way of relaxing for some people.

Personally, I don't understand why people would choose to ...

This is a solitary/creative/exciting pastime.

It's a very popular thing to do, especially with older people.

It allows you to switch off.

It exercises the mind.

You don't have to think.

artistic
competitive
express yourself
freedom
get away from it all
nature
solitary
spend time with other people
unwind

▶▶ **PART 2**

   Candidate A

• What is stressful about these situations?
• Which might be the most stressful and why?

Language bank

I can't see exactly what they're doing, but I think they're ...

It looks as though they're under a lot of stress.

I'd say this kind of stress is due partly to ... and partly to ...

There's a certain amount of danger involved in work like this.

There's always the danger that something could go wrong.

I think most performers feel nervous before going on stage, and this could be a cause of stress.

assembly line
boring and repetitive
buy/sell shares
conveyor belt
fall behind
high levels of noise
investor
make/lose a fortune
price of shares
stage fright
stock exchange
stockbroker
there's a lot at stake

▶ **PART 2**

Candidate B

• **What kind of problems do the people face?**
• **How might they be feeling in their current situation?**

Language bank

The people in the boat are probably there from choice.

Probably they feel exhilarated, even though there are dangers involved.

They may not have realised how dangerous the situation would be.

They might regret ...

In contrast, they bably has have no alternative but to do battle against the elements.

They might be facing starvation.

They are trying to protect their homes or property against flooding.

(The river) burst its banks.

drown
fishing boat
flood/flooding
in danger of capsising
rough sea
scorching heat
scratch a living from the land
sparse vegetation
starve
stormy
suffer from drought
survive
the soil is parched
water shortage
waves

▶ **1**

▶ **2**

▶ **3**

▶▶ **PART 3**

Candidates A and B

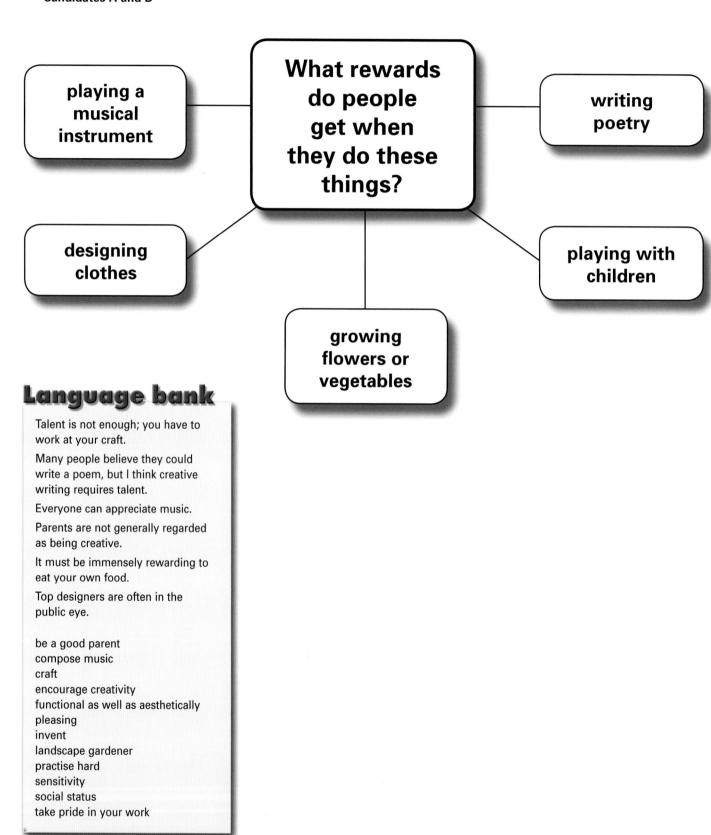

playing a musical instrument

What rewards do people get when they do these things?

writing poetry

designing clothes

playing with children

growing flowers or vegetables

Language bank

Talent is not enough; you have to work at your craft.

Many people believe they could write a poem, but I think creative writing requires talent.

Everyone can appreciate music.

Parents are not generally regarded as being creative.

It must be immensely rewarding to eat your own food.

Top designers are often in the public eye.

be a good parent
compose music
craft
encourage creativity
functional as well as aesthetically pleasing
invent
landscape gardener
practise hard
sensitivity
social status
take pride in your work

Preparing, planning and checking

▶▶ Preparing for the Writing Paper

Producing a piece of writing that fulfils a certain function is a difficult task for anybody, even in their native language. To prepare for the Writing Paper, it goes without saying that you need to have read widely. Then, you need to have studied all the basic text types you may be asked to produce, and understood the basic features that characterise them: layout, organisation, style and register. You should also practise completing writing tasks in the time allowed in the exam. Remember the criteria the examiners will use in awarding marks:

- Has the candidate achieved the purpose stated in the instructions?
- Does the text have a positive general effect on the target reader?
- Does the text cover all the content points?
- Is the text well organised and are ideas linked appropriately?
- Has language been used accurately?
- Does the text exhibit a good range of vocabulary and grammatical structures?
- Is the register appropriate for the task?
- Is the layout appropriate?

Ideally, the pieces of writing you produce should be checked by an experienced teacher who can provide useful feedback. Such feedback can help you compile a list of useful expressions, such as the useful phrases you find with the model answers in this section. You can also learn what sort of mistakes you make habitually so you can avoid them. For instance, if you find that you frequently make mistakes with a certain tense, you should consult a good grammar guide to clear up your confusion.

▶▶ Planning your answer

Perhaps the most useful lesson that experienced writers learn is the importance of planning what to write before they actually begin writing. Most good writers usually write several drafts of a text before they are satisfied with the result. Unfortunately, in the exam you do not have time to produce several drafts, and it would be a serious mistake to try: you only have time for a single draft. But you do have time to make a plan.

Always read the question carefully and make sure you understand the following:

- Who are you writing for?
- What are the points you must include in your answer?
- Does the text type have any particular layout requirements?
- Do you have the necessary vocabulary to answer the question?

Then prepare a plan or outline of what you are going to write. Its purpose is to help you, so it doesn't matter if you change it or cross things out – nobody else is going to read it. But it has to show clearly the different sections of your writing and what points you must include in which section. When you look at the plan closely, you might want to change it; for instance, something might be better in a different paragraph, or you might realise you will be repeating yourself. When you are satisfied with your outline, you will find it much easier to write your text. Planning takes time, so allow a minimum of 15 minutes for it.

▶▶ Checking

Most people make more mistakes than normal under exam conditions, so always allow at least ten minutes at the end to read through your work. Think of your task here as having two parts. First, check that you have answered the question correctly and that you have included all the information that was required. Secondly, check for mistakes in grammar, spelling, punctuation etc. You should by now have had enough experience to know where you often make mistakes – the spelling of certain words, for instance, or a particular type of punctuation.

If you need to correct something, make the correction neatly and legibly. If you need to cross out something you have written, just put one line through the word or words.

1 Essay

▶ ▶ **Exam task – Part 1**

Your class has had a discussion on the advisability of bringing the voting age in your country down from 18 years old to 16 years old. You have made the notes below:

> **Points made on the advisability of bringing the voting age down to 16 years old:**
>
> • young people are good judges
> • politicians will think more about young people's needs
> • young people will take more interest in politics

> **Other opinions expressed during the discussion:**
>
> 'Teenagers already have enough on their plates.'
> 'Young people don't trust politicians.'
> 'There aren't enough young people in parliament.'

Write an **essay** for your tutor discussing **two** of the points you made in your notes. You should **explain which point you think is more important** and **provide reasons** to support your opinion.

You may, if you wish, make use of the opinions expressed in the discussion, but you should use your own words as far as possible.

▶ ▶ **Approach**

▶ Here is a straightforward way to write an essay. If you have two main points to make, you can give your essay a clear structure by dividing it into four paragraphs.

Have a title that grabs the attention

Paragraph One – The first paragraph of an essay provides the introduction. It states what is to be discussed and why. Your main points are briefly introduced. This paragraph need not be lengthy.

Paragraph Two – In the second paragraph more background information is provided in greater detail. Your first, often strongest main point is expanded upon. Bring in and refute any arguments against your point of view.

Paragraph Three – The third paragraph provides your second key point, tying it into the theme of your essay. Again, bring in opposing points of view and support your second key point with information and background.

Paragraph Four – The fourth and final paragraph is used to summarise or conclude your essay. It shows how the two key points you have presented compare or relate to each other. It also clearly re-states your initial position from the introductory paragraph.

▶ Add quotations, statistics, facts, examples and other relevant data to support your points.

▶ The tone and register can be formal or semi-formal depending on your treatment of the topic. If your essay is written in a formal register, only bring in informal expressions when you use a direct quotation to support your argument.

▶ Punctuation is important in essays, and can be a powerful tool in expressing subtle or emphatic points. Short sentences make for a punchy style, but get irritating if they are over-used; long sentences need careful use of commas, semi-colons and dashes to achieve flow and rhythm.

Model answer

Give your text a title that will attract the reader's attention.

Should 16-year-olds have the vote?

The introduction should be short and clear.

This question was recently discussed by a group of students in Burley College, and after an hour of heated debate for and against the proposal, a conclusion was reached. I will put forward the main arguments that were considered in this discussion.

Undoubtedly the most persuasive point was that politicians would pay more attention to the expectations of teenagers. Considerable power and influence would be delivered into the hands of young people, and they would be in a position to steer policy in new directions. It is true that today there are very few politicians under the age of 30, but this new measure would certainly encourage younger people to stand for parliament.

One objection was that politicians are not well trusted these days, and 16-year-olds do not have enough experience to assess which of their local candidates would best look after their interests. But today's teenagers are sophisticated, have a huge amount of information at their fingertips, and are as well able to make judgments about politicians as any other citizen.

The conclusion can be short and should leave the reader with a clear idea of what has been described or discussed.

In the end, the discussion group voted overwhelmingly in favour of bringing down the voting age. It was felt that the new generation will have to deal with the world they inherit from their elders, and they have the right to a say in the government that will shape that world for them.

Useful phrases

Introduction

I will put forward ...

There are two main points to discuss ...

I am going to discuss the issue of ...

Main body

The most important point is ...

In addition ...

As opposed to that ...

Looking at it from another point of view ...

It is true that ...

Conclusion

In conclusion/To summarise, ...

The outcome is clear that ...

2 Formal letter

▶ ▷ **Exam task – Part 2**

A colleague of yours, Alice Watson, has applied for a job in the public relations department of a large charity, Poverty Action. You have been asked to write a letter providing a character reference for her. Indicate how long and in what capacity you have worked with her, and how her personal characteristics would make her suited for the job. Here is part of the letter you received from Poverty Action.

> The job of Public Relations Co-ordinator consists mainly of supervising PR work, and entails travelling around the country and working with various people in our large organisation. The successful applicant will need good managerial skills and be committed to the philosophy of our charity.

Write your **letter**.

▶ ▷ **Approach**

▶ A character reference is almost always addressed to the organisation where someone has applied for a job or a place to study. Generally, you should use the heading line 'To whom it may concern', rather than writing to a specific person. If the exam question asks you to refer to certain characteristics of a person, make sure you do so. You should also imagine what other information may be required, bearing in mind the position the person has applied for.

▶ All character references are formal in style. Generally, you should write at least three paragraphs: introduction, main body and conclusion.

Useful phrases

Introduction

To whom it may concern

I have been asked to write this reference for (Ms Watson).

With reference to your letter of (3rd March) …

I have known (Ms Watson) for the last (four) years …

I was her supervisor/superior in (the publicity department of) …

Main body

(Ms Watson) has always shown great dedication/commitment to her work. She has (excellent managerial skills) …

Her duties/tasks here included …

She proved to be … competent/ dependable/efficient/popular with colleagues.

Conclusion

I understand that (Ms Watson) has applied for …

I am certain that (Ms Watson) would be extremely capable …

I have no hesitation in recommending her for …

I should be very happy to supply any further information.

Please do not hesitate to contact me …

▶▶ Model answer

This is the standard heading for character references.

To whom it may concern,

Ms Alice Watson

State the name of the person for whom you are writing the reference.

Say how you know the person and explain in what way you worked together.

I have been asked to write this reference for Ms Alice Watson, who worked with me for almost four years in the Head Office of the charity *Children in Need*. I was her immediate superior in the publicity department of that organisation, so I was able to observe her work at close quarters and feel qualified to evaluate her suitability for similar positions.

Explain what sort of jobs the person did, and describe the positive characteristics she showed.

Ms Watson was extremely committed to her work and always performed to the highest standard. Her tasks included checking press releases and writing letters to a wide variety of recipients, and she displayed first-class communication skills. The executives of the organisation found her entirely trustworthy, and she always carried out her work cheerfully and efficiently. At various times of the year our department employed a number of temporary staff in order to send out appeals for donations, and in her dealings with these people Ms Watson exhibited very good managerial skills. She was also popular with the permanent staff, though she never allowed this to interfere with the work that had to be done.

I understand that Ms Watson has applied for the position of Public Relations Co-ordinator, which I imagine entails considerable responsibility. I have no hesitation in recommending her for this position, and I am certain she will prove an excellent and hard-working member of your organisation. Naturally, I would be very happy to supply any further information, so please do not hesitate to contact me if this should be required.

Refer to the person's suitability for the tasks involved in the new job.

Yours faithfully,

Emma Lyons
Public Relations Officer
Children in Need

End the letter formally.

3 Informal letter/email

▶ ▶ Exam task – Part 2

You've received a letter from someone who was a good friend at school. Your friend moved to another part of the country and you lost touch with each other. Reply to the letter giving your news and suggesting a meeting.

Now write your **letter**. You do not need to include postal addresses.

▶ ▶ Approach

▶ Be careful you understand exactly who you are writing to, and what you must include in your letter. Here, you are writing to an old friend, giving your news, although you haven't communicated for a long time.

▶ You are writing to a friend, so the register should be informal.

Useful phrases

Introduction

It was great/a lovely surprise to get your letter last week.

What a lot's happened in five years!

I was so pleased/sad to hear about …

Main body

As for me, I've been busy with …

It's been an exciting few years.

You won't believe it, but …

My main news is that …

Why don't we get together some time?

It'd be a lot of fun to meet up.

Come and stay one weekend.

Signing off

Text me on (phone number)…

Here's my email address.

Take care of yourself/Look after yourself.

Lots of love/Cheers

Hi Chris,

It was great to get your letter, and such a surprise. I can't believe it's five years since we left school – so much has happened. It seems amazing that you're married and have got a baby boy. Congratulations! But I'm sad to hear your Dad hasn't been well. Please say hello to him from me.

It's been an exciting few years for me too. I'm not married yet, but I've got a job I enjoy which involves a lot of travelling. When we left school, and you went off to college, I started work on our local paper. A couple of years ago I was offered a job in the foreign news department of a TV channel, and I'm on the move all the time. It's a steep learning curve for me because I have to keep up with international politics, and know about the geography and economy of different countries (remember I wasn't exactly brilliant at either of those subjects at school!). I think they took me on because I'm not bad at foreign languages.

Anyway, let's get together soon. I've got a week's holiday coming up and I'd love to see you and your family. How does the first week of May sound? I could easily get a train over and spend an afternoon with you.

Text me on 06009 546 385.

All the best to your wife and son. I can't wait to meet them!

Take care.

Mel

Begin with an enthusiastic reaction to your friend's letter. In a few words, comment on his/her news.

Write a mini biography for yourself. You could have fun with this part, but make it plausible - it's probably best not to go over the top.

As this is a letter to a friend, you can end informally.

4 Report

▶ ▶ **Exam task – Part 2**

An international magazine is investigating tourism in various areas around the world. You have been asked to write a report for the magazine's editors, addressing the following questions:

● How has tourism in your region changed over the last decade?

● What are the reasons for these changes?

● What problems exist and can anything be done to solve them?

Write your **report**.

▶ ▶ **Approach**

▶ Read the question carefully to see whether you should include your own opinions in the report, and if this is the case, make it clear in the report when you are describing objective facts and when you are giving your interpretation. Depending on the task, you may need to describe something, give an account or narrate an event, express an opinion, and possibly compare and contrast.

▶ You can use headings and possibly bullet points or numbered lists to make it easier for the reader to find information quickly. The introduction and conclusion can be short. You are usually asked to write a report for some sort of organisation or publication, so the language you use should be semi-formal or formal. Even if you use bullet points or numbered lists, you should write complete sentences, not just notes. Remember that in formal writing we often use the passive voice.

Useful phrases

Introduction
The following report evaluates/ describes/ presents/provides an account of …
This report aims to provide an overall view of the situation.
I shall describe the situation below.

Main body
a popular destination easy to reach by
a popular destination
easy to reach by rail/road/air
holidays to (Prague) are widely advertised
overcharging
service in hotels

It is generally accepted that …
The vast majority of visitors …
This is probably due to the fact that …
While data is hard to come by, it is thought that …

Conclusion
One measure which may improve the situation would be to introduce …
I am of the opinion that …
It is my view/opinion that …
On balance, it appears that …

▶ ▶ **Model answer**

Give your report a
suitable title. —————— **Tourism in Prague**

Introduction

The last decade has seen a dramatic increase in the number of
tourists visiting the Czech Republic in general and Prague in particular.
The following report presents a brief overview.

> Write a brief
> introduction that
> provides a few
> important facts and
> summarises what your
> report is about.

Background

Until 1989, Prague was not a popular destination for tourists from
western Europe due to a number of factors.

Use bullet points to
provide a list, but
make sure each point
is grammatically the
same; here each point
is a complete sentence.

- The city was difficult to reach; visitors often had to wait for long
  periods at border crossings.
- There was little information about trips to Prague in foreign travel
  agencies.
- Some people felt nervous about trips to countries in central and
  eastern Europe.

Changes

All the above factors have changed dramatically: Prague is now easy
to reach by road, rail and air; trips to Prague are widely advertised in
western countries; few visitors feel nervous about visiting a country in
eastern Europe any more.

> You can use semicolons
> to separate items in a
> list, but as with bullet
> points, make sure
> each item is the same
> grammatically.

Criticisms

The majority of visitors to Prague are extremely satisfied on the
whole; however, there are a few complaints about two specific areas:

- taxi drivers acting in a rude manner and, in many cases,
  overcharging.
- hotels providing less than adequate service.

Future development

The city council is at present considering stricter laws relating to
taxi drivers. Moreover, the local tourist authority is reclassifying the
hotels in the city.

Conclusion

While Prague can offer visitors a generally positive experience, there
are some issues which need to be addressed. I am of the opinion that
better regulation of taxi drivers and hotels will solve these problems.

> Make sure each section
> is clearly separated
> from the others.

5 Proposal

▶ ▶ **Exam task – Part 2**

You work at a language school that offers summer courses to students from abroad. This year the director of the school wants to hold an introductory weekend for the students. She has asked you to write a proposal for the programme. She doesn't want the weekend to cost the school very much and wants the programme to include:

- information on local facilities
- social events arranged for the students.

Write your **proposal**.

▶ ▶ **Approach**

▶ Writing a proposal is similar, to but not exactly the same as, writing a persuasive essay or producing a report.

▶ A proposal should define a problem or challenge and describe a solution that will persuade a busy, thrifty or sceptical reader to support it. Employ facts, not opinions, to bolster the argument for approval.

▶ Outline your plan or project, demonstrating possible outcomes.

▶ Any discussion of financial or other resources should present a realistic picture of the expense required.

▶ Make the proposal clear and concise, and ensure the presentation is attractive and engaging as well being well-organised and helpful.

▶ A proposal should include the following elements.

Introduction: State the background to the proposal and summarise it. (This allows a decision maker to quickly get the gist of the proposal.)

Project description: Explain why the plan or project is needed, how it will be put into effect and how it will be evaluated.

Budget analysis: If necessary, outline the financial aspects of the plan or project.

Conclusion: Summarise the proposal's main points.

Useful phrases

Introduction
In view of the fact that …
Considering the fact that …
At present, the situation is that …
My experience suggests that …

Main body
It would be helpful to students to be told …
It would be of great benefit to students if …
One possible solution would be to …
Providing the event is properly organised, it could be of great

assistance to students.
Students could also be …
You might also like to consider …
In all likelihood, …
The chances are …

Conclusion
Any teething troubles could quickly be overcome …
In conclusion, I feel (quite) strongly that this is the best way to …
In spite of/Despite the effort required, this would be a worthwhile step …

▶▶ Model answer

Give your proposal a suitable title.

Introductory weekend for foreign students

In the introduction, briefly outline the situation and indicate your position.

Previously the students' introduction to our school and town has been carried out informally, but the summer intake of students has increased to such an extent that a more organised introduction would be very beneficial.

Use simple headings to organise your ideas clearly.

Day 1

This should begin with a welcome from the director, and introduction of members of staff, followed by practical information on using local transport, banks and medical services; and a question-and-answer session.

A coffee break could also include a 'getting-to-know-you session', where students meet each other and their teachers, and are shown round the school.

In the afternoon the school coach could take the students on a tour of the town, so they find out where the local cinema, shopping centres and sports facilities are, and be given information about places of interest.

Use a variety of structures to make suggestions. For example: *would be* and *could also be*.

In the evening it would be a good idea to hold a party with a barbeque and dancing so that students could spend time with their teachers and fellow students in a relaxed atmosphere.

Day 2

A popular idea might be an afternoon coach trip to a local beauty spot.

Budget

The main expenses would be fuel and parking costs for the school coach, and food and music for the party. I think these could be taken out of the school's entertainment fund.

Conclusion

A programme like this would get the summer courses off to a flying start, and give everyone involved a lot of pleasure.

6 Review

▶ ▶ **Exam task – Part 2**

You have been watching a popular series on TV about people taking part in a competition for the best amateur photographer, and you have decided to write a review of it for your college newspaper. Say what was good and bad about the series, and whether you would recommend the second series, which starts soon.

Write your **review**.

▶ ▶ **Approach**

▶ This is for students, so it can be informal and critical.

▶ Start with an attention-grabbing opening.

▶ It can express your personal response, but should be impartial for the most part.

▶ Use the sandwich method – what was good, what was bad, what was good; or the other way round for a negative review.

▶ The review should be informative, bringing in a little background, comparisons with similar programmes.

▶ Finish by summing up your opinions and making your recommendation.

Useful phrases

The thing that struck me most was ...

The problem was (it just went on too long).

For the most part ...

Broadly speaking, ...

All in all, ...

To be honest, ...

It was the most boring/exciting thing I've watched for ages.

▶ ▶ Model answer

The great national TV photo competition

What a surprise! I loved it!

Generally state your overall opinion.

I was not thrilled when my editor told me to review this photography competition. It was going out every Monday evening for a month. What a waste of an evening, I thought. But from programme one, I was hooked.

Go into details, giving more information about your opinion.

I'm not a photographer, but the first thing that struck me was the passion of the photographers. They would put themselves into great danger, hanging off cliffs or creeping up on ferocious animals to get their picture. And all this just for the love of it. Their sheer enthusiasm made you want to rush out and buy a camera.

This was the first series, and it had its faults. Sometimes the pace dragged a bit, and there was too much technical gossip among the contributors. And I have to admit, some of the photos that made it into the later rounds seemed uninspired to me - banal or sentimental.

Give a balanced view, if possible.

The last three competitors, who were up against each other in the final round, produced some absolutely stunning work. They must have been an inspiration to the millions of other photographers in the country, and proof that the age of the gifted amateur has returned.

The programme's popularity ratings were through the roof, so of course National TV is putting on a second series. They will have listened to criticism and hopefully cut out some of the technical detail. I for one can't wait for it to begin.

Give a general conclusion or recommendation.

TEST 1

PAPER 1 Reading and Use of English

▶▶ PART 1

govern (v) to control the actions or behaviour of a person, a system, an organisation, etc.

stimulus (n) something that makes someone or something move or react

fluctuation (n) the process of varying irregularly

impose (v) to force someone or something to behave or react in the way that you want them to

at will (phr) whenever and in whatever way you want

▶▶ PART 2

pursuit (n) an activity such as a sport or hobby

sow the seeds of (phr) to do something that will cause a bad situation in the future

▶▶ PART 3

endeavour (n) an attempt to do something, especially something new or difficult

habitat (n) the place where a particular type of animal normally lives

sanctuary (n) a place where wild animals are protected

▶▶ PART 5

etching (n) a picture formed by cutting lines on a metal plate, piece of glass, stone, etc.

depict (v) to paint; to draw

on a variety of counts (phr) in several ways

sheer (adj) used to emphasise that something is very large, good, etc.

staggering (adj) extremely great or surprising

hold your own (phr) to perform satisfactorily

epoch (n) a period of history

albeit (conjunction) even though; despite

inadvertently (adv) not on purpose; unintentionally

cordon off (phr v) to enclose an area

intimidating (adj) frightening

show up (phr v) to become visible

convey (v) to communicate or make known

preliminary (n) a preparation for an event

rigid (adj) very unwilling to change ideas or behaviour

tentatively (adv) provisionally

aesthetic (adj) concerned with beauty and art

vulnerable (adj) exposed; unprotected

▶▶ PART 6

feasible (adj) possible to do

manned (adj) a vehicle with people working in it

wipe out (phr v) to destroy

precipitate (v) to lead to something to start happening

engulf (v) to surround or cover something completely

▶▶ PART 7

batch (n) a group of things

verdict (n) someone's opinion about something

naive (adj) believing only good things will happen

take off (phr v) to increase or succeed quickly

figure out (phr v) to solve; to understand

budding (adj) (someone who is) starting to do an activity and (will) probably (be) successful at it in the future

down (v) to drink or eat something quickly and finish it off

soundbite (n) a short, quotable statement

asset (n) something or someone that is useful

status quo (n) the way things are now

fiendishly (adv) extremely

preach (v) to give someone advice in a way that they think is boring or annoying

falling-out (n) a quarrel

preservative (n) a chemical that keeps food from going bad

unadulterated (adj) not containing unwanted substances

dash (n) a small amount of something

quirky (adj) unusual, especially in an interesting way

complementary (adj) complementary things go well together, although they are usually different

bust-up (n) a serious quarrel

munch (v) to chew strongly on something

stumbling block (n) an obstacle, something that causes problems and stops you from doing what you want to do

▶▶ PART 8

misconception (n) an idea based on the wrong information or a wrong understanding

coolness (n) glamour or attractiveness for other people

rating (n) measurement of how good something is

immerse (v) become completely involved in

adrenalin (n) substance produced when you are excited

do a degree (n) the qualification of a university course

brief (n) duties and responsibilities in a job

at first hand (phr) experiencing something yourself

blunder (n) mistake

flair (n) natural talent

PAPER 1 Reading and Use of English

▶▶ **PART 1**

shovel (n) a tool, similar to a spade, with a long handle and a metal plate used for moving earth, snow, etc.

buried (adj) hidden under the ground

feature (n) aspects of a person, place or thing that are important or typical

trial (n) a process of testing something to see if it works

dwelling (n) a house or other building where people live

infallible (n) never wrong; never making mistakes

disclose (n) give information that was previously secret

▶▶ **PART 2**

all told (phr) in total

insight (n) an understanding of something

▶▶ **PART 3**

engraver (n) someone who carves, cuts or etches a text, design or picture into a block or surface used for printing

dissect (v) to cut apart or separate

mount (v) to place or fix something on or in a support or setting for display or study

▶▶ **PART 5**

bewitch (v) to charm; to captivate

ball (n) large, formal party

wand (n) magic stick

convey (n) carry

smitten (adj) very attracted to, or in love

amid (preposition) in or into the middle of; surrounded by

stock (adj) commonly used

spirit (n) a mental disposition characterised by firmness or assertiveness

enduring (adj) lasting; surviving

shortcoming (n) a fault; a deficiency

sibling (n) a person with the same parents as someone else; a brother or sister

show backbone (phr) show that you are a strong character

enlightened (adj) freed from ignorance and misinformation

villain (n) a bad person, especially a criminal

empathise (v) to understand another's feelings, etc.

protagonist (n) main character in a story

make concessions (phr) allow or change something to make a situation less difficult

▶▶ **PART 7**

linguist (n) a person who knows several languages and their structure; someone who carries out research into languages

conversely (adv) the opposite or reverse of something

forge ahead (phr) to proceed with strength and speed despite problems or difficulties

periodically (adv) fairly often and on a regular basis

the point of no return (phr) a time when it is impossible to go back to an earlier situation

tonic (n) a medicinal liquid that gives energy

rub (n) a medicinal lotion or cream that is rubbed on the skin

potion (n) a strong liquid medicine

blunt (adj) frank

a lost cause (phr) something that cannot succeed

expectant (adj) pregnant

score (n) twenty

competent (adj) having the ability to do something well

consummate (adj) perfect

wary (adj) concerned about danger; cautious

▶▶ **PART 8**

enhance (v) to improve; to add to

engage (v) to take part

venture (n) an undertaking involving chance, risk or danger; a speculative business enterprise

impulsive (adj) without thinking carefully

apprehension (n) fear that something bad might happen

break (n) a piece of good luck

dabble (v) to work superficially or intermittently, especially in a secondary activity or interest

downside (n) a disadvantageous aspect

budding (adj) young and promising

down the line (phr) at a point in the future

lucrative (adj) producing a lot of money; profitable

from scratch (phr) from the beginning

avid (adj) enthusiastic; eager

the ropes (phr) knowledge about a job or situation

take the plunge (phr) decide to do something difficult

PAPER 1 Reading and Use of English

▶▶ **PART 1**

ladybug (n) American English / **ladybird** (n) British English a small flying insect, usually red with black spots

habitat (n) an area where an animal normally lives

▶▶ **PART 2**

DIY (n) Do It Yourself

reclamation material (n) useful materials or items that come from old buildings

▶▶ **PART 3**

stem (v) result from

deem (v) regard or consider

▶▶ **PART 5**

nurture (n) care and encouragement given to someone while they are growing

backlash (n) a strong negative reaction by a large number of people to something that has changed in society

neuroscience (n) the study of the human nervous system

decode (v) find out how something works

buzz word (n) word that is very fashionable

run out of steam (phr) lose energy

anecdote (n) personal story

formulaic (adj) following a formula and unoriginal

angle (v) to try to get a particular response

gender (n) being male or female

array (n) range

meticulous (adj) very careful

go for the hard sell (phr) argue in very strong terms

trait (n) feature or characteristic

pendulum (n) a weight in an old clock that swings from one side to the other; used as an image to express the idea that ideas go in and out of fashion

▶▶ **PART 7**

surmise (v) to make a reasonable guess

perch (n) a resting place or vantage point

hail (v) to greet, especially with enthusiasm

swashbuckling (adj) flamboyantly adventurous

carbon dating (n) chemical analysis used to determine the age of materials

fire (v) to fill with passion or enthusiasm

tantalise (v) to offer but not satisfy; to tempt

loot (v) to rob, especially on a large scale and usually by violence

pore over (phr v) to study carefully

wry (adj) humorous, ironic or dry in manner

aqueduct (n) a waterway made of stone blocks

intricate (adj) having many complex interrelating parts or elements

toil (v) to work hard with little reward or relief

blunder (v) to move unsteadily or confusedly

annals (n pl) a written record or collection of historical events, discoveries, etc., on a certain subject

undeterred (adj) refusing to be prevented from acting

rugged (adj) hilly; (land that is) difficult to travel over

▶▶ **PART 8**

stint (n) period of time doing something

joint (n) place where two bones join like a knee or a shoulder

treadmill (n) running machine in a gym

heel (n) the back end of the foot

ball of the foot (n) part of the bottom of the foot near the toes

wind up (phr v) find yourself in a particular situation

novice (n) someone who is new to something

resentment (n) feeling of anger that something is unfair

have a head start (phr) start in front of other people

funded (n) receives financial support

PAPER 1 Reading and Use of English

▶▶ PART 1

instigate (v) to make something happen

ingrained (adj) firmly established and therefore difficult to change

quirky (adj) unusual

gimmick (n) a clever or unusual method or object used to attract attention

▶▶ PART 2

counterpart (n) a person or thing that has the same position or function as someone or something in a different place or situation

▶▶ PART 3

foundation (n) good reason

element of exaggeration (phr) a small amount of exaggeration

venom (n) a liquid poison produced by animals such as snakes, spiders or scorpions when they bite or sting

▶▶ PART 5

slump (v) sit in a position which is not upright

posture (n) the position in which you hold your body when standing or sitting

vague (adj) not clearly defined, grasped or understood

hunched (adj) formed into a hump

osteopath (n) a person who treats physical problems by pressing and moving the bones and muscles

slouch (v) to walk, stand or sit in a lazy way, with shoulders and head bent forward

with hindsight (phr) looking back

off the mark (phr) wrong; mistaken

pilates (n) a system of exercise that increases flexibility

tilt (v) to move upwards or to the side

misalignment (n) having something in the wrong position

orator (n) someone who is good at making speeches and persuading people

reluctant (adj) unwilling

sceptical (adj) having doubts about whether something is true

debilitating (adj) describing something that makes you weak and unable to function well

▶▶ PART 7

Velcro (n) a material used to fasten clothes, consisting of two pieces of material which stick to each other when you press them together

plunder (v) to steal; to take others' property by force and in large quantity

random (adj) happening at any time; unplanned

revenue (n) income

donor (n) a person or organisation that gives something, often money

hands-off (adj) separate; detached

on tap (phr) available on demand

ornithologist (n) a person who studies birds

win-win (adj) a win-win situation is one that will end well for everyone involved in it

spur (v) to encourage someone to do something

concerted (adj) strong; intense

▶▶ PART 8

put someone off (phr v) make someone lose interest or enthusiasm for something

pepper (v) include a lot of examples of something

get to grips with an idea (phr) understand an idea

glimpse (n) a brief view of something

trilogy (n) a set of three of something – books, films, etc.

atomise (v) break something up into small particles

bounce (v) jump like a ball

anecdote (n) personal story

assertiveness (n) being self-confident

diffidence (n) not wanting to talk about yourself

glut (n) a large number of something, more than is needed

gloomy (adj) sad, unhappy

sceptical (adj) full of doubt

woe (n) problem

array (n) wide range

prolific (adj) very productive

wit (n) humour

antidote (n) something that takes away an unpleasant thing; e.g. an antidote to a poison

strive (v) try very hard to achieve something

swell (v) get bigger

facile (adj) produced without effort or careful thought

TEST 5

PAPER 1 Reading and Use of English

▶▶ PART 1

foolhardy (adj) reckless; rash

stretcher (n) something used to carry an injured person

borne (past participle) from 'bear'; responsible for

limb (n) an arm or a leg

▶▶ PART 3

eloquence (n) the ability to use language and express opinions in a fluent effective way

call into question (phr) to cast doubt upon something

mainstream (n) accepted or including most people in society

bypass (v) to avoid

distort (v) to report an event in a way that is not true

verify (v) to confirm; to say that something is true

▶▶ PART 5

draw to a close (phr) to come to an end

roam (v) to go freely over a large area; to wander

glacier (n) a large mass of ice which moves slowly down a mountain valley

submerge (v) to cover something with water

deluge (n) a flood

lush (adj) having thick, healthy growth

verdant (adj) green with vegetation growth

harpoon (n) a weapon used for hunting

mammoth (n) an animal like a hairy elephant which lived thousands of years ago and is now extinct

tusk (n) a long front tooth, such as of elephants, etc.

vessel (n) a boat

deploy (n) use

ledge (n) a piece of rock on the side of a mountain

pinpoint (v) to locate exactly

shipwreck (n) a ship that has been destroyed at sea

scathing (adj) very severe (criticism)

maritime (adj) related to the sea

aggregate (n) mineral materials, used in making concrete

quarry (v) to dig stone or sand from a quarry

dredge (v) to dig up sand and debris from a river, etc.

outraged (adj) feeling great anger

perception (n) the way a person sees something

▶▶ PART 7

field work (n) study that is done out of the classroom

patch (n) a small area

teem (v) full of living things moving around

stilts (n) wooden posts that keep a building above the ground or water

biodiversity (n) a variety of animals or plants

crawl (v) move very slowly

to be transfixed (v) to be unable to move because something has all your attention

footage (n) part of a film

germinate (v) when a seed grows and becomes a plant

adrenaline (n) a substance produced in the body when you are excited

sprout (v) grow in large numbers

nocturnal (adj) night-time

cacophony (n) mixture of loud, unpleasant sounds

lethal (adj) something that can cause a lot of harm

anti-venom (n) a medicine used to combat poison

venom (n) the poison from a snake

▶▶ PART 8

rehearse (v) practice in advance of something

interpersonal (adj) between people

babble (v) to talk without making sense

get carried away (phr) to do too much of something

go off at a tangent (phr) to leave the main point; to digress

evasive (adj) not direct, clear or frank

pedantic (adj) paying too much attention to rules and details

come across (phr v) to seem to have particular qualities

insincere (adj) not showing true feelings

prospective (adj) possible in the future

blurt out (phr v) to speak suddenly

component (n) one of several parts of a machine

swollen-headed (adj) arrogant

complacent (adj) pleased with a situation

at fault (phr) responsible for something bad

PAPER 1 Reading and Use of English

▶▶ **PART 1**

misconception (n) a mistaken idea about something

span (n) a period (of time)

plague (n) an epidemic disease causing a high death rate

appalling (adj) shocking; deeply offensive

feudal (adj) relating to a political and social system in which a king and the people of the upper classes owned the land and people of the lower classes worked it

▶▶ **PART 2**

exceed (v) to be greater than something; to go beyond the limits of something

foolproof (adj) well-designed and easy to use so that it cannot go wrong

▶▶ **PART 3**

withdraw (v) to remove

▶▶ **PART 5**

hitherto (adv) up to this time

anatomical (adj) relating to the structure of a body

instrumental (adj) helpful; causing something to happen

by-product (n) something that happens as a result of something else

outperform (v) to do better than others

on a par with (phr) as good as

ligament (n) a strong, flexible band of tissue holding bones or other body parts in place

tissue (n) a mass of cells

skull (n) the bone structure of a head

spine (n) long vertical bone running down the centre of the back

pitch (v) roll

primate (n) any animal that belongs to the group of mammals that includes human beings, apes and monkeys

tendon (n) tough, fibrous tissue connecting muscles to bones or to other muscles

calf (n) the back part of the lower leg

hypothesis (n) theory

carnivore (n) meat eater

confer (v) to give

scavenger (n) an animal that feeds on dead or decaying matter

predator (n) an animal that kills other animals to eat them

carcass (n) a dead body

vulture (n) a type of bird that eats dead animals

locomotion (n) the ability to move from place to place

contentious (adj) involving a lot of disagreement and argument

dispel (n) make something, especially a belief, disappear

▶▶ **PART 7**

glaze (v) to cover or fit with glass

ventilation (n) a system of providing fresh air

stale (adj) not fresh

outsize (adj) very large

conservatory (n) a greenhouse for growing or displaying plants

guzzle (v) consume very quickly

emission (n) gas that is sent out into the air

trim (v) to free of excess matter by cutting

tumble (v) to decline suddenly and sharply

flashy (adj) expensive and designed to attract attention

duct (n) a tube or passage in buildings, especially for air

momentum (n) strength or force gained by motion or through the development of events

lobby (n) a group of people trying to influence politicians

break (n) a deduction that is granted in order to encourage a particular type of commercial activity

dim (v) to lower the force of, especially a light

leak (v) escape

synergy (n) the extra energy, power or capability produced by combining two or more agents, operations or processes

outlook (n) a prediction for the future

come to grips with (phr) to confront squarely and attempt to deal decisively with something

tap (v) to make use of a source of energy that already exists

at the forefront (phr) the most advanced part

▶▶ **PART 8**

branch out (phr v) start to do an activity you have not done before

stray (v) move away from the place where you should be

outlay (n) money spent for something

worth your salt (phr) deserving respect because you do your job well

landscape gardening (n) the art or profession of improving the ground around a building with trees, plants, etc.

cut-throat (adj) relentless or merciless in competition

TEST 7

PAPER 1 Reading and Use of English

▶▶ **PART 1**

pollinate (v) to transfer pollen into a flower so that it produces seeds

hummingbird (n) a very small, brightly coloured bird that lives in warm climates

pod (n) a long narrow structure that grows on various plants like peas and beans, and contains seeds

fragrance (n) a pleasant smell

cure (v) to preserve food, tobacco, etc. by drying it, hanging it in smoke or covering it with salt

harvest (v) to gather a crop from the field or plantation

treat (v) to put a substance on something or use a chemical process in order to protect, clean or preserve it

exploitation (n) the use of something for profit

▶▶ **PART 2**

flourish (v) become popular and successful

▶▶ **PART 3**

zest (n) intense interest and enjoyment

▶▶ **PART 5**

blunt (adj) not sharp

talon (n) a bird's claw, especially of predators

wingspan (n) the distance from the tip of one of a pair of wings to that of the other

soar (v) to fly high through the air with no difficulty

flap (v) move up and down

diversity (n) variety

yield (v) supply, provide

incubate (v) to sit on an egg so as to hatch it by the warmth of the body

bicker (v) to argue about little things

rear (v) to help children or young animals to grow

saunter (v) to walk without hurrying

perish (v) die

antifreeze (n) a liquid used in engine radiators to lower their freezing point

coyote (n) a kind of wolf similar to a medium-sized dog found mainly in western North and Central America

shard (n) a small piece of broken glass or metal

perforate (v) to make a hole through something

carrion (n) the flesh and bones of a dead animal that is unfit for human food

juvenile (n) a youth or child; a young animal

pen (n) a small area of land surrounded by a fence and used to keep animals in

mentor (n) a teacher and friend

glide (v) to fly through the air without power

extinction (n) when a species of animal or plant completely dies out

ingest (v) consume

▶▶ **PART 7**

amenity (n) a facility that adds to people's comfort, convenience and pleasure

boast (v) to be proud of something

following (n) a group of admirers or followers

gig (n) a performance by musicians or comedians

clutch (v) hold tightly

petrified (adj) very frightened

kid (v) to make jokes

snort (n) the act of forcing air violently through the nose with a rough harsh sound

hone (v) to improve

prodigy (n) a highly talented child

flautist (n) someone who plays the flute

abrupt (adj) sudden

audition (v) give a short performance to see whether you are suitable for an orchestra, play, film, etc

abrasive (adj) rough; making people feel bad

thin-skinned (adj) touchy; sensitive to criticism

yearn (v) to have a strong desire for something; to long for something

demanding (adj) requiring high performance

clientele (n) a group of customers

daunt (v) to make afraid; to discourage

thriving (adj) successful

bare your soul (v) show your deepest most intimate feelings

precarious (adj) dependent on chance, unknown conditions or uncertain developments

draw a parallel (phr) point out similarities

breakthrough (n) an important new development of discovery

tedious (adj) boring

misconception (n) idea based on false information or a wrong understanding

reconciliation (n) end to a disagreement

erroneous (adj) mistaken

faint-hearted (adj) lacking confidence

mute (adj) silent

bystander (n) a person who sees something happening but is not involved

deference (n) behaviour that shows you respect someone or something

overheads (n) costs involved in running a business

fiddly (adj) difficult to do because of small details

plod (n) very slow speed

side-track (v) make someone do something that is different from the main thing they are supposed to be doing

afflict (v) affect someone in a harmful way

adolescence (n) teenage years; the time in life when a person changes from being a child to being an adult

trigger (n) stimulus; something that causes a change to take place

flask (n) a bottle used to store chemicals in scientific work

fluorescence (n) special light created by radiation

spectrum (n) range of coloured lights

buzz (n) excitement

yearn (v) have a strong desire for

brainstorming session (n) when a group of people all think about something at the same time to produce ideas

TEST 8

PAPER 1 Reading and Use of English

▸▸ PART 1

plain (adj) ordinary, not special in any way

dietician (n) an expert on healthy eating

fibre (n) a part of food which keeps food moving through the body; an important part of a healthy diet

intake (n) what you consume by eating and drinking

stew (n) a dish of vegetables (often with meat) that is cooked slowly in water; similar to a thick soup

▸▸ PART 2

constitution (n) the set of laws and principles that govern a country or organisation

revenue (n) the money that a business or organisation receives over a period of time

valid (adj) a valid document is legally or officially acceptable

▸▸ PART 3

conduct (v) to carry out a particular activity or process

devise (v) to invent a way of doing something

merchant (n) someone who buys and sells goods for profit

intricate (adj) elaborate; having many complex elements

issue (v) to circulate or publish; to make available

▸▸ PART 5

rope someone in (phr v) persuade someone to join an activity or to help someone, even though they may not want to do this

warren (n) a collection of buildings with many narrow passages

rack (n) a piece of furniture, usually made of metal or wooden bars, where you keep things such as bottles, tools and plates

pitch (n) how high or low a sound is

sample (n) a small amount or an example of something which you try or test to see what it is like

blaring (adj) describing a loud and unpleasant noise

brass (n) musical instruments made of metal such as trumpets and horns

mingle (v) mix

thud (n) a low sound when a heavy object hits something else

predator (n) an animal that kills and eats other animals

enigmatic (adj) mysterious and difficult to understand

olfactory (adj) relating to the sense of smell

cell (n) the smallest unit of a living substance; all animals and plants are made up of cells

anesthetise (v) give a person or an animal an anaesthetic so that they do not feel any pain

clunk (v) put something down in a heavy, awkward way

physiological (adj) the way a living thing functions

odour (n) a smell

suppress (v) control or reduce

phenomenon (n) something that happens in nature

alert (v) give a warning

musky (adj) with a strong smell

toffee (n) a hard sticky sweet made by heating sugar, butter and water together

aroma (n) a smell, usually used for a pleasant smell

reservation (n) a feeling of doubt about an idea

reluctant (adj) unwilling

implication (n) possible consequence

forthcoming (adj) going to happen in the future, probably soon

▶▶ **PART 7**

temple (n) a building used for religious worship

strip (n) a long, narrow piece of something

lap (v) gently touch

peppered (v) if a place is peppered with something it has many examples of this thing on it

complex (n) a group of buildings

superlative (n) a word praising something

unearth (v) discover

Neolithic (adj) from the New Stone Age, from about 10,000BC to 2,000 BC

acre (n) a unit used to measure land – about 4050 square metres

vibrant (adj) lively

tomb (n) a large grave; some kind of building above or below the ground to house someone who has died

underpin (v) lie behind or support

dwarf (v) to be much bigger or greater than something else

precarious (adj) not safe or certain

discard (v) throw away

pottery (n) pots, dishes, cups and so on that are made by hand with clay

coalesce (v) come together to form one larger group

acknowledge (v) give recognition to

World Heritage status (n) an official recognition by UNESCO that a place has a special cultural, historical or physical importance and because of this should be protected

UNESCO (n) United Nations Educational, Scientific and Cultural Organisation

stumble upon (phr v) find by chance

settler (n) a person who goes to live in a new place

excavate (v) to dig in the ground to look for old objects

perplex (v) confuse or puzzle

settlement (n) a place where people make their homes, especially where few or no people lived before

fate (n) the things that have happened or will happen

abrupt (adj) sudden

draw (v) attract

scrutinise (v) study carefully

eclipse (v) make something else seem unimportant

further afield (phr) further away from home

confound (v) prove something wrong

carving (n) a pattern, often artistic, made by cutting away material from something

pinpoint (v) find the exact position of something

artifact (n) something made by humans

intact (adj) in one piece, not broken up

outhouse (n) a small building outside a main building

groove (v) a narrow cut in the surface of something

▶▶ **PART 8**

indifferent (adj) having no or little interest in something

universality (n) something that is true all over the world

representational (n) showing something real

stretch (n) an area of land or water; for example, a river

grid (n) a pattern of straight lines crossing each other

lavender (n) a pale purple colour; a plant with purple flowers and a sweet smell

composition (n) the way something is assembled

flap (v) move quickly up and down

cobblestone (n) small, round stones used to make the surface of a road, especially in the past

twinge (n) a sudden, short feeling of pain

haystack (n) a large pile of dried grass in a field

grim (adj) looking unattractive and depressing

ubiquitous (adj) found everywhere

pithead (n) the entrance to a mine

pylon (n) a tall metal structure used for carrying electricity wires high above the ground

supple (adj) flexible

clasp (v) hold tightly

perspective (n) a way of looking at something

ADVANCED
TEST 1

▶▶ **PART 1**

You will hear three different extracts. For questions 1–6, choose the answer, A, B or C which fits best according to what you hear. There are two questions for each extract.

Extract One
You hear two friends talking about an experience one of them had as a volunteer. Now look at questions one and two.

Jenny: Nigel! I haven't seen you for a while! Where have you been?

Nigel: Madagascar.

Jenny: Never! Tell me about it!

Nigel: Well, you know I want to study marine biology? Anyway, I decided to get some hands-on experience while doing volunteer work, and this mate of mine put me in touch with a conservation operation called Blue Ventures in Madagascar. And off I went! We did a lot of diving to record the marine life around the reefs and monitor the effects of bleaching on the reefs themselves. Some of them were incredible – a myriad of fish of different shapes and sizes, with all these vibrant colours. Unfortunately, bleaching is wreaking havoc and threatening to destroy the coral. Now the Blue Ventures project is trying to both protect the marine life in the area and also help the local people find a way to survive. They're terribly poor, but so optimistic and friendly. It was an unforgettable experience!

Jenny: Really? Fascinating ... Did anything exciting happen while you were there?

Nigel: On one dive we saw a huge pufferfish! And then five minutes later, we actually saw a white tip reef shark! It was pretty mind-blowing. Then we ….

Extract Two
You hear two law students at Law School talking about possible future jobs. Now look at questions three and four.

Rich: I've finally decided what I'm going to do after graduation.

Jenny: I thought your uncle was taking you on in his office.

Rich: It's a prestigious firm and a good opportunity but honestly, I didn't take up law to be a solicitor on my own doorstep. The legal department in a multinational is what I'm after. I could do another year at school and get a Masters degree, but I need to be earning money.

Jenny: I thought of working in the United Nations as a Human Rights lawyer. It'd be my perfect job, but I'd need more than two foreign languages, so that's out.

Rich: Your results in Criminal Law were brilliant. Why not go for that? Top barristers make serious money.

Jenny: Yes, and it'd be really interesting if it wasn't so competitive. I don't fancy climbing my way up the ladder. Property Law is a possibility, and actually I've had an offer.

Rich: So you'll be sorting out boundary disputes and drawing up leases.

Jenny: You do make it sound exciting! But yes, I guess that's what I'll be doing.

Extract Three
You hear two friends talking about a football match that they have just watched. Now look at questions five and six.

Dave: I can't believe it! We were this close! The referee was out of order! There was no way Rooney was offside!

Tracy: Oh, come on, Dave! The replay showed that he was! Actually, I thought England were complacent. They gave away too many chances. Look at Gerrard missing that open goal. That I couldn't believe!

Dave: Don't remind me! But come on, Tracy. You can't say England played badly. Robinson made a couple of brilliant saves, and Owen had a good game. But it was the same old story: they just couldn't drive the ball home. Russia, though, were sloppy. They had no structure in their play, and Pavlyuchenko's goal was sheer luck.

Tracy: It was well executed, and you know it. Our defence just didn't see him coming. No, Russia saw their chance and took it. England were too convinced they were going to win. That's what lost them the game.

Dave: You can say that after the way Owen and Cole played?

Tracy: They were only two players, Dave. The others looked like they were strolling throughout the match. Russia might not have played well, but England were no better.

▶▶ **PART 2**

You will hear a writer talking about a book she has written on the subject of aspirin. For questions 7–14, complete the sentences.

Writer: We are all familiar with aspirin, that common household remedy which provides relief from pain. But few people are aware of just how fascinating the subject of aspirin actually is.

The key ingredient of this wonderful drug is found in several plants, and 5,000 years ago, physicians in ancient Egypt were using an extract from the bark of the willow as a cure for a variety of complaints. But it was to be many centuries before the scientific basis of this medication was understood.

Then, in the 18th century, an Englishman, Edward Stone, accidentally rediscovered the medicinal properties of willow tree extract, although he mistakenly attributed its efficacy to its bitter taste and its supposed resemblance to another drug, quinine. Later on, in 1829, a pharmacist isolated the active ingredient, salicylic acid. Unfortunately, the chemical has several undesirable side effects, the most serious of which is that it can upset the stomach.

However, at the end of the 19th century, a chemist working for Friedrich Bayer, a German company, found a way of combining salicylic acid with an acetyl group. A few years later, Bayer marketed the first aspirins, and for the next 70 years it was regarded as a miraculous painkiller. Curiously, during all that time, hardly any research was done into the way aspirin works.

Then, in 1971, groundbreaking findings were published that showed how aspirin slows down swelling and the coagulation of the blood. This means it also dramatically reduces the risk of heart disease. As you can imagine, this was exciting news. Further research showed that a third of all people at risk from a heart attack will not have one if they take aspirin regularly. Although that sounds too good to be true, most doctors now accept that aspirin really does possess these miraculous qualities. More controversially, some scientists believe that nearly everyone over the age of 50 would benefit from taking aspirin regularly as a preventative measure.

Now it seems that the active ingredients of aspirin can also be found in many organically grown vegetables – and regular consumption of such foods might be an alternative to an aspirin a day …

▶▶ PART 3

You will hear part of an interview with Stan Levin, a dance critic, about a modern ballet production involving animals. For questions 15–20, choose the answer, A, B, C or D which fits best according to what you hear.

Interviewer: Stan, you are known as being something of a conservative as far as dance is concerned, so I was intrigued when you told me you wanted to discuss Alain Platel's ballet *Wolf* on tonight's programme. *Wolf* generated a furore in certain circles when it was first performed, didn't it?

Stan: Yes, it's attracted its fair share of criticism, but it's also been welcomed as one of the most fascinating modern dance productions in recent years.

Interviewer: Some of our viewers may not have seen the ballet and they may be wondering why all the fuss, so could I ask you to describe briefly what *Wolf* is about.

Stan: Well, basically, it's about homeless people living in a disused shopping mall and returning to some sort of pre-civilised life. And it features some startling innovations, including the use of dogs as characters.

Interviewer: How do the dogs come into it?

Stan: Well, as I understand it, the pack of dogs represents this return to a primitive state. At least, that's the idea Platel is trying to convey.

Interviewer: What do you think of the idea of using animals on stage in this way? Can it be justified?

Stan: Well, more and more choreographers these days are moving beyond the traditional limits of dance, and I don't disapprove of this in principle. Many are turning to technology, for instance, using computers to plan the actual choreography.

Interviewer: Sometimes even using projections of dancers alongside the real ones …

Stan: Exactly. I find all this very interesting – take the work of Annette Sanderson in New York, for instance – but I think it's now going beyond the genre of dance and turning into something else. Whereas I think Platel is coming from the other direction, if you like, working more with improvisation and basic ensemble techniques.

Interviewer: How do audiences respond to *Wolf*?

Stan: By and large, quite enthusiastically. I think some people are surprised at how well it all works. The dogs generally keep very close to one of the characters. Apparently, the dancer works intensively with them during rehearsal, and the dogs have learned to imitate his movements. That fascinates audiences. Of course, sometimes the dogs distract attention from an important piece of dancing, but I don't feel this is a real problem.

Interviewer: Do the dogs do anything special during the performance?

Stan: No. Their main function is to add atmosphere. It's not like a circus, with the dogs performing tricks! At the same time, you realise they have been trained and are, in a sense, putting on a show simply by remaining on stage with the human performers. During the performance I saw, a member of the audience in the front row tried to call the dogs over to him, which made them look away from the dancers towards the audience. It spoiled the mood – though of course, this wasn't the dogs' fault.

Interviewer: So the dogs fulfil a kind of symbolic function in the story?

Stan: Yes and no. They are attached to one of the characters, a tramp, and we are meant to understand that they have become a pack. I must say this works rather well: you really *do* get the impression that the dogs and the tramp have bonded to form a sort of community. But for me, the most striking aspect of the production was the lurking possibility of aggression, largely as a consequence of the presence of the animals.

Interviewer: Well, Stan, I must say it all sounds fascinating. Thank you for coming along tonight and sharing your insights with us.

Stan: My pleasure.

▶▶ PART 4

This part consists of two tasks. You will hear five short extracts in which people talk about fitness and health. Look at Task 1. For questions 21–25, choose from the list (A–H) what each speaker says about his or her reasons for attending a gym regularly. Now look at Task 2. For questions 26–30, choose from the list A–H what opinion each speaker expresses about fitness and health generally. While you listen, you must complete both tasks.

Speaker 1: I play football for my local team at weekends, which is a big commitment because our club is ambitious and we're climbing up the league. I love junk food and I need to keep on the go or I put on weight. I had no trouble burning off calories when I was at college because I did some sort of sport most days, but now I've started work in an insurance company and I'm at my desk eight hours a day. I cycle to work and luckily there's a fitness club next to the company, so I work out for an hour early in the morning before I go into the office.

Speaker 2: I'm not what you'd call a fitness fanatic, but about three years ago I was knocked off my bike by a car, and I had to stay in hospital for a month. It took me a long time to regain the full use of my legs. And the physiotherapist made me promise to exercise in a gym at least three times a week. She also said I needed to stop smoking and lose weight. I think it makes sense – you can't expect to be fit if you have such unhealthy habits, can you?

Speaker 3: I suppose if I'm honest, one of the reasons I work out in the gym is that I've got to know a lot of people here, and I enjoy seeing them. Now and then we meet up outside the gym for a drink, or to go to the cinema. Of course, I do think keeping fit is important as well. Although I think it's harder for some people to keep slim and healthy. It's as though it's in the blood. I have a friend who doesn't eat much and takes regular exercise, but he's still overweight. It's as if his body doesn't want to be thin.

Speaker 4: I have to admit I'm more keen on sport than working out in the gym. But new equipment is coming out all the time and I like to have direct experience of how the different groups of muscles are exercised by the different machines. Physics and chemistry and the part they play in sport are all on the course I'm doing. I'd like a job with a major sports body when I graduate, giving advice to athletes on nutrition, devising exercise regimes for them – both are equally vital for their professional success. I also want to look into the reasons why performance drugs are part of the lifestyle of some sportspeople.

Speaker 5: My parents think I spend more time playing sport than I should, and are worried I won't get good grades. And certainly, representing my college at the national level is a major commitment, with weekly fixtures and two or more hours a day spent in the gym. But my tutors take this into account and cut me some slack when it comes to handing in assignments. I know that sporting success gives my college more status. My friends give me loads of support, I have a lot of energy and watch my diet, and I seem to be able to combine both sides of my life without sacrificing too much.

 TEST 2

▶▶ **PART 1**

You will hear three different extracts. For questions 1–6, choose the answer, A, B or C which fits best according to what you hear. There are two questions for each extract.

Extract One
You hear part of an interview with a Tai Chi instructor.

Interviewer: So, Ruth, what exactly is Tai Chi?

Ruth: Well, Peter, it's not just a form of physical exercise. The term *Tai Chi* refers to harmony in all life forces. The double-fish symbol we in the West refer to as the *yin* and *yang* symbol is in fact the *Tai Chi T'u* symbol, representing perfect balance. The dividing line between the yin and yang sections is not straight, signifying the constant flow and interaction between the two opposites. This is reflected in everyday events and activities: night becoming day, hot becoming cold or winter changing to summer, are all examples of the Tai Chi in action.

Interviewer: Fascinating! So how is this connected to the form of exercise?

Ruth: The philosophy transfers directly to the sequence of exercises that make up the Tai Chi 'forms'. Each sequence of movements is designed to bring about harmony in your body, and should flow into one another in a continuous manner. And again, balance is everything. People laugh when they see us in the park because we look as though we're dancing in slow motion! In fact, it takes years of practice and concentration to get the flow between movements close to what it needs to be.

Extract Two
You hear two people discussing taking a year off before going to university.

Sally: For me, taking a year off between finishing school and going to university was the best thing I could have done.

Mark: Yeah, too right! I had a great time. I taught English in this tiny school in China. It was unforgettable! I went off thinking that the job would be a doddle, you know, an easy way to earn some travelling money. Couldn't have been more wrong! I had to work really hard. But the thing was, I ended up loving it. The kids were great, and it was a real laugh. Of course, it had nothing to do with my studies – mechanical engineering – but it taught me a lot about how to get along with people, you know? So how about you? Why was your gap year so special?

Sally: Basically because it brought me to my senses! I'd been planning to study hotel management, and decided to use my gap year to get some practical experience by doing internship training abroad. I got placed in this hotel in Rio de Janeiro and, well, it was a real eye-opener, I can tell you! Within two weeks, I realised I wasn't cut out for that kind of thing, and when I got home, I re-applied to study marketing!

Extract Three
You hear part of an interview with an illusionist.

Interviewer: So Daniel, why become an illusionist?

Daniel: Well, I started doing card tricks in high school ... the usual story ... there was this girl I had a crush on, and not knowing how to talk to her, I tried to get her attention that way.

Interviewer: Did it work?

Daniel: For a while, but the novelty soon wore off, and this made me realise I'd have to develop my skills if I wanted to hold people's attention! Then it became an obsession. I experimented and practised every day, and I got a buzz out of the effect my tricks had on people. And it went on from there.

Interviewer: You often draw parallels between magic and film making. Why is that?

Daniel: Ah! Sure now, they're both forms of entertainment, and their success depends on creating a convincing illusion. They also demand a suspension of disbelief from the audience, and technology has helped here, through the development of special effects. The master of illusion on the stage, just like the master of the cinema, is someone who is able to use such things most effectively. You only have to watch a famous illusionist like David Copperfield to see that. In my case, I ...

▶▶ **PART 2**

You will hear part of a talk by a writer who has written a biography. For questions 7–14, complete the sentences.

Writer: I've just finished writing the biography of Robert Tewbridge, an amateur historian who achieved a certain notoriety in his day. It probably comes as no surprise that I find him a fascinating character, and I hope I've managed to convey this in my book.

One of Tewbridge's most endearing personal qualities was his fierce independence of spirit. Throughout his life, he stubbornly followed his own instincts rather than sticking to the accepted norms. He was born in Scotland, the son of a farmer. Robert's parents had ambitions for their only son, a quick-witted lad, and hoped he would study medicine at Edinburgh University, the idea being that he would return to the highlands as a doctor and set up his own practice. But Robert was determined to see the world and so, at the age of 19, he left home for London with only a few shillings in his pocket.

In the great metropolis, Robert had to find some way to keep body and soul together, and being of a literary turn of mind, he started writing for newspapers and journals. Indeed, during his lifetime Tewbridge was known primarily for his articles and essays on some of the more controversial social and political issues of the day. I was able to study most of his published work while I was doing research for the biography, but I would hardly have had an insight into the private man without access to his personal correspondence. Tewbridge wrote literally thousands of letters during his lifetime, including an astonishing number to his wife's brother, a learned chap by all accounts. The two men became very intimate, and in these letters Tewbridge felt able to be frank and honest. It was while I was reading one of these letters that I discovered how Tewbridge first became interested in history. Apparently, it was after seeing a performance of Shakespeare's *Julius Caesar*. This prompted him to begin a lifelong study of Roman history, and the fascination never left him. In fact, when Tewbridge was in his 50s, he and his wife moved to Italy, where they lived for the next 30 years, until his death, in fact. Tewbridge did not live to publish his monumental work on Rome and died without seeing his native Scotland again, but it was ...

▶▶ **PART 3**

You will hear part of an interview with Betsy Boom, owner of a chain of fashion shops. For questions 15–20, choose the correct answer, A, B, C or D which fits best according to what you hear.

Interviewer: Betsy, it's only five years since you opened your first shop, but today your chain is one of the success stories of the retail market in the UK. Perhaps one way to gain an understanding of how you managed such a phenomenal feat would be to find out a little about your personal tastes. Shopping is your business, but is it one of your pleasures? Are you an avid shopper?

Betsy: Not really, which I think helps explain the philosophy behind my stores. I mean, I like finding a bargain as much as the next person, but what I adore is trying things on – seeing how I look in outfits I wouldn't normally buy. Then there's the other aspect of shopping: going from one shop to another, being ignored in the cheaper shops or treated with disdain by aloof staff in the expensive ones – and feeling you are obliged to buy something if you've been in a shop longer than ten minutes. I can't stand that.

Interviewer: Did your personal attitudes shape the concept of your first store?

Betsy: Absolutely. I thought: wouldn't it be wonderful to go into a shop that was fun! And for me, that means friendly staff who come up to you and suggest all sorts of ideas, some of them wild, about how you might like to look. So you're persuaded to try on loads of things – but nobody minds if you don't buy them! It's more like romping around a huge fancy-dress emporium than going shopping!

Interviewer: Did the idea for your shop take off right away?

Betsy: More or less. I mean, when we opened the first place, most people who came in felt a little stunned, not sure how to respond, I suppose. But once they got used to the idea they loved it! And it was the same with the staff. I asked the assistants to be far more outgoing and upfront than usual. They were a bit shy at first, partly because they weren't sure whether customers would take it the right way or get offended and storm out. But they get quite a kick out of it now.

Interviewer: Now that success is assured, can you pick out the most satisfying aspect of the work for you personally?

Betsy: Well, it's lovely being able to turn round to all the people who said it would never work and say: 'Look! I did it!' But what never fails to thrill me is the sight of someone who isn't at all sure at first about wearing something new, and then she thinks she might as well because the atmosphere's so friendly, and in the end she's delighted by a completely different, daring outfit she'd never have tried on otherwise. It's like seeing a person discover a new self.

Interviewer: So what comes next? Where do you go from here?

Betsy: Good question. To be honest, I haven't a clue! Or at least, I do have a few ideas, but I'm being careful. The shops have worked for me, but that doesn't make me a top business brain by any means! Having said that, I'm deeply aware that I tend to be lazy. I'm quite capable of just sitting back and letting the cash roll in.

Interviewer: That doesn't sound too bad!

Betsy: No, but after a while I'd become frustrated. I know I have to take a risk and try something else, even if it fails. Otherwise my self-respect will be in tatters within a couple of years.

Interviewer: Whatever you do try next, good luck. And thanks for being with us today, Betsy Boom.

Betsy: I've enjoyed talking to you.

▶▶ **PART 4**

This part consists of two tasks. You will hear five short extracts in which people talk about environmental initiatives in the workplace. Look at Task 1. For questions 21–25, choose from the list A–H the person who is speaking. Now look at Task 2. For questions 26–30, choose from the list A–H what view each speaker is expressing.

Speaker 1: I don't think offices are environmentally friendly places at all. All that stuff that gets thrown away! People just can't be bothered to recycle paper, and they leave equipment on, wasting electricity. Our organisation sends leaflets out all the time to try and raise awareness among employees in various companies, but, well, the average worker thinks it's up to the bosses to do something. They just don't realise they could make a significant difference just by turning off computer monitors and electrical equipment at the end of the day.

Speaker 2: Fortunately, these days more people are conscious of a company's environmental image when buying products and services, which is a big change when you remember the situation 10 or 15 years ago. I think it's the hard economics of the marketplace that's making companies do something for the environment. And I've got a new generation of university students looking to me to find them an employer whose environmental concerns are similar to their own. So recruitment is harder for companies without a good attitude towards the environment.

Speaker 3: I think we should feel more encouraged about the environment these days. After all, there are some positive signs. For instance, the insurance company I work for no longer uses energy derived from the burning of fossil fuels. It uses clean, 'green' sources instead: solar energy and wind energy. We now drive company cars that run on gas fuel, so they don't burden the atmosphere with so many dangerous emissions. And considering how many of us travel all over the country every day to sell insurance, this does make a difference.

Speaker 4: One thing about environmental awareness: everyone agrees it's a good idea to encourage it. So companies benefit from a kind of association of ideas. But a business has to put real effort into making environmental initiatives work. It's no good simply introducing new regulations in the workplace. Here at Head Office, we show our employees exactly how much energy can be saved by adopting particular practices.

Speaker 5: Communication is definitely the key, because both staff and customers can easily think that environmental schemes are there simply to save money or as an advertising gimmick. Obviously, the fact that we publicise the initiatives taken by the company to support the environment enhances sales, so I'd be lying if I said it wasn't. After all, advertising is what my job's all about! But we also show our staff that we are sincere by giving them incentives to follow our environmental initiatives at work. I think that's also important.

 TEST 3

▶▶ **PART 1**

You will hear three different extracts. For questions 1–6, choose the answer, A, B or C which fits best according to what you hear. There are two questions for each extract.

Extract One
You hear two people talking about a job the man may apply for.

Keith: I've seen an ad for a job on the local paper. They want a photographer, and I've decided to apply.

Annie: Hey, that's exciting. What's the pay? Do they say?

Keith: Negotiable I expect, but it won't be much at the beginning. I'm used to living on practically nothing anyway. The thing is, they don't provide transport, and you know what my old car's like.

Annie: Hardly reliable. Hmm. What about working hours?

Keith: They don't say. I'd have to do weddings, and they're always on weekends. But that wouldn't bother me.

Annie: I think it's brilliant. Photography is one of the courses you did at college, isn't it?

Keith: I loved it but I didn't get fantastic grades for it.

Annie: I wouldn't have thought that mattered – you can learn on the job.

Keith: I'll be able to stay at home, which will be cheaper. But I'd hoped to find work somewhere else, like London.

Annie: You won't be based at home for ever, and once you get some experience on the newspaper and build up a portfolio you could have a great future – maybe even set up your own studio.

Keith: Thank you Annie, I'll definitely give it a go.

Extract Two
You hear part of an interview with Rusty Upshaw, a bossaball referee.

Interviewer: So, Rusty, how do you play bossaball?

Rusty: Ah! It's the best, you know? This sport is a combination of all the good things in life: an element of football, volleyball, trampolining, mixed together with a lot of rhythm and soul. It's also played to music, so there's an element of capoeira in there, too. Now, it's played on a court of bouncy inflatables with a net in the middle. On either side of the net there's a circular trampoline. Two teams of between three and five players aim to ground the ball on the opponents' field. Players can use any part of the body to hit the ball, but can only touch it once with their hands, or make a double touch with their feet or head. The music is optional, but it creates atmosphere and gives a rhythm to the game. And you need a good samba referee.

Interviewer: And that's where you come in, Rusty! What does a 'samba referee' do?

Rusty: He creates the atmosphere of the game. A good one is a DJ with a nice selection of music to set the pace and get the crowd in the mood. Charisma is also useful 'cause then the game becomes a show, and people love it.

Extract Three
You hear two people talking about cooking.

Ricky: I always wanted to be a chef. Food is huge in our family, and when I was a kid I'd hang out in the kitchen helping mum. My first job was in a fish restaurant – great experience, but it took me time to learn the crucial thing, which is that you've got to be very together, from shopping for the right ingredients – getting fresh stuff, going to markets – to the actual process of cooking. That didn't come naturally to me.

Eva: For me, cooking is fun. It's relaxing because if there's something on your mind, you have to forget it and just get in there – tasting it as you go along, serving it up so it looks great and seeing smiles on people's faces as they get stuck in.

Ricky: Yes, I like the excitement, not being able to think about anything else except the heat and the pan – all the smells, textures.

Eva: I cook stuff that relates to what I'm doing. Like I'm preparing for exams just now, so I'll cook up foods that are light and nutritious. And I'm trying to keep thin, so I eat a lot of chicken.

▶▶ **PART 2**

You will hear an archaeologist talking about a recent find. For questions 7–14, complete the sentences.

Archaeologist: This find was really the most astonishing stroke of luck! You see, while we know quite a lot about Roman Britain, comparatively little is known about the era before that, when various tribes inhabited different parts of the country. And then, quite by chance, builders excavating the foundations for a new motorway in Yorkshire unearthed a limestone chamber with the remains of a chariot from that period! The chariot is 2,500 years old and from it we can deduce quite a lot about the history of this region.

First of all, we know the chariot was rather special. It contained the skeleton of a man aged between 30 and 40 years old, and this suggests that the chariot served a ceremonial, not a utilitarian purpose. The hypothesis was borne out when it was discovered that it did not have matching wheels, so it could not have been used for transport. The chamber also contained the bones of over 250 cattle, and slaughter on this scale can only be explained if the person interred in the chariot was very important – a tribal leader, in fact.

Secondly, burials like this indicate a belief that in the afterlife a person would have need of his worldly possessions. Such beliefs were by no means confined to ancient Britain, of course – one immediately thinks of the ancient Egyptians. So in view of the similarities, we wonder if there had been any contact between Egypt and pre-Roman Britain.

Thirdly, we know from other sites that chariot burial was practised by a tribe known as the Parisii. These people had arrived on these shores from France, and it is not inconceivable that they were in communication with lands further south.

Finally, the finding is significant because it shows us that the Parisii inhabited regions of the country farther west than has previously been thought.

Unfortunately, the authorities have decided that work on the motorway has to continue, which means we are working non-stop in an effort to excavate as much of the surrounding area as we can in the time available. We're hoping that a place for the chariot will be found at the British Museum, if we can succeed in the very tricky task of lifting the remains out of the ground …

▶▶ **PART 3**

You will hear an interview with Fergus Reilly, a marine scientist, about the non-profit organisation he works for, Sustainable Fishing. For Questions 15-20 choose the answer, A,B,C or D which fits best according to what you hear.

Interviewer: In the studio today I have Fergus Reilly, who's a marine scientist. Fergus, your particular concern is the future of fishing.

Fergus: That's right, I work for a non-profit organisation called Sustainable Fishing, and my job is to do research into the fishing industry. Getting fish from the faraway ocean to your local supermarket is a long, complicated process these days, and what I'm particularly interested in is this process, and the problems that it causes. My organisation supports businesses which are interested in sustainable fishing – not catching more fish than the oceans can supply.

Interviewer: So, what do your campaigns involve, exactly?

Fergus: We like to make sure that customers are better informed. We want more people to know exactly what fish they're eating, and exactly how it has arrived at their dinner plate. For example, most people nowadays don't really have much idea where, when, or how their fish is caught. To some extent, the supermarkets are often to blame for this, especially when it comes to fish used in ready meals or processed food. And of course, we believe that unless customers really know what they're buying, then they won't really value the fish they eat. And this is essential.

Interviewer: OK, so tell me about most of the sea fish we usually eat. What's the situation?

Fergus: I'm afraid the situation isn't great. According to some researchers, something like 90% of the fish populations have simply gone, compared to the situation 50 years ago. But it's not all bad news. Some fish populations can grow quite quickly if they are sustained properly, and some governments and international bodies are starting to introduce new laws to help this. These laws aren't always followed, of course, and here, the most important thing is to get businesses to realise how important it is to keep our fish populations healthy and at a reasonable size.

Interviewer: I must say, I'm quite suspicious about the condition of some of the fish I see in supermarkets.

Fergus: Well, yes, I know what you mean. And this is something our organisation is tackling. We are working to improve the way fish are sold too, both for frozen and fresh fish. The truth is that 'fresh' is not a clearly defined term – it's usually described as 'not frozen or smoked'. But many customers, I'm afraid, don't really recognise 'fresh' fish when they see it. Some fish on sale – although it might look fresh to some people – can be up to a month old. Again, it comes down to customer awareness. If more people knew more about how fish were caught, and more importantly – wanted to know – then they would understand the difference between a fish that was caught recently, and a fish that was caught weeks ago. And then, of course, if customers became more aware, then the businesses which sell fish would have to change their behaviour.

Interviewer: But it must be difficult to find out exactly where a fish comes from, especially if it has been caught out in the oceans somewhere.

Fergus: We've recently started using electronic devices implanted in the fish to track them as they move from oceans to the markets. This helps us check the quality, and this is really important when it comes to threatened species. So, tagging a fish after it has been caught allows us to trace what happens to it and when. We can find out how the fish was caught, whether it was caught legally, and when.

Interviewer: It can't be that easy to motivate consumers to buy fish that's been sustainably caught?

Fergus: I'm confident that many customers do worry about our oceans, and don't mind paying a little bit more for fish which has been sustainably caught. But I don't think we should rely only on people's sense of duty. I'm sure that once good practices are being rewarded, they'll spread throughout the larger seafood market as well. The sustainable market has lots of potential for growth, which hopefully could mean reducing the serious strain on fish populations. For example, it's entirely possible to catch tuna sustainably, and manage it so that every little bit of the fish is used, and then sell it at an affordable price. This, of course, would be very attractive to most customers. We really do believe that – if we want to – we can sell fish which has been sustainably caught, at a price that customers can afford.

This part consists of two tasks. You will hear five short extracts in which people talk about children's free-time activities. Look at Task 1. For questions 21–25, choose from the list A–H the explanation each speaker gives about how his or her child became interested in an activity. Now look at Task 2. For questions 26–30, choose from the list A–H what each speaker expresses about these activities.

Speaker 1: Michael's been a member of a rugby club for two years now. He'd never played until he went to the local comprehensive, but he was hooked immediately! We were nervous at first about him getting hurt, but he's never been injured, not really. I'm glad he's got a hobby, although it *is* quite expensive. We take him to away games, which could be anywhere in the country, so petrol costs mount up. But he's learning to be one of a team, which is a good skill to have in general.

Speaker 2: Our daughter Jane's wild about skiing! Obviously, she can only actually go skiing when we're on holiday or during skiing excursions. She got the idea from a novel about some girls at finishing school in Switzerland, and kept pleading with us to let her try it. Now she's got all the equipment, which cost quite a lot – but she enjoys it so much it's worth the money. She gets anxious about the exams they have at the ski club, which is not altogether a good thing. I mean, the whole point of a hobby is that it should be fun.

Speaker 3: Dan was spending the summer with some horsy friends in Cornwall, and so of course it was inevitable that they should take him riding one day. Their enthusiasm must have rubbed off, because when Dan came home, he asked us to arrange riding lessons for him. Luckily, there's a good stables nearby, and he goes twice a week – more in the summer holidays. I'm glad he has an outdoor hobby; before he started riding, he used to get colds all the time and was rather pale, but now he's full of beans and he's got a healthy glow.

Speaker 4: I enrolled Wendy in a ballet class when she was five because our doctor told me it would help strengthen her spine, and she took to it straight away. My mother had been a professional dancer, but I don't think that influenced Wendy in any way. She goes to classes three times a week, and although she'll never be good enough to be a professional, she still enjoys it. She's become friends with some of the girls in her class, and we have a fair bit of contact outside ballet, which is nice, especially since Wendy is an only child.

Speaker 5: One Sunday night, Jim suddenly announced he was going to be a painter! My brother had been taking him to various art galleries all summer, but it seems that an exhibition of Impressionists was what really began it all. At first, my wife and I thought it was just a passing craze, and we tried to dissuade him. We thought he should have a healthy outdoor hobby. But Jim's been attending art classes for a number of years now, and I must say, some of the things he's done are very nice. He's quite dedicated to his art!

TEST 4

▶▶ **PART 1**

You will hear three different extracts. For questions 1–6, choose the answer, A, B or C which fits best according to what you hear. There are two questions for each extract.

Extract One
You hear part of an interview with a woman who has changed her lifestyle.

Interviewer: Kathy, you gave up a job with a prestigious London law firm to become an olive farmer in Greece. Why?

Kathy: Does sound rather crazy, doesn't it? But working in the City isn't all it's cracked up to be, you know. There's so much pressure on you to perform, you're frowned upon for taking a day off sick, there's the traffic, the pollution ... the list is endless! It all got on top of me, and I suddenly realised how unhappy I was. My husband Kostas suggested moving to Greece for a while. I liked the idea, but I realised that I wouldn't be happy doing nothing but playing housewife. Then, while I was surfing the et, I came across a site on olive growing, and it clicked. We made a few contacts, and found this lovely plot on the slopes of a mountain. Within six months, we'd left our jobs, put our furniture in storage, and moved. And I've never looked back!

Interviewer: And you're surprised by that?

Kathy: Yes. I thought I'd get bored, and miss the buzz of being in court. But it hasn't happened. I'm too busy! There's a lot more to olive farming than meets the eye, and if you want to be organic, there are rigorous procedures to follow. Great fun, though ...

Extract Two
You hear part of a radio discussion in which two teachers are talking about teaching poetry.

Mark: I think the main problem with teaching poetry is not so much the attitude of the students, but that of the teacher.

Marjory: How do you mean?

Mark : Well, teachers know that a lot of students are going to ridicule the lesson, so they are reluctant to teach it from the outset, which in turn is unlikely to inspire students!

Marjory: Oh, come on, Mark! I know some very good teachers who love their poetry lessons! I think the problem lies elsewhere. We need to break away from the 'I teach, you learn' dynamic in order to make the poetry class work. Kids need to be given the freedom to respond to a poem without too much 'guidance' from the teacher.

Mark: But the teacher has to point them in the right direction, surely! Otherwise some of them will understand next to nothing!

Marjory: What 'right' direction? You see, one of the limitations of saying we're going to teach poetry is just that – we 'teach' it. When perhaps we should just present it, and allow students to respond to it in their own way. Then they will learn to enjoy poetry ...

Extract Three

You hear two people talking about an unusual kind of competition.

Jake: It was incredible, really. I was driving through Wasdale, on my way back from the meeting, and I saw all these cars parked outside this pub in the middle of nowhere! So I thought, this one must be good, and stopped for a bite.

Sarah: Hm! But three hours later ... !

Jake: Well, I wasn't to know it was the World's Biggest Liar Competition in there! I mean, I'd never heard of such a thing! But it was excellent! Some of the stories! Half of them deserved a prize just for being so clever!

Sarah: So, how does the competition work?

Jake: Well, contestants make up a tall story – based on true events so that it sounds convincing – and try and deceive the people who are judging them. The story that won had us rolling about with laughter. It started out as a tale about a fishing trip, and ended up in a German submarine off the coast of Scotland! Brilliant! Oh, yeah! And do you know who was sitting next to me? Rowan Atkinson! Mr Bean himself!

Sarah: Really? Did you talk to him? What's he like?

Jake: Hah! Got you! Sarah, you're so gullible sometimes! I just might go in for that competition myself next year.

▶▶ **PART 2**

You will hear part of a talk by the director of a sports academy. For questions 7–14, complete the sentences.

Helen: I'm Helen Waterman, director of the Waterman Sports Academy, a school that helps promising young athletes fulfil their dreams. We coach youngsters who want to swim faster than anyone else in the world and children who dream of running the marathon at the Olympic Games one day.

I've coached many athletes in my life, going back to the day when the daughter of a friend announced she had entered for the long jump in an amateur athletics event. I enjoyed coaching her, and that was the start of my career. I also became interested in sports medicine at about that time, when my nephew fell off his bike and hurt his back. He'd been a keen athlete before his accident, but unfortunately, he never really got over his injury sufficiently to get back into serious training. That's when I realised the importance of sports medicine, and the staff of the academy includes two doctors.

Perhaps at this point I should answer a question often asked by young people when they enrol at the academy: how important is an athlete's build? Well, nobody can deny that build does matter, and one cannot hope to be a world-class long-distance runner, say, if one is built like a weightlifter. But other factors also play a vital role. For a start, good general health and fitness. These are important, even in sports where you might not think they are a priority. In shooting, for instance, athletes have to be fit to lower their heart rate. This enables them to fire between heart beats and so achieve maximum accuracy. At the academy, we encourage healthy eating habits. Without a proper diet, young athletes cannot achieve their optimum physique. Nor will they have the energy for training. Then there's the role of technology in sports. These days, athletes cannot compete successfully at the highest level without access to state-of-the-art equipment.

I've already mentioned sports medicine, and it goes without saying that young athletes need to be able to consult specialists in case of an injury. But above all, at the academy we stress the importance of attitude. Without the will to succeed, you may as well not bother to take up any sport seriously. In my opinion, it is this that ...

▶▶ **PART 3**

You will hear part of an interview with Jon Kennedy, who works on oil rigs. For questions 15–20, choose the answer, A, B, C or D which fits best according to what you hear.

Interviewer: My interview today is with Jon Kennedy, an engineer who works on an oil rig. Jon, please tell us about your work.

Jon: I'm a field engineer and I've worked for several companies. With my current employers, I spend most of my time in the office, planning things, but I often go onto the rig, where I manage a project for a number of weeks. I work offshore, on floating oil rigs – my job is basically to prevent the accidents that you might occasionally see on the news. It's a fascinating job.

Interviewer: Tell us about your fellow workers in the oil industry.

Jon: Most people I work with are not highly educated. I don't mean than in an insulting way. I just want to say that this is a tough job, and you get your hands dirty. And most highly educated people are not interested in this kind of heavy work. And it's not to say that my colleagues aren't smart. They are – very smart. But they're not academics. And that's fine. They're good, honest people. There's a growing number of women oil engineers, but they're still in the minority. They say it's not easy for them to work in such a male-dominated environment, which is a shame, but I hope they don't give up, because it's a great career.

Interviewer: You must be proud of the engineering involved. It's breathtaking.

Jon: Breathtaking and pricey. It can cost around $1 million per day to operate an oil rig, when it's fully functioning. And it can take up to half a year to set it up so that it's drilling down in deep water. It's an expensive, complicated set up. We've got nearly 10 kilometres of pipe going down into the sea. We use GPS, and sonar. And our rigs are safe. Really safe. Even in the middle of a hurricane – and actually I was out in a hurricane recently – the rig is stable and can keep drilling, and doesn't lose its position. And that was in 30-metre high waves, and 70 kilometre an hour winds. We kept on working.

Interviewer: How do you reach the ship?

Jon: We use a helicopter. It's super exhilarating the first couple times you do it, but when you get used to it, it's just normal. Some people just sleep the whole ride. We have to wear ear protection, because helicopters are loud. Then, we arrive on the rig, and we go through the two-hour safety briefing. We need to pay attention to it, even if, like me, you've heard it a dozen times. Then there's some paperwork. Then I'm free to meet colleagues, sleep, eat, and so on.

Interviewer: Do a lot of people work on the rig?

Jon: Lots. Around 200 workers can be working on a rig. Most are employed by the rig company, not the oil company. There are only a few oil company representatives, and in my current job, I'm one of them.

Everyone tries to be friendly and relaxed with everyone else on the rig, but you know, I've got the oil company logo on my shirt and that means everyone treats me differently. Once on this project, I made a big mistake, said something stupid. But the crew just shrugged it off. But, in my last job, the crew didn't treat me with such respect. If I made a mistake, I was out through the door in a second!

Interviewer: What gives you most enjoyment in your current job?

Jon: I look after very complicated equipment. I do risk-assessments and look for possible problems in the drilling gear. The underwater equipment is what goes wrong most often, and when it does go wrong, it costs a lot – hundreds of dollars every minute, so there's a race against time to fix a problem when it occurs. We work hard. It's stressful when you start doing this job, but after a while things get easier and you get used to it. You get to enjoy the drama of it all. Some people even find it addictive to get an adrenaline rush. I don't much like the physical risks. If you're scared of heights, then working on a rig can be pretty scary. Especially when you're working outside at night. If you fall off the walkways in the dark, then … well, no-one's going to find you again. But that's also something you get used to. And you learn to trust your colleagues. If you don't, then you stop working on rigs.

▶▶ PART 4

This part consists of two tasks. You will hear five short extracts in which people talk about their experiences at the theatre. Look at Task 1. For questions 21–25, choose from the list A–H what each speaker says about the show he or she enjoyed most. Now look at Task 2. For questions 26–30, choose from the list A–H the view each speaker has about why theatre is an interesting medium.

Speaker 1: The first time I went to the theatre, I was 12, and my mother had to drag me along. But it was a fantastic play – a murder mystery – and I was entranced. Ever since then I've enjoyed the theatre, and I go whenever I can. I love the atmosphere you get at a good play, as if you are all in an enchanted circle for the two or so hours the play is on. I don't think you get that feeling in the cinema.

Speaker 2: When I was at university, I saw a production of a comedy by Tom Stoppard called *After Magritte*. It was absolutely hilarious! I liked it so much that I went back the next night with two friends! There were some very simple jokes, there was slapstick humour, and there were some very witty lines. I don't think you'd get that in a film these days – the cinema has become so formulaic. For me, it's the theatre's ability to jolt you out of your complacency that makes it so special.

Speaker 3: As a child I saw a performance of the musical *My Fair Lady* with my Aunt Emily. My family weren't sure I'd enjoy it, but the actor playing the lead was marvellous! He could sing, his acting was great – he dominated the whole performance. I do some acting myself – I'm in an amateur dramatics society – and I love watching the way different actors go about interpreting a role. It definitely helps me when I have to take on a big part.

Speaker 4: My most memorable theatrical experience was a performance of Shakespeare's *Romeo and Juliet*. I went because we were studying it at school. I didn't expect to be affected, but to my intense surprise I was in tears at the end! That's when I finally understood how magical the theatre is. Seeing a play on stage is special; all the emotions come across to the audience if it's a good production. While you are watching there's a suspension of disbelief, and what's happening on the stage becomes real, at least for a while.

Speaker 5: I'd read a review of a production of *Antigone* by Sophocles in a very small theatre, so I went along. The acting was excellent, and because you were so close to the actors you felt very involved in the play – it became a sort of personal experience, as if you were in the play yourself! I suppose what I've come to love about the theatre is that no two performances are ever exactly the same: the actors do not always deliver their lines in the same way and there are subtle differences of timing and interpretation.

 TEST 5

▶▶ PART 1

You will hear three different extracts. For questions 1–6, choose the answer, A, B or C which fits best according to what you hear. There are two questions for each extract.

Extract One
You hear part of a radio programme in which a man is being interviewed about an unusual sport.

Interviewer: Chris, I must admit, I was a bit bemused when I heard about cheese rolling. Tell us about it.

Chris: Well, it's an event that takes place on May Bank Holiday Monday every year in Gloucestershire. Basically, a large Double Gloucester cheese is rolled down the hill, and a bunch of idiots like me try to catch it. Whoever gets to the bottom of the hill first wins.

Interviewer: It sounds easy! But isn't it dangerous?

Chris: Well, the hill is really steep and the surface is rough and uneven. It's not so bad if it's dry, but if it's been raining and the ground's muddy, it can be tough. You get tangled up in the grass, and it's difficult not to fall. People have had to be carted off to hospital with broken limbs or concussion. But it's great fun, and people come from all over. The last three years, an Australian woman has won the women's race, and they've set up a similar competition down under.

Interviewer: So what advice would you give to someone wanting to take part for the first time?

Chris: Wear sturdy football boots or walking boots, pad yourself out in hardwearing clothes, and have fun!

Interviewer: I think a suit of armour would be more suitable for me! Now …

Extract Two
You hear two students on a business course talking about a book they are studying.

Mike: Sue, you know that book *Starting in Business*? I've just finished it and I thought it was pretty good.

Sue: Yes, bits of it were useful. My father's a businessman and I've learnt quite a lot from him, like what you have to do to register as a company, all the legal stuff, so I left that section out. But it was inspiring to read about companies that started from scratch and thrived. The book chose its examples well and it did a good job of analysing them. I could have done with something about getting good terms from suppliers – practical hints.

Mike: Maybe that only comes with experience. I got a lot out of the book, but all the business jargon was a bit distracting, and the acronyms – a pain to have to look them up. And the index could have done with being checked – the page references were wrong sometimes. But it was all a good length and relevant.

Sue: Yes, it included most of the information we need to know, and apart from the problem of looking things up and finding your way around, it was well written.

Extract Three

You hear two people talking about yawning.

Man: So what you're saying is yawning actually wakes us up?

Woman: In a sense, yes. It's been known for a while that when we yawn, both our heart rate and blood pressure increase, but for a long time scientists believed its purpose was purely to increase our intake of oxygen. Research has proved that this is not true, and psychologists have put forward a theory that yawning helps make us more alert. That's why we yawn when we're tired or bored. It's our body giving us a warning, or 'wake-up' call, if you like.

Man: Interesting. So why is it if one person starts yawning, pretty soon all the people around are also at it?

Woman: Well, the same psychologists have a theory for that, too. They suggest that some kind of empathic mechanism in our brain is triggered when one member of the group yawns. It may be a way of keeping everyone in the group awake and on the alert. Monkeys do it as well. It seems that, instead of encouraging us to sleep, yawning is trying to do the opposite!

Man: OK, I'll buy that. But what about yawning during exercise? I sometimes yawn while I'm running, …

▶▶ **PART 2**

You will hear an astrobiologist talking about her work. For questions 7–14, complete the sentences.

Astrobiologist: When I tell people what my particular branch of science is, I often get funny looks. In a way, I understand because astrobiology is the study of life on other planets. Well, obviously, life has not been discovered on other planets, which would appear to make astrobiology a science without a subject! However, everything we know about life on our own planet suggests we have to try to understand if there are any universal requirements for life to evolve, as well as the processes involved in evolution. Consequently, astrobiologists are deeply interested in the beginnings of life on Earth. Once we know more about what happened on home ground, as it were, we will be in a better position to understand any life forms we may one day find on other planets.

When most people think of extraterrestrial life, they conjure up images of so-called 'higher' life forms: they imagine humanoid creatures or bizarre and probably dangerous animals of some kind. But if we consider the whole history of life on Earth, a very different picture emerges. For billions of years the only forms of life on the planet were organisms consisting of single cells. It was only about 550 million years ago, during the geological period we call the Cambrian, that the seas suddenly became filled with a whole array of multi-cellular life.

So how do humans fit into this time frame? Well, human-like creatures first appear in the fossil record about five or so million years ago: in geological terms, this is just a blink of an eye compared to the long history of life on Earth. And *Homo sapiens*, our own species, has only been around for about 130,000 years. The point is if we do find life on other planets, it will almost certainly be relatively simple – of the sort that populated the Earth for most of its existence so far.

And of course, we must be prepared for these life forms to look very different from life on Earth. We must not forget that many modern life forms came about as a result of chance, their fate shaped by floods, continental drift and comet or meteor strikes. It is interesting to reflect that if a giant asteroid had not hit the Earth and wiped out the dinosaurs, they might still be ruling the planet and we might never have evolved …

▶▶ **PART 3**

You will hear part of a radio interview with Pete Birtwhistle, a playwright. For questions 15–20, choose the answer, A, B, C or D which fits best according to what you hear.

Interviewer: This evening on *Arts Alive* I'm talking to Pete Birtwhistle, whose new play, *Time Talking*, has just opened at the Court Theatre in London. Pete, thank you for joining us.

Pete: Glad to be here.

Interviewer: Before we talk about your new play, I'd like to ask you how you started writing for the theatre in the first place. I think I'm right in saying that your background isn't exactly typical for a playwright?

Pete: I suppose you could put it like that! You see, I was a miner until my mid 30s, but then my health got bad and I had to leave the pit. But the theatre was the last thing on my mind! I don't think I'd ever been to a play – apart from taking the kids to pantomimes at Christmas – and I wasn't even curious about it: I didn't feel it had any bearing on me and my life at all.

Interviewer: So what prompted you to write your first play?

Pete: Doctor's orders. Being out of work was terrible – it really got me down when I realised I had to stop working down the mine, and in the end I was in such a bad way that my local GP sent me to a psychiatrist. She suggested I write a story about what had happened to me, how I felt about working in the mine and then having to leave. All therapy, really. Well, of course, it was pretty hard at first, writing a play from scratch.

Interviewer: Getting the dialogue and story right, I imagine?

Pete: Funny you should say that. I started off thinking I could invent a group of characters and have them put forward different views. But when I sat down to write, I couldn't get them to do what I wanted, no matter how hard I tried. In the end, I discovered I had to let them do and say what *they* wanted.

Interviewer: What do you mean, exactly?

Pete: They took on a life of their own. So I had to sit back and let them go whichever way they wanted. And once I let myself give them that freedom, the play wrote itself. The odd thing is I feel all the characters I create are part of me, so I'm revealing different aspects of myself.

Interviewer: Is that the most profound effect writing has had on you?

Pete: I think so, yes. Practical things have changed as well, of course – we've just bought a new house – but material benefits are fairly peripheral in the end.

Interviewer: Turning to your new play about time travel – isn't that an unusual theme for the theatre?

Pete: Definitely! But it's not deliberate. I mean, I don't go round looking for novel subjects just to be different. It's more a case of finding an issue that doesn't have easy answers, a topic that stretches you when you start thinking about it.

Interviewer: I hear you're going to start work on a screenplay for a film in the next few months. Is that an exciting prospect?

Pete: Yes, but there are so many stories of films that never get made, writers and directors who throw themselves into the task of making a film and then get terribly disappointed when it all falls apart. So I have to watch out that I don't take the whole thing too seriously …

▶▶ PART 4

This part consists of two tasks. You will hear five short extracts in which people talk about tracing their ancestors. Look at Task 1. For questions 21–25, choose from the list A–H what each speaker says about the discoveries he or she made. Now look at Task 2. For questions 26–30, choose from the list A–H the emotion aroused in each speaker by these discoveries.

Speaker 1: The first bit of new information was quite exciting. It turned out my grandfather's only brother had slipped out of the house one day when he was about 16 and disappeared! At first, the family thought he'd gone off to Australia, but it turned out that he'd joined a circus and become a clown. Romantic, isn't it? I managed to track down his descendants, and I found out they were all circus performers, too. It's fantastic to know that the two branches of our family are in touch again.

Speaker 2: I wanted to know something about my roots, and with a name like O'Dwyer, I knew I probably had some Irish ancestors. Eventually, I did find out a bit about them, though this is going back to the end of the 19th century. It was my great-grandparents who came over to the States because life was so hard back home. People were starving in Ireland – literally. And apparently, my great-grandmother's family were worse off than most. I get furious at the idea of ancestors of mine having to leave their homes because they were so hungry.

Speaker 3: After a lot of work I established that one branch of the family exists to this day in Australia, though regrettably the background to the story is a distressing family row. Apparently, my great-grandmother's brother wanted to marry a girl his family didn't approve of, so he just walked out and never came back. He ended up in Australia with his wife, and his parents never saw their grandchildren. A family tradition has it that his mother died of a broken heart. Imagine a family being torn apart by something like that!

Speaker 4: One of my ancestors seems to have been a pretty crazy guy, loving to take risks. He found life on a small island rather dull, and at the age of 18 said goodbye to his family and sailed to South America. His first job was on a ranch, herding cattle. The workers spent their free time playing polo, a fast and dangerous sport. My ancestor had an accident where his leg was crushed between two colliding horses. I admire him enormously for his bravery because with his badly injured leg he went on to work as a surveyor plotting the boundary between two states in the most inhospitable region you can imagine.

Speaker 5: There was a story passed down in the family that we're distantly related to an aristocratic family from Scotland, complete with an estate, manor house and so on. Well, it turns out that my great-great-grandmother really did live in a posh house, but only because she was a servant to the family who owned it! It wasn't exactly what I had been expecting, and it took me a while to get over it, but now I can see the funny side of the whole business.

ADVANCED TEST 6

▶▶ PART 1

You will hear three different extracts. For questions 1–6, choose the answer, A, B or C which fits best according to what you hear. There are two questions for each extract.

Extract One
You hear part of an interview with a head teachers about the environmental policy at her school.

Interviewer: Your school is well known throughout the US for being environmentally aware.

Teacher: That's right, it's a challenge to keep our reputation. Last year, we had a lot of success negotiating with local farmers and growers to supply our caterers with organic food. Our latest project, which we're doing with classes in the Science and Technology department, is to construct a method of processing our waste so we can re-use it. We were the first school to install solar panels so that we wouldn't have to rely so much on oil.

Interviewer: Aren't the initial expenses high?

Teacher: Yes, and it'll be a few years before we start seeing even a small financial advantage, but we're getting an immediate benefit from the sense of purpose our initiatives create in the school community. As yet, the parents are slow to change to a greener lifestyle, but their children are deeply committed to carrying on what they have learnt here into their adult lives. All this brings us media attention, which I have to admit can be hostile as well as enthusiastic.

Extract Two
You hear an interview with a man talking about his first day at work.

Interviewer: Today's speaker has just started work with a big software company, and he's going to talk about his first day in the office. Colin …

Colin: I wasn't prepared for how daunting it'd be walking through the door for the first time. In reception they gave me a badge and reeled off directions to my department. I got there a few minutes late because it's a massive building. My supervisor was there waiting for me, and took me round to introduce me to everyone in the team. I was so nervous, I immediately forgot who everyone was, which didn't help. I felt less tense when she took me to my computer and told me what I had to do, but I was exhausted by the end of the day.

Interviewer: Some of you will soon be in Colin's situation, and would probably like some information. Colin's got a blog, but if you want guidance from him on a confidential basis, you should get in touch with him through me – I'll give you details shortly. For other job tips, contact our producer through our usual email address.

Extract Three
You hear part of an interview with a film maker, Tony Dupois.

Interviewer: Tony, you went to film school, yet many directors I've spoken to recently suggest that it's a waste of time. What's your view?

Tony: Well, my family had no background in film, so film school put me in touch with the right people. Yes, the curriculum was sometimes too rigid, hindering true creativity, but the important thing is that I met like-minded people, and was inspired by what was happening around me. But I can see that for someone whose father's an actor or director himself, film school could seem limited in scope. Dad's already their inspiration, while mine was one of my professors. He mapped out the whole film-making process for me, making everything seem possible.

Interviewer: Regarding your films, Tony. I find your characters fascinating. Even the bad guys in your films have a subtlety to them. A fine example is Carl Fraullet in *Games of the Gods*, who commits a heinous crime, then spends the rest of the film battling with his conscience.

Tony: It's vital that my characters are convincing human beings, not just stereotypes. There are many facets to the human psyche. Not one of us is completely good or completely bad. I wish my characters – all of them – to convey this …

▶▶ PART 2

You will hear an archaeologist talking about an experience he had in South America. For questions 7–14, complete the sentences.

Archaeologist: A couple of years ago I was working in an ancient Aztec city in South America. This city is becoming more and more popular with visitors, and I was part of a team employed to map out the city and its environs. We were half-way through our contract when we were approached and asked if we could come up with some ideas about how best to conserve the site, because it was feared that the increasing numbers of visitors could be damaging it. The worst damage is caused by the mere presence of people. Their breathing makes the air very humid, which causes the plaster on the walls to crumble. At the time I'm talking about, this was one of my special interests, so I was only too pleased to undertake the job.

Anyway, one day I had to go into one of the minor tombs – we were making a survey of it because the authorities were going to build a coach park nearby, and we had to ensure the tomb wouldn't be damaged any further by the construction work. To my horror, the tomb was in a worse state than we thought it would be. There were signs of recent erosion, apparently caused when an underground stream flooded. But it was when I was climbing into the tomb itself that disaster struck. The stones underfoot were loose, you see, and I twisted my ankle. I fell awkwardly and rolled down a slope. I heard a terrible cracking noise, rather like a pistol shot, and I

knew I had fractured my leg. The pain was excruciating, but once I got over the initial shock I became far more worried about the fact that it was now dark outside, which would lessen my chance of being discovered. As the hours went by, I began to feel very cold and pretty scared, but in the end I was incredibly lucky. A tour guide was out for an evening stroll and just happened to come close enough to hear me shouting from the hole in the ground, so he alerted the rest of the team. The break wasn't too bad, fortunately, but the whole thing was quite a frightening experience …

▶▶ PART 3

You will hear part of an interview with Professor Hector Williams. For questions 15–20, choose the answer, A, B, C or D which fits best according to what you hear.

Interviewer: Professor Williams, I know you've made a special study of artificial languages. I suppose most people think of Esperanto when this subject comes up, but is Esperanto the most widespread of the various artificial languages in existence?

Williams: I think that's the case today, yes, but you must remember that the idea of an artificial language isn't new. Esperanto dates back to the 1880s, but even in medieval times people were fascinated by the idea of a language created by man. Of course, their aims would have been quite different back then.

Interviewer: What do you mean?

Williams: Well, in the Middle Ages there was a theory that the universe was constructed on logical principles and that everything in it could be classified and named according to a regular and logical system. Ultimately, the nature of the universe itself could be understood through a language created in this way.

Interviewer: That all sounds rather complicated. Would such a language be easy to learn?

Williams: That one wouldn't have been, no, but there were other artificial languages that did have this goal. One man, for instance, struck by the fact that the notes of the musical scale were known by the same syllabic value all over the western world, felt this could be of use in the creation of a universal language, so he invented words based on the syllables *do, re, mi, fa* etc.

Interviewer: Was there the same kind of logic behind Esperanto?

Williams: In a way, and if I may digress for a moment, I must confess that the first time I heard it, Esperanto did seem musical to my ears. I think it was because the syllables of Latin origin aroused in me vague memories of the operas my father used to play on the gramophone when I was a child. Anyway, the man who came up with Esperanto, Dr Zamenhof, wanted his artificial language to be easy to learn, so he chose word stems and roots from major European languages, hoping they would sound familiar to most Europeans. And most experts believe he did a remarkably good job in that sense. A person with average linguistic skills can gain a working knowledge of Esperanto in a matter of months.

Interviewer: So do you feel it could have a future as a universal language?

Williams: To be perfectly honest, I don't. And there are a number of reasons for this. I have some sympathy with those who claim that the words of an artificial language seem one-dimensional, as it were, because they don't have any flavour derived from past usage; no word could have connotations in such a language. And this is not just a theoretical problem; it really does make the language seem rather mechanical.

Interviewer: You'd describe advocates of Esperanto as idealists then, would you?

Williams: Possibly – though that isn't such a bad quality! In my experience, people who have taken the trouble to learn Esperanto are marked by a refreshing enthusiasm for the task; I imagine many language teachers would be delighted to have students with such single-minded determination to master the details of a language. The difficulties with imagining Esperanto as the language of the United Nations, say, or the European Union, are not based on any deficiencies among the speakers.

Interviewer: Well, you've mentioned one problem with artificial languages; what others are there?

Williams: The fundamental difficulty is psychological. For the vast majority of the world's population, the sense of self is inextricably bound up not just with location but also with what is aptly referred to as their mother tongue. So any attempt to replace that native language meets with very strong resistance – and that is why I am convinced that the applications of an artificial language are very limited.

Interviewer: Professor Williams, thank you for being with us.

Williams: My pleasure.

▶▶ **PART 4**

This part consists of two tasks. You will hear five short extracts in which people whose jobs involve traveling talk about their work. Look at Task 1. For questions 21–25, choose from the list A–H what job each speaker has. Now look at Task 2. For questions 26–30, choose from the list A–H the view each speaker expresses.

Speaker 1: This is my first job and I love it, especially as it quite often involves trips overseas, for trade fairs or to visit suppliers. I like learning languages and practise them whenever I get a chance, though generally most of the people I talk to want to practise their English on me. However, I persist and it gives me a kick when they say 'But you're not bad!' I spend a lot of time on planes, which actually I don't find boring. There are movies to watch or I can work on my laptop. The only thing is, my friends get fed up with me being away so much.

Speaker 2: I think it must be because of the way I was brought up, but I'm never happier than when I'm on the road. My father and mother worked for a newspaper, reporting on foreign affairs, and we lived in five different countries during my childhood. I loved learning about other cultures and got a lot of ideas for my compositions from that. Anyway, I've not been able to settle since I grew up, and get itchy feet if I'm too long in one place. There are four of us, all good friends, and we go wherever we're asked to play, carrying our equipment and sometimes even sleeping in our old van.

Speaker 3: I seem to have been living out of a suitcase since I was 17. It's tough because I have to adapt to different climates, there's often the problem of jet lag, and

I've got to stay super fit even if I'm spending up to 24 hours on an plane. But sometimes we get a week off between fixtures somewhere exotic and then our hosts sometimes take us to see the wildlife and local beauty spots. We're always told we're ambassadors for our country, and that's a role I enjoy because I never have any difficulty getting on with the people I meet. But I wouldn't mind spending more time at home.

Speaker 4: I got my dream job straight out of college. But I find myself staying late at work too often, because I get absorbed in what I'm doing and lose track of time. So it's a good thing when a call comes through from a client whose system has broken down and they need it fixed now. It can be anywhere in the country, and whatever time of day it is, I have to get on the road. I'm not always able to crack the problem, which is frustrating, but at least I have a change of scene. Because of the equipment I carry, I usually take the company car, which is great.

Speaker 5: I'm not that confident in my work because I'm new to it and get nervous if I'm called to some high-level event. When there's a discussion underway, the pace hots up and there's no time to decide between one word or another. Most of my work is in this country, but I occasionally have to fly to conferences that include foreign delegations. Mostly, people manage without me, but if they get stuck because of some obscure jargon in a treaty, for example, and start arguing about the meaning, I step in and clarify things, which is very satisfying. My supervisor comes with me, and I'm always glad to have her support.

 TEST 7

▶▶ **PART 1**

You will hear three different extracts. For questions 1–6, choose the answer, A, B or C which fits best according to what you hear. There are two questions for each extract.

Extract One
You hear two people talking about the sport of go-karting, racing small motor vehicles.

Scott: I've got a busy weekend – I'm going to a couple of karting events.

Judy: Will you be racing?

Scott: Actually, I've given that up. I used to do a lot of racing, but training takes up too much time. And it's not just driving, you've got to be very fit. I'm mainly behind the scenes now, sorting out competitors and starting times, doing safety checks – you know. I love the technical side of things and I'd rather be looking after the machines than doing admin work, but at least I can get into events free.

Judy: It's so expensive now, isn't it? Whether you're a driver or a spectator. I go to the children's events because my kids are crazy about karting, and they're turning into great little drivers. I don't mind spending the money if I think they'll be safe on the roads - to me it's an investment. There was a track near us, which meant we could go out pretty often, but the company moved it closer to town. I suppose that's where most of the business is.

Extract Two
You hear part of a radio programme in which an interior designer is giving advice on colour in the home.

Interviewer: So, tell me, Eugene, why shouldn't I paint my bedroom orange? It's my favourite colour, after all!

Eugene: Well, *you* might look lovely in orange, but on the walls of your bedroom? Orange is a wake-you-up, vibrant colour that stimulates and inspires. It's hardly going to *relax* you! No, what you want in your bedroom is a subtle shade of blue or green to promote tranquility. Or why not try a creamy yellow, which is optimistic and happy, without being too intense and dramatic?

Interviewer: OK. So what about the kitchen? I spend a lot of time there.

Eugene: Well, here you *could* use orange to create a lively atmosphere that will inspire you to create wonderful meals!

Interviewer: Mm. My cooking needs all the inspiration it can get! Now what about the living room? I find this room difficult to decorate because it's not just a communal room. It's also got a wild combination of colours in upholstery and paintings.

Eugene: Of course, if you've got lots of pictures on the wall, you need to tone down the colour behind them. Beige and brown can create a warm, welcoming atmosphere, and offset the colours in your paintings nicely. But you're so right. This is usually the most difficult room to get right.

Extract Three

You hear a conversation between a man and a woman about something that has happened.

Patrick: … so I'm driving along the road when out of nowhere, this old man starts to cross the road in front of me! It was pitch black, and he just walked out from behind the parked lorry! I had no time to stop, so I swerved out across the road and hit the Ford coming in the opposite direction!

Helen: Goodness, Pat!

Patrick: I couldn't believe it! The driver of the Ford started ranting and raving at me, but then the old man – who was pretty shaken himself – came up and apologised and offered to pay for damages, so the other driver calmed down a bit.

Helen: What did the police say about it?

Patrick: Well, they arrived fairly quickly, and a couple of other people stopped and asked if we needed help. I was feeling dizzy – shock, probably. The other guy was OK, except for a couple of bruises. But the police, well, they were more concerned about the lorry having been parked in such an awkward place. I think the driver's going to be in for it. They were OK with me, though. The old man's statement really helped. It's a good thing he admitted it was his fault.

Helen: You were lucky none of you got badly hurt!

Patrick: I know.

▶▶ PART 2

You will hear part of a talk by a writer who has written a book about bread. For questions 7–14, complete the sentences.

Announcer: Here in the studio with me today on *Food Matters* is Algernon Lacey, who's just written a book called *Half a Loaf* about that most basic of foods: bread. Algernon, what first aroused your interest in the subject?

Algernon: My grandmother, actually. One day she was describing to us how she used to make bread in the old days, and I was interested enough to start doing some research. I found out that all the big manufacturers use the same process to make bread these days. Even the supermarket chains, who think it makes them look good if customers see bread baking in their stores, use the same ingredients as everyone else. 98% of bread is made in this way – that's all the bread on sale in this country except for the products of small independent bakeries. And this process is a basic departure from the traditional techniques. You see, bread used to be made by allowing the yeast to ferment in water, which takes a few hours. But the modern method uses rapid mixing to shorten the time necessary for fermentation. This method is preferred because it saves money: less flour is needed to make bread. Unfortunately, there is a downside: you need a lot more water and fat, which makes the bread less wholesome. And since it's the fermentation process that gives bread its natural flavour, the modern method would produce rather tasteless bread if a great deal of salt weren't added. Some modern bread is also given a coating of calcium propionate to make sure it doesn't go stale. The loaf will last for a couple of weeks that way. But of course, there's a problem here, too – an increasing number of people are developing allergies to bread and wheat products, and I think there's a connection. The modern method doesn't ferment the ingredients properly, and it's hard for consumers to do anything about this because bread-making methods are dictated by the large supermarkets, who don't make a profit on bread. They don't even sell it at cost price. They're prepared to lose money to bring customers into their stores. So they dictate the methods used in the big bakeries.

▶▶ PART 3

You will hear part of a discussion between Velma Andrews, a lawyer, and Sergeant William Bailey, a police officer. For questions 15–20, choose the answer, A, B, C or D which fits best according to what you hear.

Interviewer: Today on *Legal Issues* we have Velma Andrews, a lawyer, and Sergeant William Bailey, a police officer who helps to run a scheme which trains police officers in the art of giving evidence in court. William, perhaps I can start by asking you why this training scheme is necessary?

William: Well, you must remember that in a criminal case the police have gathered evidence to show that someone – the defendant – is guilty of a crime. And the defendant's lawyer is trying to show that this evidence is wrong or unreliable. Now, the way the defence lawyer goes about doing this can be very tricky. For instance, the first time I gave evidence in court 25 years ago, the lawyer for the defence made me look like a right fool. He annoyed me by interrupting me all the time, and when I tried to argue with him I got confused, and the people in court laughed at me. That made my evidence look bad. I simply had no idea what I was up against.

Interviewer: Velma, you are a defence lawyer; do you agree with William?

Velma: Absolutely. A police officer has to learn how the system works. You must get used to the idea that the lawyers are just doing a job, and even if it seems they are attacking your honesty in a rude or brutal manner, they have nothing against you as an individual.

Interviewer: It must be hard to think like that when you're giving evidence and some lawyer is trying to trip you up.

Velma: It is, but a police officer has to develop the right attitude. You need to think of your evidence as one piece in a jigsaw puzzle, the picture being the whole case against the defendant. If you start giving opinions about other pieces, other parts of the case that aren't your responsibility, it weakens the case as a whole. Your piece of the puzzle is the only thing you should think about!

Interviewer: Do you find Velma's advice helpful for police officers on your training scheme, William?

William: Definitely. For a young officer, appearing in court is an intimidating experience. It's hard to get used to the system. I mean, there are two lawyers, one acting for the defendant and one for the crown, and in the courtroom they are adversaries but they probably know each other professionally. They may even go off together after the trial and have dinner. As if it were all a game!

Interviewer: Would you advise William's trainees to treat a court case as a game, Velma?

Velma: I would tell them to remember that the defence lawyer is trying to discredit them and their evidence. One tip to help you develop the right attitude so you don't get drawn into an argument with the lawyer is to stand so you're facing the judge, and direct all your answers to the bench. That should make it easier to avoid any sort of personal exchange with the lawyer.

Interviewer: William, is your training scheme having results?

William: Yes. I think police officers are more confident in court. And this is not just about making people less nervous! I've seen some pretty terrible things happen in court. You get an inexperienced officer who starts arguing with the lawyer and ends up making the judge and jury think there's something wrong with the police case – there's a risk that dangerous criminals might be found not guilty and set free. That's the main reason why officers need this training.

Interviewer: Velma Andrews and William Bailey, thank you.

▶▶ PART 4

This part consists of two tasks. You will hear five short extracts in which people talk about wind power. Look at Task 1. For questions 21–25, choose from the list A–H the attitude each speaker has towards wind power. Now look at Task 2. For questions 26–30, choose from the list A–H what each speaker says about the alternatives to wind power.

Speaker 1: I've just been reading about some sheep farmers in Wales who were losing money and looked into a different way of earning a living. So they took the plunge and decided to set up a wind farm. But apparently, some neighbours resented the fact that they'd had a brilliant idea and capitalised on it. As a result, there was a good deal of opposition to the farm in the area. However, I did think it was an encouraging story, especially since wind farms aren't as expensive to set up as, say, it is to build a hydroelectric station. That's why so many people are interested in going into them.

Speaker 2: The whole issue is an emotional one, but it's the *look* of these wind farms that's causing the greatest outcry, it seems to me. I know quite a few people in rural areas are getting together and starting wind farms to serve their local community, and though I think they have the best of intentions, it does seem that they're going about it the wrong way. Wind turbines are not a reliable source of energy and still need a substantial backup, which can only be satisfactorily provided by fossil fuels at present.

Speaker 3: I find it odd that people object to having wind turbines miles offshore, where nobody except a passing ship would ever see them. What's wrong with that? After all, it's a question of using fossil fuels, other renewable energy sources or nuclear power. Obviously, there's no real future in fossil fuels, but I can't see any feasible way of generating enough electricity from wave power or hydroelectric stations either, at least not in this country. Which leaves the third option, though we have to make sure sufficient safeguards are in place.

Speaker 4: I get quite angry about the whole question, actually, because everyone goes on about how wonderful wind power is, but there's only enough wind to generate electricity about 30 per cent of the time. I think the whole method is fundamentally impractical. And the irony is that we could save more energy than wind can ever generate if we could make better use of existing coal and oil supplies. If only the government would formulate sound energy conservation policies and implement them!

Speaker 5: There's been a lot of talk about birds flying into turbines, and that has turned a lot of people against wind energy. But if you look at the figures, you'll see that the number of birds killed in this way is insignificant. On the other hand, I think we have to see wind power in perspective as just part of a move towards energy from renewables. We can't rely on any *one* source; a combination of wind, hydroelectric and solar power will be needed before we can realistically talk about replacing fossil fuels completely.

 TEST 8

▶▶ PART 1

You will hear three different extracts. For questions 1–6, choose the answer, A, B or C which fits best according to what you hear. There are two questions for each extract.

Extract One
You hear two college friends discussing a lecture they have just attended.

Mark: That was interesting, wasn't it?

Suzy: And useful. I'll be applying for jobs soon, and I only ever thought of working near home for my first job. But I've had my horizons opened up now.

Mark: My dream is to work for myself, maybe have my own company. But I want to get experience first, travel to as many countries as possible getting jobs as I go. And I was really encouraged by what he said.

Suzy: He was a bit serious, though. I like speakers who tell a few jokes.

Mark: Well at least he didn't talk down to us. And he let us interrupt him if we wanted to know anything or wanted him to give more details. I appreciated that because there was a lot to take in.

Suzy: He certainly listened to us carefully and explained things we weren't clear about.

Mark: I wish he'd given out some notes for us to take away, but he's got a website and I expect everything's on that.

Extract Two

You hear part of a radio programme in which two people are discussing growing herbs.

Interviewer: So, Jerry, what useful tips have you got for us on growing herbs?

Jerry: Well, now, listeners will be delighted to know that herbs are not at all hard to grow. The ideal situation is to have a herb garden, of course. Or you could dedicate a corner of your garden to herbs – perhaps plant them in a knot pattern. They can be a very attractive feature. But if you don't have much space, you needn't feel deterred. Herbs grow just as nicely among other plants. In fact, they can help keep unwanted bugs at bay in vegetable patches. Growing basil among tomato plants, for instance, has a two-fold purpose: it acts as an insect repellent, and it adds flavour to the tomatoes. Some herbs can also be grown on kitchen windowsills or in window boxes. They're very versatile.

Interviewer: How many different kinds of herbs are there?

Jerry: Well, they fall into two main categories. There are your annuals – these grow and die in one season. Basil, parsley and dill are good examples, and all of these are widely used in cooking. Perennials, on the other hand, such as rosemary and thyme, grow year in, year out, and can make attractive borders for your flower beds.

Extract Three

You hear two friends talking about job interviews they recently attended.

Susan: What happened at your interview?

James: I was told to arrive at nine, and everyone must've been told the same time because when I got there, there was this small room packed with people, all waiting to be interviewed.

Susan: Poor you!

James: It didn't really bother me. Some people looked a bit panicked, though. Then I talked to a woman for 10 minutes. I was expecting a panel of interviewers, so at first I wondered if I'd come to the right room. But it was all right. She'd read my CV and had some pretty pointed questions ready for me, which I hope I answered well enough.

Susan: I did OK, I think, except I arrived an hour early. It was a complicated journey and I set off at some ridiculous time. Then I just sat there getting nervous. Anyhow, the interviewers asked me what I knew about their product, and I'd read up all about it. I had my CV on a presentation slide – my brother's a graphic designer and he did it for me, though I think it was a bit over the top for them.

▶▶ **PART 2**

You will hear an anthropologist talking about a recent find. For questions 7–14, complete the sentences.

Anthropologist: A most exciting discovery has been made in a remote region of Ethiopia, and I don't think it's too much of an exaggeration to say this may change the way we think of evolutionary history! Last winter an international team of anthropologists unearthed some fossil hominid skulls that have been reliably dated as being 160,000 years old. Three of the skulls – two belonging to adults and one to a child – were in quite good condition, but fragments of other skulls were also found. Now, this in itself isn't the exciting part because skulls of hominids – we use the word to mean species similar to our own – have been found that are considerably older than this. But it seems that these people were our direct ancestors, whereas the older hominid skulls are from species which died out. To put it simply, the fossils were the skulls of *Homo sapiens*, the species to which modern humans belong.

Another reason why this discovery is causing great excitement in the world of anthropology is because it ties in with other research indicating that we are not descended from Neanderthals at all. You see, the Neanderthals only vanished from the the fossil record about 30,000 years ago. So if the hypothesis is correct, it paints a fascinating picture. For an incredibly long time, tens of thousands of years in fact, at least two different species of humans co-existed on the planet, and then – for reasons we don't understand – the Neanderthals became extinct.

It is also interesting that a number of tools were found near the fossil skulls in Ethiopia, and it may well be that these people's superior technological skills allowed them to drive the Neanderthals away. Moreover, there are suggestions that they lived in groups, and there is a close correlation between advances in human development and social interaction. This may explain why *Homo sapiens* prevailed as the dominant human species! On the other hand, I must remind my listeners that the distant origins of mankind, those early days lost in the mists of prehistoric time, continue to be a mystery. Nobody really knows what happened – which naturally makes my work even more fascinating.

▶▶ **PART 3**

You will hear an interview with Marianne Nolan, a surfing champion. For questions 15–20, choose the answer, A, B, C or D which fits best according to what you hear.

Interviewer: You've been junior surfing champion since you were 13, but now at 18 you'll be entering senior championship events for the first time. How do you feel about this?

Marianne: I don't know. It's scary, but it's also something I'm looking forward to. I'm going to take things easy, though. The people who I'm going to be surfing against, well they are all more experienced, they're older. So I'm not expecting to go through and win. But, I just want to give it a shot and do my best.

Interviewer: These days there are more women in competitive surfing than in the past. But do women still have to work harder?

Marianne: It's to do with showmanship. Women's surfing and men's surfing is not the same. There are lots of differences. The women are probably more athletic, and more interesting to watch, but up to now I think they took less risks than the male surfers. But I think, recently, things have started changing, and now you can start to see the women surfers doing some pretty exciting things, which puts them more on a par with the men, which is great. And I think slowly, we're going to see men and women surfers becoming more equal – doing the same things. You know, men and women, there's never been a difference in quality when it comes to professional teachers or trainers in surfing, so it's great that the gap is being narrowed in the competition, too.

Interviewer: You started surfing as a small child. In your opinion, have things changed for girls in your generation of surfers?

Marianne: Sure, I really think they have. When I was growing up, we were all really optimistic. We were always encouraging each other, supporting one another. And it made me want to try harder and go further in my sport, I think, the attitude that my generation has. But of course, we have to be grateful for all the women who came before us. Because, of course, without them, and the work they did, we wouldn't be here surfing now – not as an international sport, anyway.

Interviewer: People have started to see you as one of the most promising surfers.

Marianne: Well, that's nice, of course! It's flattering. But, also, it's a big responsibility. It means I can't let my supporters down. And really, I'm just doing my own thing – following my own path. Who knows if I can actually get to win a world championship. I'd love to, of course. I'll try my hardest, and if I succeed, great. But, you know, I'm just happy that I can do something that I love doing. Not everyone can do something professionally that they are passionate about. But I can, and that means a lot to me.

Interviewer: You've just finished college. Any other plans for what you might do later?

Marianne: I once had ambitions to be a singer, but, you know, I'm not that much of a singer! Just in the car, maybe, or in the bath. I do have plans to go to college, and I'd like to work in a school, as a teacher. I like working with kids. But surfing has taken up so much of my time recently. When I've finished competing, though, I'd like to go back and finish my education.

Interviewer: What has surfing taught you?

Marianne: Surfing has taught me how to be flexible. The sea is like life – it's always changing, never the same. You have to react and change your plans quickly. You can't take things for granted. There are always going to be surprises. Of course, sometimes you win, sometimes you lose. So you have to be able to deal with the losses, to pick yourself up and start all over again. There's no point feeling bad if you lose or focusing on the negative side of things. Just carry on and try again. The important thing is to have a can-do attitude, believe in yourself. If you can do that, anything's possible.

▶▶ **PART 4**

This part consists of two tasks. You will hear five short extracts in which people talk about holidays that went wrong. Look at Task 1. For questions 21–25, choose from the list A–H the person who is speaking. Now look at Task 2. For questions 26–30, choose from the list A–H what each speaker is expressing.

Speaker 1: I was looking forward to meeting up with my friends again. My family had hosted the two girls, and it was exciting to visit them in their home this time round. The trip over went smoothly, and on the first evening we all walked round the town, which was beautiful. Everything was so different – the architecture and the shops. When we went back to their house for supper I asked for a dish without meat. That was a problem, which surprised me because the two girls knew I was vegetarian. I mainly had eggs all week, which spoilt things a bit. I was as polite as possible, but I was glad to get home.

Speaker 2: I wanted to spend a vacation in the Scottish Highlands. I knew how treacherous those mountains can be at any time of year, so I signed up with a company that promised a week of hiking, 'led by people with years of experience in the region'. I arrived at the place where we were supposed to meet at the time it said on the programme. The rest of the party was there, but not the experienced leaders. They eventually turned up, with the excuse they'd been given the wrong schedule. 'Not good enough,' I thought, wondering what else the company had got wrong, and I had that nagging doubt the whole week.

Speaker 3: As a student, I have long summer holidays. I love travelling but can't afford to go far during that time. But there are ways round that problem, and I offer my services as a grape picker or a nanny in return for my airfare and food and lodging. Last summer I was offered a place on an archaeological dig in Australia. Fabulous, because that's my subject. But when it came to getting the papers I needed to travel, there was so much delay I missed my flight and couldn't get another one for five days. I had nothing to do except hang about in my flat, wondering if I'd ever get away.

Speaker 4: I'm a tolerant person, generally easy-going if people mess up, but one time, I really lost it. I don't have a huge salary, but I wanted to give my girlfriend a treat for her birthday. I saw an ad by a hotel company for a long weekend trip round three of their hotels, sampling the creations of their famous chefs. It was a special offer, not too pricey, and it sounded wonderful. The food lived up to its reputation, but in one hotel the restaurant service was terrible. I made things worse by yelling at the waiter, instead of complaining in a civilised way. I'm not proud of myself for that.

Speaker 5: I love sailing and every summer, four of us rent a boat and spend a week on the water. It's hard work because we cook and sleep onboard, and there's always a lot to do. Last year we found out that the boat hire company we used had gone out of business, so we decided to have our holiday by the sea instead of on it, bought a tent and found a spot in a pretty, isolated bay. It was similar to being on the boat, except there wasn't enough to do, and we ended up fed up with each other and arguing because we were bored. Fortunately we've made up since.

TEST 1

PAPER 1 Reading and Use of English

▶▶ **PART 1**

1 C **2** D **3** A **4** C **5** D **6** B **7** A **8** C

▶▶ **PART 2**

9 not **10** such **11** other **12** be **13** One **14** how
15 as **16** with

▶▶ **PART 3**

17 incredibly (adjective to negative adverb)
18 majestic (noun to adjective)
19 keeping (verb to noun)
20 beneficial (noun to adjective)
21 stimulation (verb to noun)
22 criticized criticised (noun to verb)
23 extensive (verb to adjective)
24 daily (noun to adjective)

▶▶ **PART 4**

25 you (ever) happen (1) + to be (1)
26 had Paula reached (1) + the gate than (1)
27 it was Mark (1) + who/that wrote (1)
28 though (1) + it may be (1)
29 to tell the truth (1) + will/would mean (1)
30 may/might/could have got lost (1) + as/since/because (1)

▶▶ **PART 5**

31 A: Incorrect. They are 'extremely rare', not 'unique'.
B: Incorrect. They are etchings, not paintings.
C: Incorrect. The images are not compared to other cave art in Britain.
D: Correct. 'But more importantly, the Church Hole etchings are an incredible artistic achievement.'
32 A: Incorrect. This is not stated or implied in the text.
B: Incorrect. The point made is that Ancient Britons 'were part of a way of living, thinking and seeing the world' that spread across the continent, which is not the same as saying that they hunted over large areas.
C: Correct. 'Britons were part of a way of living, thinking and seeing the world that had spread right across the continent.'
D: Incorrect. Britons were 'at least as sophisticated as' people in Europe.
33 A: Incorrect. The discovery of the images was made public, but the writer does not suggest this should have been avoided. She implies the images should have been protected.
B: Correct. 'As a result, some etchings may already have been adversely affected, albeit inadvertently, by eager visitors.'
C: Incorrect. The text states that many people *knew* about the etchings within hours of their discovery, but it does not say that they *visited* the cave within hours of the discovery.
D: Incorrect. Measures were taken too late to prevent damage that had already been done, but the text does not say that the measures themselves are ineffective.

34 A: Correct. 'However, the Church Hole images are modifications of the rock itself, and show up best when seen from a certain angle in the natural light of early morning.'
B: Incorrect. 'They had been looking for the usual type of cave drawing or painting'
C: Incorrect. The text does not mention the time of day when the initial survey took place.
D: Incorrect. The text does not suggest that the brightness of the light was a problem.
35 A: Incorrect. This statement does not express the conclusion Dr Samson draws about the function of the etchings.
B: Incorrect. They intended the images to be visible in the early morning.
C: Correct. 'I think the artists knew very well that the etchings would hardly be visible except early in the morning.'
D: Incorrect. The text mentions 'rituals involving animal worship', but this does not mean that ice-age hunters kept animals in the cave.
36 A: Incorrect. It is implied that we can make inferences, but we cannot 'insist on any rigid interpretation'.
B: Incorrect. Dr Caruthers does not think their function 'can be determined with any certainty', but she does not imply they serve no particular purpose.
C: Incorrect. Saying someone knows 'so little' is not the same as saying they know nothing.
D: Correct. 'We should, in my view, begin by tentatively assuming … while of course being prepared to modify this verdict at a later date.'

▶▶ **PART 6**

37 D: Writer A's view is: 'The early manned space flights generated genuine interest around the world, but who really cares nowadays …?' Writer B's view is: 'it seems to have lost its appeal for many people'. Writer C's view is: 'People with a vested interest will say that human space flight is important for the prestige and glamour of space exploration and for the way it draws young minds into science and technology' but that it would be more exciting to invest the money in science education.' So, A, B and C don't believe manned space flight is inspirational these days. Writer D, however, says: 'people do not feel excited when they see robots launched into space. Computers attached to a rocket will not stimulate the imagination or the enthusiasm for space exploration.' This implies that manned space flight is what inspires people.
38 D: Writer B's view is that one day there will be a major disaster and 'the human species may only survive by settling in a new home. If we are to form colonies on the moon or other places in space, we have no alternative but to go there ourselves.' Writer D says: 'In the long term, we need to find out whether we can survive outside the Earth's orbit. It's a question of species survival.'
Writer A says: 'Who really believes it will ever be feasible to … migrate to these places in the event of a catastrophe?' Writer C says: 'The idea that humans will ever be able or want to settle on the moon or anywhere else in space is unthinkable.' So, writers

A and C have similar views which are opposed to those of writers B and D.

39 B: Writer A's view is: 'The only thing we bring back is knowledge and robots outperform astronauts in that respect … they can collect and retain far more information.' Writer C's view is: 'So much of the investment in manned missions goes into keeping astronauts alive and safe that the really useful science takes second place', implying that unmanned space missions are better for research. Writer D's view is: 'satellites, robots and other technology are probably better than astronauts at collecting information from space.' So, writers A, C and D think that unmanned space is better for research than manned missions. Writer B accepts that 'Robots tend to be good at certain tasks like collecting data.' But then writer B goes on to say that some 'experiments that can only be conducted in space require the physical and intellectual dexterity and skills only humans possess.' So, writer B's view is different from those of A, C and D.

40 C: Writer A says: 'They (robots) are cheaper to put into space, they can stay there longer and they can collect and retain far more information.' Writer C says:, 'So much of the investment in manned missions goes into keeping astronauts alive and safe that the really useful science takes second place.' So C agrees with A that manned space flight is less cost effective than robots and other technology. Writer B says 'Space exploration, whether manned or not, is hugely expensive' and writer D says 'we do need to explore space, whatever the financial implications.' So, neither says that one is more cost effective than the other.

▶▶ **PART 7**

41 C: Link between 'asked their customers for a verdict' in the previous paragraph and 'We had a bin that said "yes" and a bin that said "no". Also, link between 'We quit our jobs the next day' and the information that they struggled for nine months to get the business started in the next paragraph.

42 G: Link between 'nine months living on credit cards and overdrafts before they sold their first smoothie' and 'They found that the finances were the basic stumbling block.'

43 B: Link between 'What was the recipe for this startling success?' and 'Probably something to do with pure unadulterated ingredients with a dash of quirky advertising.'

44 A: Link between 'This was when they discovered the truth about the majority of so-called natural fruit drinks' and 'Most are made from concentrated juice with water.'

45 F: Link between 'Wouldn't it be great to make it easy for people to get hold of this natural fresh goodness?' and 'So, at another festival in 2004, the Innocent team tried extending their range of products into desserts.' Also, link between 'a big tub of ice cream' in F and 'we simply froze some of our smoothies' in the next paragraph.

46 D: Link between the question at the end of D 'Was there ever a temptation in those early years to sell up and

go and live on a desert island?' and the answer 'We didn't rule it out completely.'

▶▶ **PART 8**

47 C: 'When I told my father I'd decided to study French, he said, "Are you sure? Wouldn't something more substantial be better?"'

48 D: 'languages defeat them and that seriously narrows their options. I'm glad I'm not in their shoes.'

49 B: 'I hear lots of people saying "I'd like to have another language but it's beyond my abilities." The truth is, though, that anyone can learn a language.'

50 A: 'my coolness rating definitely shot up, which has been nice'

51 B: 'one thing it's given me , … is a greater awareness of my strengths and weaknesses in Spanish.'

52 C: 'I once committed a major blunder in an office in Japan. Had I spoken Japanese, I would have known not to do it, and would have avoided a couple of very awkward days afterwards.'

53 D: 'To be honest, I hadn't considered myself unusual'

54 A: 'I interpret at conferences. That gets my adrenaline going'

55 C: 'candidates who are multilingual tend to be more adaptable and open-minded'

56 B: 'I had no idea what I was going to do with it when I finished. I was by no means the only one from my course in that position, and there's a similar thing in other countries'

PAPER 2 Writing

▶▶ **PART 1** (*suggested answers*)

Question 1
  Style: Semi-formal or formal
  Content: 1 Give a general overview and state your opinion.
       2 Explain the advantages of the two methods.
       3 State any possible disadvantages.
       4 Sum up, giving a recommendation for further action.

▶▶ **PART 2** (*suggested answers*)

Question 2
  Style: Neutral or semi-formal
  Content: 1 Suggest that the radio station will be beneficial.
       2 Give details of possible programmes you would begin with.
       3 Outline the support you would need.
       4 Sum up your proposal.

Question 3
  Style: Semi-formal or neutral
  Content: 1 Introduction: explain what you will write about.
       2 Give an example of one good thing.
       3 Give a second example of some good things.
       4 Give an example of some disadvantages.
       5 Conclusion, stating whether Paul should leave his village.

Question 4

Style: Semi-formal or formal

Content: 1 Introduction: give some relevant information about your region.

2 Describe people's attitude to public transport, giving examples.

3 Describe what action is being taken to improve use of public transport.

4 Conclusion: express your view on the situation.

PAPER 3 Listening

▸▸ **PART 1**

1 C   2 B   3 A   4 B   5 A   6 C

▸▸ **PART 2**

7 ancient Egypt   8 willow tree extract   9 1829
10 stomach   11 German company   12 research
13 fifty/50   14 vegetables

▸▸ **PART 3**

15 B   16 A   17 D   18 D   19 C   20 A

▸▸ **PART 4**

Task One
21 B   22 H   23 A   24 D   25 F

Task Two
26 G   27 F   28 H   29 D   30 B

 TEST **2**

PAPER 1 Reading and Use of English

▸▸ **PART 1**

1 B   2 D   3 C   4 A   5 B   6 D   7 C   8 A

▸▸ **PART 2**

9 may/might   10 but   11 apart   12 far   13 any   14 into
15 every   16 as

▸▸ **PART 3**

17 originated (noun to verb)
18 inventor (verb to noun)
19 undisputed/indisputable (verb to negative adjective)
20 initially (adjective to adverb)
21 invariably (adjective to adverb)
22 discoveries (verb to plural noun)
23 updated (noun to verb)
24 inconclusive (verb to negative adjective)

▸▸ **PART 4**

25 as/so long as (1) he did (1)
26 came up with (1) the idea (1)
27 having our living room (1) done up (1)
28 to being (1) spoken to (1)
29 on the point of (1) calling him (1)
30 no circumstances (1) am I (1)

▸▸ **PART 5**

31 A: Incorrect. It is implied that this is Ellen MacIntosh's view, but it is not the writer's view.

B: Incorrect: 'simplicity' refers to the 'stock, two-dimensional characters', not the stories themselves.

C: Correct. 'Indeed, although her comment does make one wonder why simplicity of this sort should be out of place in a story for children.'

D: Incorrect. This is not stated or implied in the text.

32 A: Incorrect. This is a true statement in itself but it is not what Ellen objects to.

B: Correct. 'Instead of standing up to her cruel stepmother … Cinderella just waits for a fairy godmother to appear and solve her problems. But wouldn't you want a daughter of yours to show more spirit?'

C: Incorrect. The two sisters are 'absurd', which is not the same as saying they are figures of ridicule. Also, this is not what Ellen objects to.

D: Incorrect. This is implied in the text, but it is not what Ellen objects to.

33 A: Correct. 'In these versions for the silver screen, the Cinderella character … persists in not showing much backbone.'

B: Incorrect. This is not stated or implied in the text.

C: Incorrect. This is not stated or implied in the text.

D: Incorrect. This is not stated or implied in the text.

34 A: Incorrect. 'In the majority of film versions, the heroine has a profession', but the text does not indicate whether she is successful in her profession.

B: Incorrect. 'marrying her prince' is used metaphorically, to imply that Cinderella will 'live happily ever after', not that she will become a real princess.

C: Incorrect. This is not stated or implied in the text.

D: Correct. 'In the majority of film versions, the heroine has a profession and is even permitted to continue working after marrying her prince – this is the 21st century, after all.'

35 A: Correct. 'Most children … empathise with the protagonist … challenge.'

B: Incorrect. The text does not state or imply that little girls like to be challenged themselves.

C: Incorrect. This is not stated or implied in the text.

D: Incorrect. This is not stated or implied in the text.

36 A: Incorrect. This is not stated or implied in the text.

B: Correct. 'This can be seen in the original story of Cinderella …. She has to grow spiritually, and by maturing, she becomes attractive to the prince … In the later versions, this element is missing.'

C: Incorrect. This is not stated or implied in the text.

D: Incorrect. This is not stated or implied in the text.

▸▸ **PART 6**

37 D: Reviewer C's view is that the selection is too limited: 'The bulk of the music Levitin talks about, however, is pop. Classical music, or modern music in that tradition, is sometimes referred to in patronising terms, but …'. Reviewer D says: 'The choice of music to illustrate his arguments … draws so strongly on Levitin's own musical preferences that some readers who do not share his musical tastes may feel lost,'

which also suggests that he feels it should be more balanced.

In contrast, reviewer A refers to a sensitive choice of familiar tunes and songs which he uses to illustrate concepts and theories, and reviewer B refers to different musical genres but makes no comment about how well Levitin uses them as examples.

38 B: Reviewer A refers to 'a number of small errors obvious to a knowledgeable musician'. Reviewer B refers to a subject which is 'excessively complex' but makes no reference to any errors. Reviewer C mentions 'flawed accounts of certain aspects of musical acoustics and music theory', and reviewer D mentions 'misleading descriptions of significant research work'. So, A, C and D all refer to mistakes, while B does not mention any problems with accuracy.

39 B: Reviewer D thinks Levitin's references to himself can be unhelpful: 'regular reference to his own career in music – as a musician, producer and neuroscientist – is well-intentioned, but there are times when we could do with fewer funny stories and more attention to detail.' Reviewer B says 'Levitin's anecdotes about famous musicians he has met and played with are worth passing over', also suggesting criticism of some of the personal content.

By contrast, reviewer A says Levitin makes the subject more interesting by explaining 'against the background of his own intriguing narrative', and reviewer C says that Levitin 'wisely weaves in stories about music-making and working with musicians to make the science easier to relate to'.

40 A: Reviewer A says that 'in trying to keep things simple for a non-specialist audience, as far as technical terms are concerned, Levitin too often ends up dumbing down', which is a criticism of the style. Reviewer B says the book 'goes out of its way to make the general reader feel at ease', and makes no criticism of the writing style. Reviewer C says that Levitin sets 'jargon aside in favour of everyday terminology', and implies this is a good thing. Reviewer D says 'it is to Levitin's credit that this book contains clear, well-informed explanations', and it should be 'accessible to the non-specialist'. So B, C and D all praise the accessible style of the language used in the book.

▸▸ **PART 7**

41 E: Link between 'As many as 1,000 languages have died in the past 400 years. Conversely, the handful of major international languages are forging ahead' in the previous paragraph, the description of the status of the world's major languages today, and the description of what is happening to many languages in the following paragraph.

42 G: Link between 'several linguists around the world who are determined to document as many of the remaining endangered languages as possible' and what this involves: 'This often means trekking to some of the most inaccessible parts of the Earth …'.

43 F: Vocabulary link between 'region' and 'area' - between 'A great number of languages in the greater Himalayan region are endangered or have already reached the point of no return' and 'There are about 200 languages spoken in this area, but only a few have been properly described'.

44 D: Link between the specific reference to the two old women who were the last speakers of a language suddenly appearing at a conference, and the acknowledgment that 'particular stories like this can be fascinating'.

Also, the question at the end of D, 'Why look back instead of forward?', is answered in the next paragraph when Kortlandt asks: 'Would you ask a biologist looking for disappearing species this?'

45 C: Link between 'Language is the defining characteristic of the human species. These people say things to each other which are very different from the things we say, and think very different thoughts, which are often incomprehensible to us' in the previous paragraph and 'If you want to understand the human species, you have to take the full range of human thought into consideration'.

46 A: Link between 'All this knowledge could be lost if the tribes and their languages die out' in the previous paragraph and 'This is one of the things worrying linguists working in Fiji in the South Pacific. There are hundreds of known remedies in Fiji's forests.' in A.

Also, link between 'There are possibly scores more yet to be discovered' in A and 'We will only be able to find them and benefit from their properties through … ' in the following paragraph.

▸▸ **PART 8**

47 A: 'now I can really understand why someone's using a certain technique or piece of equipment'

48 C: 'I'm considering either expanding – more shops, managers and so on – or diversifying, perhaps producing my own surf boards'

49 B: 'The classes themselves aren't terribly lucrative, but I supplement my income …'

50 D: 'and the next thing I knew, my wife was urging me to set up my own company'

51 B: 'Then someone at an organisation called Business Link … suggested advertising on the internet!'

52 A: 'If I hadn't realised that early on, I probably would have carried on dreaming that my big break would come.'

53 B: 'I couldn't work out how to find people who would pay for their children to attend the kind of courses I wanted to run.'

54 C: 'He said he wanted to sell up and I jumped at the chance to buy the business from him!'

55 D: 'I had to take a very deep breath before I finally took the plunge.'

56 B: 'I studied medicine, but when I finished medical school I had a sort of crisis. I knew I couldn't go on with it!'

PAPER 2 Writing

▶▶ **PART 1** (*suggested answers*)

Question 1

Style: Semi-formal or formal
Content: 1 Give a general overview and state your opinion.
2 Explain the advantages of the two methods.
3 State any possible disadvantages.
4 Sum up, giving a recommendation for further action.

▶▶ **PART 2** (*suggested answers*)

Question 2

Style: Semi-formal or formal
Content: 1 Give a general overview, introducing the topic of the report and explaining where your region is.
2 Give some key findings of your report.
3 Give some details, explaining how young people feel about history and culture in the region.
4 Describe how this might change in the future.
5 Conclusion: end with a summary of the report findings.

Question 3

Style: Semi-formal or formal
Content: 1 Introduce yourself and the general problem.
2 Describe the events of what happened.
3 Describe how you feel, and how your holiday was affected.
4 Describe your feelings about the service.
5 Explain what you would like to happen next.
6 Finish the letter appropriately.

Question 4

Style: Neutral or semi-formal
Content: 1 Say which film you have chosen to write about.
2 Describe the book on which the film is based.
3 Use examples from the film to discuss the characters and plot.
4 Say how you think the film compares with the book.

PAPER 3 Listening

▶▶ **PART 1**

1 C   2 B   3 A   4 C   5 B   6 A

▶▶ **PART 2**

7 an amateur historian   8 farmer   9 a doctor
10 articles and essays   11 personal correspondence
12 wife's brother   13 Roman history   14 Italy

▶▶ **PART 3**

15 A   16 B   17 C   18 D   19 A   20 A

▶▶ **PART 4**

Task One
21 G   22 E   23 B   24 C   25 F

Task Two
26 D   27 H   28 C   29 E   30 G

TEST 3

PAPER 1 Reading and Use of English

▶▶ **PART 1**

1 C   2 A   3 B   4 D   5 C   6 B   7 A   8 D

▶▶ **PART 2**

9 not   10 in   11 as   12 why   13 whole   14 though/if
15 the   16 Such

▶▶ **PART 3**

17 increasingly (verb to adverb)
18 originally (noun to adverb)
19 unsuitable (verb to negative adjective)
20 censorship (verb to noun)
21 growth (verb to noun)
22 tendency (verb to noun)
23 critical (noun to adjective)
24 sophistication (adjective to noun)

▶▶ **PART 4**

25 no matter (1) how hard (1)
26 seem to be (1) taken into consideration/account (1)
27 placed the blame (1) on him/John (1)
28 take back (1) what I said (1)
29 despite the fact that (1) it was (1)
30 accused Joe of (1) leaving his (1)

▶▶ **PART 5**

31 D: Correct. The prefix *back* in *backlash* means something returning or coming back to something. Options A and C are about new things and B is about 'inner workings'. D is about a 're-evaluation' – thinking about something again. *Lash* means 'hit' or 'strike', so a backlash is hitting back, a negative reaction. The word *reaction* in the first sentence of the second paragraph, and also the main point made in the second paragraph, give a further help in working out the answer.

32 C: Correct. 'Accelerated the widespread reaction' and 'gave way to cries that the simplification of science, in particular of neuroscience, often by science journalists, was once again to blame'.

33 A: Correct. 'Angling for high-profile speaking work' is similar to 'concerned with eye-catching statements and colourful anecdotes' which the reviewer expresses disapproval of in the previous paragraph. The words 'too many of the popular neuroscience writers write as though …' suggests a criticism, and elsewhere in the text, the reviewer makes it clear that he admires Prinz's approach, so he may well disapprove of something that Prinz is not doing.

34 D: Correct. In paragraph 5, we are told that 'for years, the field of linguistics has been heavily influenced by Noam Chomsky's notion of a universal grammar'. 'For years' and 'heavily influenced' suggest it is an established theory. Also, in paragraph 6, we are told that Prinz suggests a 'different explanation' from Chomsky. In challenging Chomsky's thinking, he is expressing a 'controversial' view, which means a challenge to the majority view.

35 A: Correct. 'Instead of going for the hard sell, Prinz admits that all he hopes to do is raise the possibility that this alternative theory might be true. This lends his work an air of maturity.'

36 B: Correct. 'The nature/nurture pendulum has swung back and forth over thousands of years.'

▶▶ PART 6

37 A: Writer A says: 'There is no alternative but to opt out of further growth.' Writer B says 'it is tragic that growth has such a bad name' and calls for 'more resources and better technology rather than less', so B is in favour of continued economic growth. Writer C asks whether we should 'give up on economic progress' but says that the reality of this is 'unimaginable'. Writer D says 'the way forward, then, is to tackle excessive consumerism and its associated ills ... while the world economy carries on growing'. So, B, C and D are in favour of continued growth, while A opposes it.

38 B: Writer A says: 'ever-increasing consumption adds little to human well-being. In fact, ... it positively impedes it.' Writer B says: 'increases in economic output have brought enormous benefits ... surely, greater general well-being,' and calls for continued growth. Writer C says: 'The more we have, the less satisfied we are.' Writer D says: 'life in some of the world's most technologically advanced nations, while abounding in consumer products, has evidently not been enhanced in terms of personal relationships, meaningful work and other key values for well-being – indeed, it's quite the opposite.' So, A, C and D argue that economic growth past a certain point does not bring well-being, or happiness. Therefore, writer B has a different opinion on this issue.

39 C: Writer B says 'we need more resources and better technology rather than less. We should invest in high tech energy production, sea walls to resist flooding and other practical engineering-based solutions.' Writer C says economic progress is 'unimaginable' and we should apply 'our technological expertise to overcome our difficulties, with massive projects to harness solar, wind and wave power.'
Writer A is against economic growth and says we need 'to fundamentally rethink the uses to which we put our technological expertise'. Writer D admits there are problems in the 'world's most technologically advanced nations', but does not refer to 'the use of technology'.

40 D: Writer A calls for 'much tighter regulation of advertising, which incites wholly superfluous consumption'. Writer D says 'the way forward, then, is to tackle excessive consumerism and its associated ills by various reforms such as greater control of advertising'.
Writer B mentions controlling or eliminating advertising as part of 'received wisdom', which is different from A's opinions. Writer C believes that 'even wholesale reform of aspects of modern economies like advertising, the cheerleader for consumerism, is unlikely to be accepted'.

▶▶ PART 7

41 G: Link between 'but then, the explorers realised it could have been a platform where Inca priests stood and watched the path of the sun' in the previous paragraph and 'So, a decision was made to battle on through the thick jungle.'

42 F: Link between 'Machu Picchu' and 'But that staggering discovery took place over 100 years ago'.

43 C: Link between 'waiting to be found' in the previous paragraph and 'According to these experts, what we now know as Peru has hosted advanced civilisations for as long as almost anywhere else in the world.'

44 A: Contrastive link between 'by no means everything there has been unearthed' in the previous paragraph and 'Far from it'.

45 D: Link between 'in danger of being ruined forever' in the previous paragraph and 'These worries mean it is fortunate that the urge to discover ruins swallowed by the jungle is still strong'.

46 B: Link between 'The best explorers spend time reading the accounts of the Spanish conquerors, studying maps and talking to local people ... Raising funds to pay for the work is also part of the challenge' in the previous paragraph and 'The importance of this kind of preparation is underlined by Hugh Thompson'.

▶▶ PART 8

47 B: 'We made several false starts. One skydiving group agreed to take part and then pulled out. Then we had trouble recording the interviews and organising the data. At one stage I wasn't sure it would ever happen. I suppose it's good to know that research can be like this.'

48 C: 'It was intimidating at first ... I did eventually feel part of the team, though. It was good to know they valued my contribution and respected me.'

49 A: 'It was brilliant being able to ask them about their work – and challenge it sometimes.'

50 D: 'Some of it went over my head, of course, but I asked a friend of my dad's, who's a doctor, to simplify some of it.'

51 C: 'They didn't pay me but I was expected to show up on time and do an eight-hour day, just like everyone else.' There is no resentment in Katie's comments, however. She believes she has a head start on some of her fellow students in having had an authentic taste of life as a scientist.'

52 B: 'I'm glad I was working on something I was curious about. If I hadn't been, I wouldn't have got nearly so much out of it.'

53 A: 'The implications for runners were obvious and the findings were soon made known more widely.'

54 D: 'Tariq regards himself as fortunate to be interested in a subject that attracts a lot of attention in the media at large, as well as scientific circles. It means the research is well-funded, and scientists involved have the money and time to dedicate to students like Tariq.'

55 A: 'He sustained knee injuries, which kept him off the track for months. Rather than becoming discouraged, however, Eric turned to science and landed a voluntary stint in a sports research unit in his summer holidays.'

56 B: 'Angela assumed that learners would base the degree of trust they placed in an instructor on levels of experience and perhaps appearance. What novices reported, though, was that it mainly related to the way the instructors talked.'

PAPER 2 Writing

▶▶ **PART 1** (*suggested answers*)

Question 1:
Style: Semi-formal or formal
Content: 1 Introduction: describe the situation you are going to discuss.
2 Describe the advantages of working from home.
3 Describe any disadvantages.
4 Discuss the two most important advantages and give your reasons.
5 Conclusion: end with a summary of your views.

▶▶ **PART 2** (*suggested answers*)

Question 2:
Style: Formal
Content: 1 Introduction: introduce yourself and explain the basic idea.
2 Describe the benefits of the music festival (e.g. it would bring a lot of money to the town).
3 Describe the possible programme types and possible locations.
4 Outline some possible disadvantages and how you would deal with them.
5 Conclusion: end with a summary of your proposal.

Question 3:
Style: Formal
Content: 1 Introduction: state the purpose of the report and what you are going to write about.
2 Describe the recreational opportunities.
3 Describe the cinemas and theatres.
4 Describe the cafés and restaurants.
5 Discuss whether the leisure facilities are suitable, and whether it is a good idea to open a new hotel there.
6 Conclusion: end with a summary and some recommendations.

Question 4:
Style: Informal
Content: 1 Introduction: greet your friend and explain what you are writing about.
2 Describe what you were doing before the accident.
3 Describe the accident – give details to make it sound interesting.
4 Describe what other people were doing and how they reacted.

5 Describe your experience with the police – make it as lively and interesting as possible. Try to make your friend feel as if he/she was there with you.
6 End the letter with an appropriate goodbye.

PAPER 3 Listening

▶▶ **PART 1**

1 B **2** A **3** C **4** A **5** A **6** B

▶▶ **PART 2**

7 a (new) motorway **8** skeleton **9** ceremonial **10** cattle **11** leader **12** France **13** west **14** the British Museum

▶▶ **PART 3**

15 B **16** B **17** D **18** A **19** D **20** C

▶▶ **PART 4**

Task One
21 A **22** H **23** G **24** E **25** B

Task Two
26 F **27** D **28** B **29** H **30** C

TEST 4

PAPER 1 Reading and Use of English

▶▶ **PART 1**

1 A **2** C **3** A **4** B **5** A **6** A **7** D **8** B

▶▶ **PART 2**

9 which **10** many **11** According **12** other **13** addition **14** Besides **15** little **16** own

▶▶ **PART 3**

17 misconceptions (noun to negative plural noun)
18 comparison (verb to noun)
19 fatalities (adjective to plural noun)
20 solitary (noun to adjective)
21 occurrences (verb to plural noun)
22 unpleasant (verb to negative adjective)
23 underestimated (verb to verb)
24 precautions (noun to plural noun)

▶▶ **PART 4**

25 highly likely (that) (1) this novel will (1)
26 insisted (1) on us/our staying (1)
27 no matter (1) what time it may/might (1)
28 no account (1) am I to be / must I be / should I be (1)
29 it not been (1) for Mark (1)
30 will have started (1) by the time (1)

31 A: 'I was brought up to think that the preferred way of dealing with aches and pains is to do nothing and hope they'll go away, but I eventually allowed myself to be dragged along by a friend of mine to talk to an osteopath.'

32 C: 'I had regularly been told … that I tend to slouch in chairs but had thought bad posture was something one was born with and could do nothing about. With hindsight, it's hard to believe just how far off the mark I was.'

33 C: 'It trains you to use your body less harshly and to carry out the sorts of movements and actions that we do all the time with less effort.'

34 D: 'The key is learning to break the bad habits … a habit the body has formed which can be hard to break.'

35 B: 'Frederick Matthias Alexander, an Australian theatrical orator … found in his youth that his voice was failing during performances … He worked on improving it with dramatic results.'

36 B: The text as a whole.

► ► **PART 6**

37 A: Writer A says that all the investment will 'end up stimulating the economy eventually'. Writer B says that 'research suggests that few former hosts have experienced long-term economic gains. Indeed, certain cities like Montreal and Los Angeles have taken decades to pay off the debts.' Writer C says that 'critics … often focus on the more easily measurable economic implications which suggest that the Games are not a viable proposition, but the Olympics are not just about money,' which implies that the writer believes the Games do not bring economic benefits on balance. Writer D says that 'past experience suggests the financial costs tend to outweigh the benefits anyway'.
So, B, C and D believe the Olympics do not bring economic gains, but writer A claims there are long-term gains.

38 C: Writer B says: 'There is also the chance for everyone, the younger generations in particular, to observe elite athletes, and therefore sporting excellence, exercise and fitness become cool things to aspire to'. Writer C says: 'There is the sporting legacy too, with the greatest athletes from around the world inspiring mass participation.'

39 D: Writer A says: 'proof of a capacity to rise to the challenge can pull the country together, make it feel good about itself'. Writer B says the Olympics 'inspire a local feel-good factor, enhancing a sense of pride in belonging to a city and country …'. Writer C says the Olympics 'present an opportunity to showcase, domestically …. the notion that the city possesses the know-how and manpower to manage a hugely complex international event'. Writer D says: 'research reveals significant regional resentment about all the attention from government, the media and other organisations being directed at one city. So much for pride in one's country.'

So, A, B and C all suggest there is positive effect on the sense of national identity, whereas D says there can be 'resentment', which is not positive.

40 C: Writer A says that 'the international media focus on the Games can also lift the host country's profile to another level'. Writer C says the Olympics 'present an opportunity to showcase …. to the world at large, the notion that the city possesses the know-how and manpower to manage a hugely complex international event …'. So, both A and C suggest the host city's international reputation will be improved.

► ► **PART 7**

41 B: Link between 'a vast library of unread books, and the plundering of nature is comparable to the random discarding of whole volumes without having opened them and learned from them' in the previous paragraph and 'it's the already opened texts that attract the majority of us, however'.

42 D: Link between 'it's undoubtedly expanding. There are definitely more and more people seeking wildlife experiences now' in the previous paragraph and 'this growth …'. Also, link between 'People want to discover nature at first-hand for themselves – not just on a screen' and 'There's no way to compare seeing an animal in the wild with watching one on TV'.

43 G: Link between 'a concept that comes under the broad label of 'ecotourism' in the previous paragraph and 'it's a term which is overused, but the principle behind it …'. Also, link between 'it also extends to consideration of the interests of people living in the places that tourists visit' and 'In practice, this means that many tour operators, guided by ethical policies, now use the services of local communities, train local guides and have close ties to conservation projects' in the following paragraph.

44 E: Link between 'Rekero has established its own school – the Koyiaki Guide School and Wilderness Camp – for Maasai people in Kenya' in the previous paragraph and 'they have largely been excluded from the benefits brought to the region by tourism. This initiative is a concerted effort to enable them to take up jobs and also run programmes themselves.'

45 F: Link between 'some organisations even allow tourists to take part in research and conservation' in the previous paragraph and 'Earthwatch is a nonprofit international environmental group that does just that. 'Participation in an Earthwatch project …'.

46 A: Link between '… Dr Matthias Hammer, calls an "adventure with a conscience". Volunteers can visit six destinations around the world and take part in various activities including snow leopard, wolf and bear surveys and whale and dolphin research' in the previous paragraph and 'He is confident that, if done properly, this combination of tourism and conservation can be 'a win–win situation'.

47 C: 'The intensity of Park's search makes for a less than relaxing read, and, in all probability, there will be readers who fail to make it past the first couple of chapters.'

48 D: 'A leading writer in what could be called the 'anti-self-help self-help' genre – which happily seems to be swelling.'

49 B: 'It aims to be a practical, how-to guide for maximising co-operation, but ends up a sort of unsystematic self-help book: listening is as important a skill as presentation of your own ideas; discussion need not reach agreement but can teach us new things; assertiveness is valuable, but so is politeness and diffidence. All true, but don't we know it already?'

50 A: 'Peppered with insights that may never have been expressed quite like this before but which make you want to scrawl 'yes' in the margins on almost every page.'

51 D: 'Doesn't offer facile instructions for living a happy, easy life … we have to stop searching for firm answers and quick fixes.'

52 C: 'If *Teach Us to Sit Still* does well, we could be in for a glut of writing by people who don't have much wrong with them, yet still write about it at length.'

53 D: '*Help! How to Become Slightly Happier*, his previous book, comprised a series of short sections, each a page or two long, which presented an idea fairly quickly. *The Antidote* has just eight chapters and each one explores a subject like success and failure in detail.'

54 B: 'The trouble is it all feels atomised itself. Sennett's argument seems to bounce from place to place … ends up a sort of unsystematic self-help book.'

55 D: 'Many self-help books these days would shout 'Yes!' Oliver Burkeman isn't so sure.'

56 A: 'Sometimes you think you're just getting to grips with an idea, only for it to slip away.'

PAPER 2 Writing

▶▶ **PART 1** (*suggested answers*)

Question 1:

Style: Semi-formal of formal
Content: 1 Introduction: describe the situation you are going to discuss.
2 Outline the arguments for conducting this survival exercise.
3 Describe which arguments you think are more important and give reasons.
4 Conclusion: end with a summary of your views.

▶▶ **PART 2** (*suggested answers*)

Question 2:

Style: Neutral or semi-formal
Content: 1 Say which films you have chosen to write about, and which one you enjoyed most.
2 Explain why you enjoyed one film more than the other one.
3 Describe each film, giving examples of the actors, story, effects, etc.
4 Conclusion: end with a summary of your views.

Question 3:

Style: Informal or neutral
Content: 1 Introduction: greet your friend and explain why you are writing.
2 Describe how long you have been in the job and what you do.
3 Explain your feelings about starting a new job. Give examples of your experiences.
4 Give some suggestions to your friend.
5 Finish your letter with an appropriate goodbye.

Question 4:

Style: Formal
Content: 1 Introduction: state the purpose of your report and give some details of the zoo you are writing about.
2 Describe the green spaces in your area and what wildlife lives there.
3 Describe the condition of the green spaces.
4 List some things which could be done to create more green spaces.
5 Describe the effects of doing these things.
6 Conclusion: end with some recommendations for future action.

PAPER 3 Listening

▶▶ **PART 1**

1 C **2** C **3** B **4** A **5** B **6** C

▶▶ **PART 2**

7 (long-distance) running **8** long jump **9** nephew
10 build **11** shooting **12** proper diet **13** equipment
14 attitude

▶▶ **PART 3**

15 A **16** C **17** A **18** D **19** B **20** B

▶▶ **PART 4**

Task One
21 F **22** D **23** G **24** C **25** A

Task Two
26 C **27** H **28** D **29** B **30** F

PAPER 1 Reading and Use of English

▶▶ **PART 1**

1 D **2** A **3** B **4** C **5** C **6** B **7** D **8** C

▶▶ **PART 2**

9 longer **10** which **11** having **12** There **13** like **14** to
15 One **16** with

▶▶ **PART 3**

17 eloquently (noun to adverb)
18 conceivable (verb to adjective)
19 disrespect (noun to negative noun)
20 influential (noun to adjective)
21 discredited (verb to negative verb)
22 incorporated (adjective to verb)
23 unmodified (verb to negative adjective)
24 disprove (noun to negative verb)

▶▶ **PART 4**

25 would benefit (1) from (taking/having) (1)
26 no time (1) were we (ever) aware (1)
27 had not/hadn't been (1) for that accident (1)
28 are on (very) good terms (1) with (1)
29 can't have been (1) put (1)
30 had her bag (1) snatched (1)

▶▶ **PART 5**

31 C: 'all that remains to tell us that it was once lush and verdant – and inhabited – is the occasional stone tool, harpoon or mammoth tusk brought up from the seabed by fishing boats'

32 C: 'bathymetry can now deploy computers, satellite positioning equipment and special software to create accurate and remarkably detailed maps'

33 A: 'She is however, scathing about the scale of financial support' and 'it's an absolute scandal that we know so little about the area just off the country's shores'

34 B: 'The idea shared by many people in Britain of their country as a natural island kingdom will be challenged … It remains to be seen how far this new awareness is taken on board, however.'

35 D: 'In addition, commercial applications are a real possibility.'

36 A: 'mapping the seabed will also identify places where rare plants and shellfish have their homes. Government legislation may prevent digging at such sites'

▶▶ **PART 6**

37 A: Reviewer A says Griffiths uses 'excessively poetic, at times, absurd language'. Reviewer B says her argument is 'passionately and eloquently expressed'. Reviewer C says her theory is 'fluently and vividly delivered'. Reviewer D describes a 'rare vitality and admirable energy in Griffiths' writing'. So, B, C and D all say positive things about the style of writing, but A's comments are critical.

38 B: Reviewer A says: 'Jay Griffiths draws the familiar but erroneous conclusion that traditional societies and tribes treat nature and children better than modern ones ... the claims she makes about children's development are too often illogical and unsupportable.' Reviewer B says that Griffiths pursues it (her idea) in ways that simply don't hold up.'

39 D: Reviewer A says that Griffiths fails to provide an analysis of the data in the UNICEF report on children's well-being. Reviewer B says that Griffiths is 'guilty of selective deployment of the data'. Reviewer C also finds fault with Griffiths' use of the data: 'She refers to a UNESCO report on children's wellbeing … that report, however, finds that well-being depends on many factors …'. Reviewer D mentions the use Griffiths' makes of the UNICEF data but is uncritical. The result, as the UNICEF surveys of well-being that Griffiths quotes reveal, is a generation of children who are unhappy and unfulfilled.'
So, D is the only reviewer who is uncritical of the way Griffiths uses the UNICEF report.

40 C: Reviewer B says that Griffiths 'regards children as originally innocent and good, and that these characteristics are suppressed by the restrictions imposed on them. As parents have known for millennia, however, children are far more complex than that.' Reviewer C says that Griffiths believes in 'the innate purity of children and a need for them to be close to nature, mystery and risk and be gloriously free', but that she 'ignores all the science that shows that children are, in fact, far from being the simple innocents of romantic tradition'. Reviewers A and B discuss what Griffiths says about the way children are brought up but neither refer to Griffiths' depiction of children's basic nature.

▶▶ **PART 7**

41 E: Link between 'But what does it mean to be a field scientist?' in the previous paragraph and 'By and large, they work outdoors, and are interested in pretty much everything from discovering new species to the effect of obscure parasites on ecosystems.'

42 C: Link between 'The air is hot and thick, the trees are densely packed, and everywhere is teeming with life' in the previous paragraph and 'This morning, for example, a square half metre of mushrooms sprouted on the dirt floor of my kitchen. My favourite time here is in the early evenings. It's finally cool enough to be comfortable.'

43 F: Link between 'Each family has a *finca* in the forest, a wooden home on stilts' in the previous paragraph and 'They have their own traditions, too.' Also, the contrastive link between treating the woman with a snake bite and 'But my normal life here as a work experience student revolves mainly around my personal research' in the following paragraph.

44 A: Link between 'I am trying to establish exactly which species are here, where and when I can find them, and what condition they are in' in the previous paragraph and 'To do this, I walk slowly along several paths in the forest, accompanied by a local guide, and at night equipped with a torch.'

45 G: Link between 'Research is like this – laborious and monotonous – but it can be rewarding too' in the previous paragraph and 'And the thing is to imagine being the person that has made a discovery: the person who first questions something, investigates and then contributes to the vast catalogue of information that is science.'

46 D: Link between 'very few matching my desire to explore and investigate wildlife' in the previous paragraph and 'The reality is, however, that to make your way you need to build up a range of contacts and a portfolio of work.'

▶▶ PART 8

47 D: 'Preparation is of extreme importance; things like finding out what form the interview will have … will you be talking to one person or a panel?'

48 A: 'But I got carried away and went off at a tangent, which made a bad impression.'

49 C: 'They believed in being casual … people all used first names with each other.'

50 C: 'I was so relieved it was over that I just smiled and blurted out: "No thanks!"'

51 D: 'Another question interviewers sometimes ask … is about mistakes you have made. … admit that you were at fault.'

52 B: 'Firstly, a candidate should not learn a speech off by heart; you will come across as insincere.'

53 C: 'A candidate should decide in advance on at least ten things to ask the interviewer.'

54 D: 'Actually, it's not so much what people say … as the way they sit, how they hold their heads, whether they meet the interviewer's eye.'

55 B: 'I wondered if perhaps I had been too direct, but I later discovered … they were impressed by my enthusiasm and ambition.'

56 A: 'The other lesson I learnt was that if you are asked to talk about things you aren't good at, you shouldn't be evasive. You could mention something that can also be a strength.'

PAPER 2 Writing

▶▶ PART 1 (suggested answers)

Question 1:
Style: Semi-formal or formal
Content: 1 Introduce your essay, and explain what you are going to be writing about.
2 Describe the different methods for encouraging students.
3 Discuss which two methods you think are more useful. Give reasons, and if appropriate, explain why other methods are less useful.
4 Conclusion: end with a summary of your views.

▶▶ PART 2 (suggested answers)

Question 2:
Style: Informal
Content: 1 Introduction: greet your friend and say how nice it was to meet again.
2 Describe the party and the feelings you had about it.
3 Give details about the things you enjoyed.
4 Suggest ways of meeting in the future.
5 Finish your letter with an appropriate goodbye.

Question 3:
Style: Formal
Content: 1 Introduction: describe the situation you are going to discuss.
2 Describe the current dress code in the workplace you are writing about.
3 Outline the advantages of a casual-dress day.
4 Outline any disadvantages.
5 Conclusion: end with a summary of the pros and cons, and offer some recommendations for future action.

Question 4:
Style: Neutral or semi-formal
Content: 1 Introduction: explain which film you are talking about and which series it is a part of.
2 Describe what is good about the film.
3 Describe what is not good about the film.
4 Describe how well it fits with other films in the series.
5 Conclusion: summarise your views about the film.

PAPER 3 Listening

▶▶ PART 1

1 C **2** B **3** A **4** B **5** B **6** A

▶▶ PART 2

7 subject **8** on Earth/earth **9** extraterrestrial life **10** organisms **11** (geological) period **12** five million/5,000,000 **13** (very) different from **14** (the) dinosaurs

▶▶ PART 3

15 A **16** D **17** C **18** B **19** A **20** C

▶▶ PART 4

Task One
21 B **22** C **23** G **24** A **25** D

Task Two
26 E **27** A **28** F **29** G **30** H

TEST 6

PAPER 1 Reading and Use of English

▶▶ PART 1

1 A **2** C **3** B **4** D **5** C **6** D **7** A **8** C

▶▶ PART 2

9 as **10** which **11** how **12** such **13** order **14** among **15** each/every **16** far

17 originated (noun to verb)
18 inhabitants (verb to plural noun)
19 livelihood (verb to noun)
20 unpredictable (verb to negative adjective)
21 traditionally (noun to adverb)
22 temporarily (adjective to adverb)
23 guidance (verb to noun)
24 reputedly (noun to adverb)

▶▶ **PART 4**

25 was/has been (1) put down to (1)
26 only (1) I had asked (1)
27 pulled through (1) because/as/since (1)
28 objected to (1) what was being said (1)
29 your father, (1) rather than me/I who (1)
30 thought (that) the school (1) was vandalised (1)

▶▶ **PART 5**

31 D: 'An article published in the prestigious scientific journal *Nature* sheds new light on an important, but hitherto little appreciated, aspect of human evolution. In this article, Professors Dennis Bramble and Daniel Lieberman suggest that being able to run was a crucial element in the development of our species.'

32 A: 'When it comes to long-distance running, humans do astonishingly well. They can maintain a steady pace for many kilometres, and their overall speed is at least on a par with that of horses or dogs.'

33 B: 'When we run, it is this ligament that prevents our head from pitching back and forth or from side to side. Therefore, we are able to run with steady heads, held high.'

34 C: 'Then there are our Achilles tendons ... which have nothing to do with walking. When we run, these tendons behave like springs, helping to propel us forward.'

35 B: 'What evolutionary advantage is gained from being good long-distance runners? One hypothesis is that this ability may have permitted early humans to obtain food more effectively. ... evolved in order for our direct ancestors to compete with other carnivores for access to the protein needed to grow the big brains that we enjoy today.'

36 C: 'At the very least, I hope this theory will make many people have second thoughts about how humans learned to run and walk and why we are built the way we are.'

▶▶ **PART 6**

37 C: Reviewer A says the film 'is likely to appeal to younger audiences,' but 'whether this will prompt them to go back and read the novel ... is highly questionable.' Reviewer B says: 'There may be an element of wanting to attract teenage viewers.' Reviewer C says: 'The great hope is that all the noise and visual excitement will persuade younger viewers to try reading the novel.' Reviewer D says: 'Audiences, especially perhaps younger ones, will undoubtedly be attracted by the visual and auditory glamour, but they will miss out on what makes the novel great.'

So, reviewer C is the only one who is hopeful that the film will encourage younger people to read the novel.

38 A: Reviewer C says the 'musical soundtrack is a mix of period pieces, contemporary rap and dance tunes which somehow hang together and support the excesses.' Reviewer A says that 'the soundtrack mixing 1920s orchestral pieces with hip hop and modern pop works a treat.'

So, C and A both say positive things about the appropriacy of the music. Reviewers B and D make negative comments.

39 D: Reviewer B says: 'The narrative is unchanged but rather squeezed in, but then it is rather slight in the novel anyway.' Reviewer D says something similar: 'It's not that he makes substantial changes to the narrative in the film; the original has a thin plot anyway, and the film is largely faithful to it.' Reviewers A and C both feel the narrative is 'drowned out' in the film.

40 B: Reviewer A says: 'Baz Luhrmann's attempt fares little better ... this sense is largely drowned out by the lavish excess, the fancy camerawork and the general superficiality in this film.' Reviewer B says: 'There is no reason, however, why a film of the same story shouldn't take on a different style and this is what Baz Luhrmann does, largely to good effect.' Reviewer C says: 'director Baz Luhrmann's version is a loud confection of colour, lights and noise from start to finish – but the film's overblown nature drowns this message out.' Reviewer D says: 'With his exaggerated operatic style, Luhrmann is the wrong director to shoot F. Scott Fitzgerald's small but perfectly formed novel.'

So, reviewers A, C and D are all critical of the director's style. Reviewer B recognises that it is different from the original book, but thinks it works.

▶▶ **PART 7**

41 E: Link between the general description of BedZED homes and where they are.
42 F: Link between 'buildings can be made to be environmentally friendly' and 'this essentially means finding out how to increase efficiency in the least complicated manner possible.'
43 G: Link between 'receiving more and more attention' and 'this has been coming from Asia'.
44 A: Link between 'it would be relatively easy to reduce the energy consumption of most of our buildings' and 'it would be possible to achieve a great deal simply by using existing technologies.'
45 B: Link between 'European Union' and 'Governments elsewhere in the world'.
46 D: Link between 'Interesting initiatives have been taken in other parts of the world too' and the descriptions of initiatives in India and Sweden.

▶▶ **PART 8**

47 C: 'At first, I was surprised at how much paperwork I had to deal with.'
48 A: 'I figured I'd better not stray far from what I was familiar with ... I've deliberately kept the operation small-scale.'

49 B: 'I had a ready-made clientele, in the shape of former colleagues and people they recommended me to.'

50 D: 'I do almost all my work from home, using email, video conferencing and other online tools.'

51 C: 'I'd always thought that working outdoors would be brilliant.'

52 A: 'the outlay for office equipment was low.'

53 C: 'I've also been invited to write articles about gardening for a couple of magazines and websites, and I definitely want to do more of that in the future.'

54 D: 'The sector's very cut-throat, and when we got a new boss he decided to make his mark.'

55 B: 'Any personal trainer worth their salt should attend training courses on a regular basis to familiarise themselves with the latest developments in sports science – there's lots of really good research these days about things like running techniques, nutrition and rehabilitation from injury.'

56 A: 'A change in the way self-employed people complete their tax returns was due to be introduced, and I had an idea for some software showing people how to go about it.'

PAPER 2 Writing

▶▶ **PART 1** (*suggested answers*)

Question 1:
Style: Semi-formal or formal
Content: 1 Introduction: describe the topic and what you are going to write about.
 2 Describe the various reasons for having business sponsorship of your school.
 3 Describe the reasons which would be most important to consider.
 4 Describe any disadvantages to these reasons.
 5 Conclusion: summarise your views.

▶▶ **PART 2** (*suggested answers*)

Question 2:
Style: Formal
Content: 1 Introduction: describe the topic and what you are going to write about.
 2 Describe the three different questions which were discussed.
 3 Describe the opinions which were raised, and any agreements or disagreements.
 4 Describe the outcome of the discussion.
 5 Conclusion: summarise the main information in your report.

Question 3:
Style: Informal or neutral
Content: 1 Introduction: greet your friend and explain why you are writing.
 2 Describe the summer camp you were working with and what you had to do.
 3 Describe the positive and negative sides of the experience. Mention the relationships you had with the people you worked with, as well as your social activities.
 4 Make some recommendations for your friend.
 5 Finish with an appropriate goodbye.

Question 4:
Style: Neutral or semi-formal
Content: 1 Introduction: explain what concert you are writing about, and what type of concert it was.
 2 Give details of the things you enjoyed.
 3 Describe what you found disappointing.
 4 Conclusion: summarise your views.

PAPER 3 Listening

▶▶ **PART 1**

1 C **2** B **3** A **4** B **5** C **6** B

▶▶ **PART 2**

7 map (out) **8** conserve the site **9** humid
10 coach park **11** an underground stream
12 (loose) stones **13** leg **14** tour guide

▶▶ **PART 3**

15 D **16** D **17** B **18** A **19** C **20** B

▶▶ **PART 4**

Task One
21 F **22** A **23** C **24** D **25** G

Task Two
26 H **27** E **28** F **29** B **30** A

TEST 7

PAPER 1 Reading and Use of English

▶▶ **PART 1**

1 C **2** D **3** B **4** A **5** B **6** D **7** C **8** A

▶▶ **PART 2**

9 which **10** What **11** only **12** no/little **13** whose
14 case **15** over **16** as

▶▶ **PART 3**

17 influential (noun to adjective)
18 inspiration (verb to noun)
19 generosity (adjective to noun)
20 restless (noun to negative adjective)
21 medical (noun to adjective)
22 admiration (verb to noun)
23 enthusiasm (verb to noun)
24 outcry (verb to compound noun)

▶▶ **PART 4**

25 complete/total/absolute disregard (1) for her (1)
26 never discovered (1) who the murderer (1)
27 (me) against (1) calling Leo (1)
28 leaving/having left the office (1) did I realise (that) (1)
29 will never (1) live it (1)
30 are being (1) looked into by (1)

PART 5

31 C: 'Their appeal begins to become evident when they take flight' and 'can soar effortlessly for hours'.

32 D: 'From studying wild condors, they already knew that if a pair lost an egg, the birds would often yield another. So the first and sometimes second eggs laid by each female in captivity were removed'.

33 B: 'As a result, the scientists, zookeepers and conservationists who are concerned about condors have bickered among themselves over the best ways to rear and release the birds.'

34 B: 'At times they landed on people's houses and garages, walked across roads and airport runways, sauntered into park visitor centres and takeaway restaurants, and took food offered by picnickers and fishermen.'

35 A: 'The real key to successful condor reintroduction, he believes, lies in properly socialising the young birds as members of a group that follow and learn from older, preferably adult birds.'

36 C: The article as a whole. A is discussed in the first paragraph only, and D is addressed in paragraphs 3, 4 and 5. Paragraph 5, however, goes on to describe new measures taken to avoid the failures, and the meaning of option C includes this as well as the problems.

PART 6

37 D: Reviewer A mentions 'intriguing portraits of memory champions'. Reviewer B says 'It's a delight to travel with Foer into the geeky, largely male subculture of the competitive memorisers'. Reviewer C says 'it's an entertaining story'. Reviewer D says that what these competitive memorisers have to memorise is utterly trivial.'
So, A, B and C's have a positive attitude, whereas Reviewer D regards the competitions as 'the dreary world of mental athletes'.

38 C: Reviewer B says that Foer's 'account of the neurological functions of memory … is generally sound and up-to-date, with one notable exception. The idea that all our past experiences are stored somewhere in the brain, waiting to be retrieved, is now largely disputed by scientists.' Reviewer C says: 'Foer is not a neuroscientist, but his treatment of the subject is balanced and faithful to the science, apart, that is, from suggesting that all memories are permanently retained, though not always re-activated; studies now suggest that memory is very much subject to change.'

39 A: Reviewer A says that 'At times, it feels a little too friendly, with the science in particular deserving a linguistically more formal and detached approach.' Reviewer B says the book is 'delivered in clear, lively prose'. Reviewer C says Foer gives 'lucid, accessible explanations of a complex subject'. Reviewer D says that 'Foer proves he has a gift for communicating quite complex ideas in a manner that is palatable without being patronising'.
So, B, C and D say positive things about the way Foer writes. Reviewer A is the only one who is critical of his writing style.

40 A: Reviewer C says: 'If a self-help, brain-training guide is what you are after, look elsewhere.' Reviewer A says that the book is not ' a self-improvement manual.' Reviewers B and D make no comment about whether the book would be useful or not for people who want to improve their memory skills.

PART 7

41 G: Link between 'They have been together for two years now, slowly but steadily building up a loyal following, and there is little doubt that tonight's gig will be a success' in the previous paragraph and 'It is an enviable position to be in, especially for someone who, like Marjorie, has managed to make a living in a notoriously precarious profession'.

42 A: Link between 'I'm scared of the audience … I freeze up when I look at them' in the previous paragraph, and 'To help her with this, she reaches for her sunglasses. Wearing them … is one of the methods she uses to control her nerves.'

43 D: Link between 'two careers not normally associated with each other' in the previous paragraph and 'As if this combination wasn't unusual enough'. Also, link between 'she's a vet by training' in the previous paragraph and 'she suddenly decided to sell her thriving practice'.

44 F: Link between 'I was satisfied with my life' and 'contentment of this sort' in the following paragraph.

45 C: Link between 'it was as if she was hearing music for the first time' in the previous paragraph and 'I thought I'd gone to heaven'.

46 E: Link between 'Oddly enough' in the previous paragraph and 'the other curious factor'.

PART 8

47 C 'I talked to my psychology professor, an expert on child development, and she said: 'Why don't you fill the gap yourself? … my mentor's encouragement made all the difference.'

48 D: 'That buzz was a faint echo of the moment, over 200 years ago, when the pioneering chemist Humphry Davy first electrolysed molten potash and was rewarded with a spray of brilliant flashing droplets of potassium.'

49 A: 'I remember attending a talk years ago, at which the speaker, a distinguished biologist, was continually challenged by the audience … This lack of deference is by no means exceptional.'

50 D: 'Few of us are likely to come close to a discovery on that level, though it's something many yearn for.'

51 B: 'Working out the project details was fiddly and time-consuming. Then it slowed down even more, to a dull plod, as I checked and rechecked things.'

52 D: 'The unexpected turns up in little ways in day-to-day research and each time a miniature brainstorming session ensues, where adjustments are made to the research direction.'

53 A: 'The absence of a natural forum for scientists to describe their emotions in their work can lead to the erroneous view that we don't have any. In fact, we usually make a huge emotional investment in our work.'

54 B: 'It was reassuring to be reminded of the importance of my research subject.'

55 A: 'I had a long argument with a fellow biologist about a particular set of experiments ... A week later, we sent mutually apologetic texts and made up.'

56 C: 'Slightly apprehensive. It wasn't until then that I realised it was exactly what I wanted to do – move into a subject that was rather unknown territory to me. I was taking a risk.'

PAPER 2 Writing

▶▶ **PART 1** (*suggested answers*)

Question 1:
Style: Semi-formal or formal
Content: 1 Introduce the topic of the essay and what you will write about.
2 Outline the seminar you attended, and the points raised.
3 Discuss which methods you think are more important.
4 Give reasons for your opinion, and also mention why other methods are less important.
5 Conclusion: summarise the views mentioned in your essay.

▶▶ **PART 2** (*suggested answers*)

Question 2:
Style: Formal
Content: 1 Begin the letter appropriately and explain why you are writing.
2 Outline the situation and describe the general events. Describe the damage caused by the fire, and that you had to stay in temporary accommodation.
3 Explain the reasons for the fire.
4 Enquire about the possibility of compensation.
5 End your letter appropriately.

Question 3:
Style: Semi-formal or formal
Content: 1 Introduction: describe why you are writing this proposal.
2 Introduce the idea of the festival in more detail. Explain its purpose.
3 Describe how the event could be organised.
4 Outline some ideas for making the festival interesting.
5 Conclusion: finish by making some recommendations for future action.

Question 4:
Style: Formal
Content: 1 Introduction: describe why you are writing this report.
2 Explain the background to your recent experience and why you went.
3 Describe the enjoyable things about the visit.
4 Describe any less enjoyable things, and any difficulties.
5 Conclude your report by summarising the problems and making recommendations for change.

PAPER 3 Listening

▶▶ **PART 1**

1 C **2** A **3** B **4** A **5** C **6** A

▶▶ **PART 2**

7 chains **8** ninety-eight percent/98% **9** a few/several hours **10** flour **11** (rather) tasteless **12** stale **13** allergies **14** lose money

▶▶ **PART 3**

15 A **16** C **17** D **18** B **19** C **20** A

▶▶ **PART 4**

Task One
21 D **22** E **23** A **24** G **25** B

Task Two
26 C **27** F **28** A **29** H **30** D

TEST 8

PAPER 1 Reading and Use of English

▶▶ **PART 1**

1 D **2** B **3** A **4** C **5** A **6** D **7** B **8** C

▶▶ **PART 2**

9 due/down **10** how/where **11** besides **12** despite **13** which **14** every **15** whether **16** against

▶▶ **PART 3**

17 inconvenience (adjective to negative noun)
18 transactions (verb to plural noun)
19 tendency (verb to noun)
20 transferable (verb to adjective)
21 financiers (noun to plural noun)
22 accompanied (noun to verb)
23 withdraw (verb to verb)
24 widespread (verb to compound adjective)

▶▶ **PART 4**

25 was taken aback by (1) the warmth (1)
26 is not/isn't worth (1) trying to talk/talking (1)
27 (that) the job involved/would involve (her) (1) travelling (1)
28 it not been (1) for (1)
29 may/might/could have accidentally/accidentally have (1) taken (1)
30 was only (1) when she/Sara took off/after she/Sara took off/had taken off (1)

▶▶ **PART 5**

31 D: 'I left not much the wiser about what was going on.'
32 B: 'We call dull thuds 'heavy' and associate them with large objects, even though the sound itself has no size or weight.' The association of a sound, 'thud', with a word that describes size or weight, 'heavy', and the suggestion that it 'would have helped

our ancestors decide whether to run away from predators based on how big they sounded, without stopping to look them over', is an example, or illustration, of the point made in the last sentence of the second paragraph: 'Our senses mingle more often than we realise, collaborating to help us make sense of the world more easily.'

33 C: This fact refers back to the final part of the previous paragraph: '... even sound and smell sometimes form an unlikely pairing.'

34 A: 'They only intended to measure how olfactory tubercle cells in anesthetised mice responded to smell. But during testing, Wesson noticed that every time he clunked his coffee mug down next to the experiment, the mouse cells jumped in activity.' The noise of the coffee cup hitting the table was not a planned part of the experiment; Wesson noticed by chance the impact it had on the mice.

35 C: 'The results were interesting: piano was regularly paired with fruity scents. Musky smells sounded like brass.' The words 'regularly paired' indicate that the associations were consistent.'

36 B: 'The consequences of these advances are worth considering … One day, will you be routinely ordering a coffee with a soundtrack to bring out your favourite aromas? Come to think of it, that could be one notion you hope coffee shops chains don't get round to.'

▶▶ PART 6

37 C: Scientist B says: 'the idea that it would divert resources from conservation rests on a false assumption. The truth is that money invested in high tech solutions would not otherwise be available for the protection of wild environments and species; it would probably go into such activities as plant research for commercial use.' Scientist C says: 'the funds required (for de-extinction research) would not alternatively be available for conservation but would instead be directed at some other cutting edge field like medical science.'

38 D: Scientist A says: 'It would revolutionise the way we think about science … It would deliver a profoundly hopeful message.' Scientist B says that major breakthroughs can 'restore our faith in science, progress and even in ourselves. Species revival would show that science can be used for good, not simply to feed our lower appetites.' Scientist C says: 'it is likely to widely welcomed and will help create a favourable climate for science.' Scientist D says de-extinction 'reinforces the idea that advanced science can solve all our problems', which is dangerous because it 'distracts us from safeguarding out planet's biodiversity for future generations.' So, A, B and C suggest de-extinction research will lead to positive attitudes towards science, while D suggests it will lead people to rely too much on science.

39 A: Scientist A says: 'Revived species would also help to restore a great deal of ecological richness.' Scientist B says that we need to 'think through carefully … how we would re-introduce species into nature. The ecosystem of a vanished species will have changed since it last inhabited it, and anyway, its extinction almost certainly resulted from the deterioration of its natural habitat.' Scientist C is worried that re-introducing species into the wild 'would require changing the biodiversity of huge geographical areas.' Scientist D makes a similar point to scientist C that animals became extinct because of 'changes in the environments they depended on', and also that de-extinction work would be a distraction from conservation of endangered ecosystems. So, A predicts positive consequences for the environment, while B, C and D focus on environmental problems.

40 B: Scientist A says: 'Knowledge and techniques developed for de-extinction would also be directly applicable to living species that are endangered, so conservation would benefit.' Scientist B makes a similar point: 'We could also apply what we learn from it (de-extinction) to efforts to conserve living species.' Scientist C mentions that breakthroughs in de-extinction may create a positive attitude towards science but does not mention specific research contributions to any other field of science. Neither does scientist D.

▶▶ PART 7

41 D: Link between 'green, hilly landscape' in the previous paragraph and 'this remote place'. Also, link between 'archaeologists had completely overlooked' and 'What had escaped their attention was …'.

42 F: Link between 'covers more than six acres of land' and comments about the size and how impressive it was. Also, the following paragraph refers back with 'this architectural marvel'.

43 A: Link between beliefs and the purpose of the great structure being 'unknown' and the contrast that 'one thing archaeologists are sure of …'. Also, the link between something that remains a 'mystery' and the contrast expressed in 'What is clear is that …' in the next paragraph.

44 G: Link between the idea that the discovery has 'revolutionised our understanding of the period' in the previous paragraph and the 'need to turn the map upside down when considering the Neolithic era'. Also, link between the idea that 'Orkney was the centre of new ideas' and 'these innovators' in the next paragraph.

45 C: Link between 'cattle, pigs and sheep and hunting and fishing' in the previous paragraph, and 'the bones of domesticated animals alongside those of wild deer, whales and seals'. Also link between information about the age at which people died and how long people lived and 'however … they lived long and well enough …' in the next paragraph.

46 E: Link between being given World Heritage status and 'this recognition'. Also, link between the Ness of Brogdar being selected for study and the idea that people had assumed 'it was a natural feature' in the next paragraph.

▶▶ PART 8

47 D: 'Nowadays a great deal of art doesn't generate strong feelings in me one way or another.'

48 C: 'That's exactly what Bernd and Hilla Becher have done for industrial architecture. The German artists spent decades travelling around, obsessively

catologuing those grim, ubiquitous structures – gas
cooling towers, pitheads, pylons.'

49 B: 'It throws you into the 19th–century city with its wide
boulevards and grand buildings.'

50 A: 'I think it must signify influence as well as a self-
contained perfection of form ... a painting by Monet,
who changed the way painters in the west saw and
depicted light.'

51 D: 'The way Picasso uses Cubist techniques to break
up their bodies and present different perspectives
allows him to give us that detail. It's abstract but at
the same time manages to convey the humanity of
the moment in a wonderfully touching manner.'

52 C: 'I can't look at any such structures in real life
without thinking of their photographs. I have several
pinned to the walls of my studio. As a sculptor, I'm
fascinated by their shape and form.'

53 A: 'While I can see beauty in, say, a bronze sculpture
from the Benin kingdom of West Africa, I have no
idea whether it was influential in its own culture, or
typical, or what.'

54 B: 'The slippery shining cobblestones in the road give
me cold toes, and I can smell the damp wool from
all those coats ... I experience a twinge of envy.'

55 D: 'It's something that absolutely everybody has
experienced and witnessed. Today, thousands of
depictions will be made of this all over the world,
most with a camera.'

56 C: 'Think of Monet with his haystacks at the end of
the 19th century, or Turner with his sunsets several
decades before: once you've seen their paintings,
you never look at those things in the same way.
That's exactly what Bernd and Hilla Becher have
done for industrial architecture in the last 50 years.'

PAPER 2 Writing

▶▶ **PART 1** (suggested answers)

Question 1:
   Style: Semi-formal or formal
  Content: 1 Introduction: describe why you are writing this
      essay.
      2 Describe the discussion you attended and what
      points were raised.
      3 Outline the methods which could be focused on.
      4 Discuss which two methods you believe are
      most important, and why.
      5 Conclusion: summarise the points raised in
      your essay.

▶▶ **PART 2** (suggested answers)

Question 2:
   Style: Formal
  Content: 1 Introduction: describe why you are writing this
      report.
      2 Describe the club you belong to and the trip
      you went on.
      3 Describe how the club's money was well-spent
      on this trip. Give some examples of why the
      trip was beneficial.
      4 Conclusion: summarise the findings of your
      report, and make suggestions for future action.

Question 3:
   Style: Formal
  Content: 1 Introduction: explain why you are writing this
      letter, and give some brief information about
      yourself.
      2 Describe your local area and how you know it
      so well.
      3 List some examples of your knowledge of the
      local area. Concentrate on places and parks.
      4 Summarise why you would be good for the
      job. Add any other personal qualities which
      might be important to know about.
      5 Finish your letter appropriately.

Question 4:
   Style: Neutral or semi-formal
  Content: 1 Introduction: explain which novel you are
      writing about, and that it is something that
      people enjoy reading.
      2 Outline the successful features of the book,
      giving examples of its characters, story, style,
      etc.
      3 Outline any weak points of the book. Again,
      give specific examples.
      4 Describe the book's success, and why people
      enjoy it.
      5 Conclusion: summarise the main points of
      your review.

PAPER 3 Listening

▶▶ **PART 1**

1 C   **2** A   **3** C   **4** A   **5** A   **6** B

▶▶ **PART 2**

7 winter   **8** two/2   **9** direct   **10** not descended
11 became extinct   **12** tools   **13** groups   **14** a mystery

▶▶ **PART 3**

15 D   **16** A   **17** B   **18** C   **19** D   **20** A

▶▶ **PART 4**

Task One
21 B   **22** E   **23** A   **24** G   **25** H

Task Two
26 D   **27** G   **28** F   **29** A   **30** C